WITHDRAWN

STUDYING PEOPLE

STUDYING PEOPLE

A Primer in the Ethics of Social Research

by
ROBERT D. REECE

and
HARVEY A. SIEGAL

with a Foreword by
JAMES M. GUSTAFSON

MERCER

ISBN 0-86554-220-1
ISBN 0-86554-221-X (paperback)

Studying People
Copyright © 1986
Mercer University Press, Macon, Georgia 31207
All rights reserved
Printed in the United States of America

Library of Congress Cataloging-in-Publication Data
Reece, Robert D.
Studying people.

Bibliography: p. 217
Includes index.
1. Social sciences—Research—Moral and ethical
aspects.   2. Social scientists—Professional ethics.
3. Participant observation.   4. Privacy, Right of.
I. Siegal, Harvey A.   II. Title.
H62.R366   1986   174.9301   86-18059
ISBN 0-86554-220-1 (alk. paper)
ISBN 0-86554-221-X (pbk. : alk. paper)

CONTENTS

FOREWORD

Reece and Siegal have a clear and overriding purpose in this book, namely to provide a pedagogical device that induces students to think ethically. The context in view is specific: the ethics of social research. But the procedures used in this sustained exercise could appropriately be used in other specific contexts.

The literature on ethical theory and on "applied ethics" has grown enormously in the past two decades. The proliferation of journals and textbooks has reached a point at which it is difficult for busy teachers and students to sustain a command of the literature. Many teachers are frustrated in their efforts to find a book that combines the introduction of critical ethical distinctions with cases or narratives out of human experience. Some books begin with chapters on various types of ethical theory and then apply the theories to the matters at hand; this is often seen to be unsatisfactory since theory and application become somewhat separated.

This book is quite distinctive in the way in which concepts, important ethical distinctions, and narratives are related. It is written to evoke and sustain the interest of the reader. It is not "narrative ethics" in the sense of telling stories that give shape to character; rather, it uses intriguing narratives to elicit critical reflection. The reflection is elicited from the narratives in such a way that the reader becomes aware of a moral quandary; the proper concepts and distinctions are introduced at a place and time that make them most significant to the reader. Theory and concepts are not introduced in such a way that the thinking of the reader is done for her or him; there is no way in which this book can be used as a moral notebook to resolve uncertainties in social research.

The book is written in a way that brings to consciousness many aspects and dimensions of moral experience. It shows how certain principles and rules pertain, but it also describes the conflicts of responsibilities and loyalties that the researcher often experiences. The social matrix of difficult moral choices and the internal stresses they create for the participants enrich and distinguish this book. This book does not confine itself to moral theory, but instead addresses the concept of a moral life. Pedagogically this is effective since readers emphathize with persons in the circumstances described; the authors make one "feel" the burden of moral conscientiousness as well as sort out ways in which resolutions can occur.

Footnotes and bibliography can lead the reader to the sources that back this book and to further exploration of a more technical sort.

One gets a very strong impression that two very good teachers are deeply motivated by their calling, and are sharing their skills with others who are equally dedicated to helping students learn—in this case to think ethically.

James M. Gustafson

PREFACE

This book evolved from a relationship that began nearly ten years ago when we became colleagues in a newly established medical school. We came from very different backgrounds and experiences, one from religious studies with a concentration in ethics and the other from sociology with experience in ethnographic studies of deviant populations. At the medical school, we worked closely in shaping a humanities and social science program. Around and through it, we spent hours in conversation about our disciplines, our interests, and ourselves. As our appreciation and understanding of each other grew, we discovered that there were, despite our differences, many areas of agreement.

One of those was a concern for the ethical issues faced by those who study people and their behavior. Much more has been written on this subject than was available when we began this project, but we think the topic has still not received the scholarly attention it deserves. More importantly, ethical questions are never answered perfectly and permanently. Our ethical standards and our procedures for protecting human subjects need continual scrutiny.

Because nothing is so complex as human beings and what they produce, we believe that no single perspective can provide an adequate understanding. To get people from different perspectives and disciplines to sit down and reason together is itself exciting. It is part of what a university is about. We hope this book will encourage such a dialogue about ethical issues. Ethics is not boring, and our goal is to stimulate an active interaction with the book and a lively discussion among its readers about the ethics of social and behavioral research.

Our own thinking and work, of course, rests on the work of countless people whose influence is so pervasive and subtle that we probably do not recognize all the sources of our ideas. We acknowledge in gratitude our debt to those individuals, living and dead, who have taught us through their writings. We are especially grateful to those who directed our formal education, who taught us by precept and example, who guided our thinking, but who, in their wisdom, allowed us to make mistakes from which we have also learned.

We thank Thomas McElhinney for reading an early draft of the manuscript, and we especially appreciate Thomas Shannon for his careful and thoughtful reading of a later draft. Their comments and suggestions and encouragement at critical stages of our work have helped us immensely.

We express our deepest affection and gratitude to our families who have suffered with us, and sometimes because of us, during this venture. Finally, we wish to thank Wright State University and Mercer University Press for supporting us and our work.

I

INTRODUCTION

1

What's the Problem?

The twentieth century has seen the blossoming of scientific research, and the fruits of the wedding of science and technology are
evident all around us. Daily, we are adding to our knowledge and using
it in wonderful new technological feats. A late arrival to this "wedding"
is the scientific study of human behavior. All of this new information
has brought with it a questioning of values and beliefs. What is good?
What is valuable? What is unethical? Is anything unethical? Who makes
these decisions? How are they made?

We generally assume that knowledge is good. We tend to believe that
the more information we have, the better we are able to choose from the
various alternatives. We may hope that with enough knowledge, hard
choices become unnecessary. We may hope that with enough information anyone can make the proper decision. Sometimes that is true. As a
nation we invest enormous resources to acquire knowledge. It has been
said that we have frantically turned every stone and poked into every
dark corner and recess in our relentless search for truth.

This observation about our age seems fairly accurate. A few centu-
ries ago, people thought an exceptional person such as Leonardo da
Vinci, or the "Father" of psychology, Wilhelm Wundt, knew "all there was
to know about everything." The validity of this claim is not important.
It clearly indicates how manageable the body of knowledge *was thought
to be.* Today no one would presume to claim mastery of even a single
subject. A continuing "knowledge explosion" is an established part of
our world. Corresponding to it is an ignorance explosion that makes us
increasingly prone to rely on experts who know a great deal about one
field, and perhaps very little about anything else. Much like an atomic
chain reaction gone out of control, we are bombarded every day with new
facts, new methods, and, most importantly, new questions that demand
answers. Not the least of these questions is about us: our bodies, our
minds, and our behavior.

Our primary concern in this book is not whether it is good to have
knowledge. We are mainly interested in *how* we obtain knowledge and

what we do with it. On the one hand, when we are dealing with questions about the natural world, we do not worry about how we gather information. A rock or stone has no feelings, so if a geologist wants to subject it to strong acid or wants to shatter it with a hammer, we do not object because no one is harmed. The same can be said about the biological sciences. Work with bacteria, fungi, or protozoa, for example, causes little concern, at least in our society. Because these simple creatures lack feelings, we sense we cannot harm them. On the other hand, the issue becomes cloudier when dealing with animals like ourselves, such as mammals. If we study these creatures, what kinds of obligations do we have? Can we pretend that they, too, are immune to pain? Do we have an obligation to restore them when the experiment is completed? Despite a lengthy history of research with animals, the issue—what our responsibilities are to other creatures—has not been resolved.

The argument becomes even more complex when we study ourselves. Most people in our society assume that human beings should not normally be subjected to harmful experiments in our quest for knowledge. The obscene biomedical experiments conducted on human subjects by the Nazis remain a blot on the conscience of humanity. Unfortunately, our record in the United States is not free of blemishes. Withholding medical treatment from people in order to observe the long-term, progressive effects of disease; performing unnecessary or even harmful surgery on mentally ill or retarded people; administering powerful drugs without consent—all of these have occurred. Because we are concerned about such cases, we have established methods of protecting the health and well-being of people in scientific and social experiments.

Nevertheless, it took years to develop these mechanisms. Difficult issues were confronted, and the process continues. Biomedical research provided the first arena in the debate over the use of people for experimental purposes. Some experimenters, in their zeal to acquire information, were apparently unconcerned about the care or well-being of their subjects, who ironically became the "objects" of the research. More recently, some of these concerns have surfaced in other research involving human subjects. Psychological experiments that examine a person's reaction to a stressful situation and sociological studies of deviant (and illegal) behavior without subjects' consent raise serious questions regarding appropriate methods and limits of social and behavioral research. There is a growing sense that the difference between using human subjects in biomedical and social-behavioral research is only a matter of degree. Both involve a risk of harm; the difference is that medical experimentation may cause more obvious physical harm.

Potential injury in social-behavioral research shifts from gross bodily damage to more subtle, but no less important, harm through mental anguish, anxiety, fear, unnecessary embarrassment, and social or economic damage. Much of our discussion in this book will focus on the individuals whom the social or behavioral scientist is studying and the people close to them. But we are also concerned with the whole context of research—the relations of researchers to subjects, to colleagues, to funding agencies, and ultimately to society as a whole.

As the subtitle indicates, this book is about *ethical* issues in social and behavioral research. It is not our intention to provide definitive answers to these difficult questions. We hope to help our readers ask the right questions and to provide guidance in thinking about these questions. The book is a study in applied ethics, not ethical theory, and this has two important implications for our book. First, though we will introduce important material and perspectives from the long history of ethical thought, we cannot hope to completely resolve the fundamental problems raised in the continuing debate about ethical theory. Second, we are genuinely concerned with helping the reader to achieve sound judgments about right and wrong in social research. Our purpose is practical rather than theoretical.

In general, applied ethics has at least has two purposes. At the individual level, the goal is to help the concerned person make moral decisions. The broader social goal is to increase awareness and understanding and so contribute to the development of better social norms. Even those with the best intentions need established guidelines. Clearly defined norms can also help ensure that even those who are less sensitive to moral issues will behave acceptably. Some of our readers can relate directly to the first goal because they are engaged in research. We hope that all are concerned with the second, since the establishment of appropriate standards governing research is important both for researchers and the public.

The book is intended primarily for academic use. Our goal is to assist you in thinking about ethics, using as little technical jargon as possible. We anticipate that most of our readers will be students and instructors in ethics classes or in social and behavioral sciences classes. We want you to involve yourselves in thinking creatively about the ethics of research. Actively participate in classroom discussions of these issues. This may be difficult at first because the student is usually forced into the passive absorption of information. To help you become involved, we will present a series of fictionalized cases in which researchers must make choices about whether to continue a study or how to proceed. We have designed the cases to focus on certain issues which deserve discussion.

Through commentary on these cases, we raise a variety of ethical issues, define some basic ethical concepts, and offer a perspective. Only a few issues are selected from each case, with no pretense of being exhaustive. We invite you to use the cases to explore more deeply the other issues that we only touch upon.

Different readers will undoubtedly highlight different aspects of the cases. Classroom dialogue should increase your appreciation for the ethical dimensions of research. Readers with little background in formal ethics should gain some understanding of the nature of ethical theory and its use in analyzing moral problems. Those with only a vague notion of what social and behavioral scientists do will learn about social research and the ethical problems it presents. Social-science students are challenged to think of better methods of conducting the studies we present. Finally, we hope that our readers will become better informed and more concerned citizens because of our effort. Let us begin our inquiry together by looking at the first case.

ENTERING THE CULT OF DEATH

"I guess I've got a lot on my mind," Don replied to Jenny's look of concern and the gentle squeeze of her hand. The bustle of activity and friends in the Rathskeller—called "The Rat" by all the students at State U.—did little to displace the nagging doubts that were creeping, with increasing regularity, into Don Clark's mind. Somehow the scene at The Rat—all the chatter, the familiar burgers, the loud music—didn't seem real today. "It's almost like my body is sitting here next to Jenny, but my mind is somehere else, kind of looking down at me . . . weird!" Don thought.

Jenny was concerned. She caught herself chewing the ends of her long, brown hair, something she always did when she felt nervous. She had known Don for more than two years, since their introductory sociology course. They had been almost inseparable since they returned to State last fall. Now they were nearing the end of their senior year. "I'm really worried!" Jenny thought.

Their plans for the future looked good. Don had applied to several fine graduate programs in sociology, and his grades and recommendations were sure to get him into one of the better schools, probably with a healthy fellowship despite the tightening of scholarship funds. Jenny's major in chemical engineering and her standing in the top ten percent of the class were sure to land her a good job anywhere. The semester had started well. Jenny's classes were difficult but satisfying. She delighted in working through experiments and equations. Everything fit together so neatly, without a lot of loose ends and uncertainty. Campus life was fun, too. She had lots of friends, so much to do, no hassles, and now she had Don. Life couldn't be better.

But the past few weeks had been difficult, ever since Don had started his senior project. Jenny turned over in her mind the recent changes. Don had lost weight, he'd been looking tired and preoccupied so often, and he'd been spending more time on the project, which meant less time together. She wondered what he'd been doing with all that time.

At first Don had seemed so excited about his senior project. Jenny had tried to share his enthusiasm, but she found it difficult because the neat rows and columns of computer printout were so much more understandable to her than the lengthy notes Don took and that "weirdo cult" stuff that he was studying. Don talked about "meanings," "symbols," and "interpretations from the standpoint of a group member." These things didn't make a lot of sense to Jenny. Despite all the hours she and Don argued, Jenny still wasn't sure sociology was a science, especially when Don insisted that in order to really understand what was happening, he had to experience the same things the people he was studying did. "I guess it's an important assignment," Jenny thought. "After all, it is a senior honors project. But it shouldn't dominate our whole life."

Don glanced at the clock on the wall and then looked over at Jenny. "She's pretty," he thought. "Small, with long, shiny, brown hair. She's always so clean, I bet she'd shower ten times a day if she could." Images of the night before rushed into his mind. How unlike Jenny were the Disciples of Necromancy (or "Necrons" as they called themselves). The "hags" or "weird sisters," as the female members of the cult were called, seldom bathed. Bathing, Don had discovered, was reserved as a prelude to a special event, the "Ritual-of-One." Don's only similar experience had been his interview with a few members of a Hell's Angels-type motorcycle gang. For members of some counterculture groups, dirt seemed a matter of prestige, even honor. Now here he was getting more and more deeply involved with the Necrons.

"Gotta shove off to class now," Don said absently to Jenny and was stung by the look in her eyes. "I'll see you tonight. . . . No, I've got that meeting tonight. It may be late."

Jenny started to protest, but the look on Don's face froze the words before she could even get them out. Don kissed her lightly on the head, gathered his books, and ambled out. "I wish I could help," Jenny thought. "I'm so worried about him. I don't even know who to talk to, or even how to talk to Don about what he's doing. And people think engineering is complicated!"

"Complicated, that's the word for it," Don found himself saying almost aloud. Professor Kincaid made it seem so easy. A sociological study was just a series of discreet steps, the professor had said. The researcher is a finely tuned instrument that collects, receives, processes, categorizes, and analyzes data. "Neat, clean, and simple," Don snorted under his breath. "But Kincaid knows his stuff," Don confessed to himself. "I guess if there is anybody I would want to be like, it'd be Rob Kincaid." His field studies of junkies and prostitutes were already classics, and his lectures made you feel as if you were right on the street with him. "Besides, it's Kincaid's recommendation that's gonna get me into Zenith for my Ph.D., and that's where I really want to go. I've got to do a good job on this Necron study."

Don could feel his anxiety level rising as he sat in class thinking about it. He remembered how he'd felt when he had presented the prospectus to the class. Professor Kincaid had stopped just short of saying it was the class's only really exciting project. Everyone else was doing the usual survey of State U. students, asking about marijuana smoking, premarital sex, or attitudes about the new nuclear-power plant under construction in the next town. He remembered how the other students had whipped around and looked at each other when he said that he was planning a study of the Necrons! He even felt that the professor was a little envious. The Necrons had shown up around campus about a year and a half before. Nobody knew much about them, and he was going to discover what the group was all about.

Portington, the city where State U. is located, was like many other towns with a large university. There were the usual campus accompaniments: the line of book and record stores, student bars, and cafes. The campus was in the oldest part of town with the cheapest real estate surrounding it, thus accentuating the tendency for fringe elements to cluster around it. The university had collected an assortment of neighbors; motorcycle gangs, a couple of communes, and a halfway house for recovering drug users were located within a stone's throw of campus. Like many other campus communities, State U. had its share of exotic types. A large group of former students who never finished their degrees still stayed around enjoying the college atmosphere, going to concerts, speeches, and exhibits. The campus green had once been the gathering spot for Portington's hippies, and the occasional Krishna disciple still wandered through.

Then the Necrons began appearing. No one paid much attention at first, but before long both students and faculty began noticing these folks walking around in long midnight-black robes with a tiny blood-red death's head over their hearts. No one ever saw them talking to anyone, nor did they pass out tracts, or do anything like other religious groups around campus. Instead, they walked the streets, either singularly or in pairs—gaunt, hollow-looking people in long, black robes.

Students soon wondered what went on inside the "Crypt," as the Necrons' house had been dubbed by the campus community. Like everything else about them, it was mysterious. This big, old house, identical to so many others around it, had been transformed by the Necrons. They had painted the entire house black. Even the windows had been blackened. All of the vegetation, even the weeds growing around the house, had been removed and students had noticed members of the group carefully removing tiny blades of grass as they appeared. Some students claimed they had witnessed one of the Disciples spreading salt on the ground to keep anything from growing. But like everything else, the novelty wore off and the general interest of the campus community turned elsewhere. Nevertheless, enough mystery remained to spark the interest of Don's fellow students when he presented his prospectus.

The prospectus, Don had to admit, was well-prepared. He did his homework and made an organized presentation on cults and other exotic groups. The apparent secretiveness of the group, he had argued, meant that a straightforward interview study would be unlikely to provide usable data. Then, with just the right touch of superiority, he explained how only a participant observation study would produce an in-depth, complete understanding of this socially isolated "deviant" group.

Don smiled as he remembered how Dr. Kincaid had reminisced about his own first participant study. He recalled the feeling of warmth as he sensed his classmates' envy and Kincaid's approval. That feeling didn't last long. Although Jenny was pleased to hear about Dr. Kincaid's approval, she wasn't thrilled to learn how much time the study would take. She was also a little worried that Don might get hurt in the process. Don admitted that he felt a touch of guilt now because he had delighted so much in regaling her with slightly embellished stories of Dr. Kincaid's adventures in his participant research with narcotics addicts.

As Don sat in class thinking about the beginning of his study, he remembered how he had gone back to his old notes from Professor Hollister's class in sociological methodology, especially the lectures on qualitative and field-study methods. The more he read, the more uneasy he became. How was he to get access to the group? How could he face his classmates and Dr. Kincaid if he couldn't? Don's discomfort increased as he saw classmates busily at work tabulating their questionnaires.

Don's decision to penetrate the group covertly was made almost by accident. As his anxiety rose, Don felt increasingly paralyzed. Should he simply approach members of the group and say, "I'm a sociology student doing a study of various religious groups," and ask if he could study them? What would happen if he were rejected out of hand? He couldn't admit failure. Not knowing what to do, Don left his apartment one evening almost on an impulse and walked over to the Crypt. He strolled up and down the street a few times. It was a lovely autumn night, slightly warm and balmy with just a sliver of moon in the sky and a hint of wood smoke in the air. He walked back and forth several times and then turned abruptly and approached the house. He felt nearly suffocated as he walked up the path toward the Crypt's porch. All the adjacent houses were lighted; the Crypt looked like a monstrous, black mountain looming in front of him.

"Well, here goes nothing," Don thought. "Why didn't any of those profs ever tell us it would be like this?"

As Don approached the front door, it opened without his even knocking. One of the Disciples stood in the doorway and said in a simple, flat voice, "You have arrived." Don didn't know what to say; a million thoughts fluttered through his mind. Should he introduce himself? Should he say he wanted to study the group? Should he do nothing at all? Don stood there feeling uncomfortable, even a little foolish. The house was quiet, although he could detect some movement in an adjacent room. Almost before he knew it, Don had followed the Disciple into the house. The lighting in the front room was provided by two candles on the far side of the room. Don was told to sit on a low, backless bench just inside the room, and was left alone. After a short while, Don began exploring the room. There was nothing really to see—just an empty, musty-smelling room with a couple of candles burning in it. Don went back to the bench and began thinking about the project all over again. "Well, I've come this far; I'm sure I can wait them out," he decided.

After an hour or so, a Disciple emerged from a doorway on the other side of the room and slowly approached Don. The Disciple was in the usual black robe. The figure paused in front of Don. The person's back was to the candles, making it impossible to determine the Disciple's sex. The pause seemed to go on forever, and Don could feel his heart beating in his chest.

Finally, the Disciple said in the same flat tone, "You have arrived."

Don was at a loss for something to say, and he stammered something like "Yes. . . . " Then Don heard himself saying, "I want to be here. . . . I think I want to join."

"You must wait," the Disciple replied and nodded his head toward the bench where Don had been sitting. Don returned to the seat, and the Disciple silently left the room. Don sat on the bench for a few hours and, after nothing happened, he left the Crypt.

The following night, Don returned and the same sequence of events occurred. The Disciples he encountered would not speak to him, but he didn't feel as though he was being turned away either. Again, this second night, Don spent a few hours at the Crypt and then returned home.

On the walk home, Don began to consider his experiences with the group. He knew he would have to go back, but he realized that sooner or later he would have to say something that would make the Disciples want to accept him. Sometime during the third day Don hit upon the idea of inventing a recent suicide attempt and a mystical experience associated with it. Once he got the story started, embellishing it was easy.

His hunch proved right. The third night, after his initial greeting and wait, two robed and hooded Disciples entered the room. Speaking slowly and wringing his hands, Don began telling his made-up story of a suicide attempt by an overdose of sleeping pills and a mystical vision in which he had experienced the truth of death. Don said there was something familiar and comforting about the Necrons, and that he longed to belong to a group that could understand his feelings and share his experiences.

Don was told to sit, and one of the members of the cult lit a small, foul-smelling candle and placed it on the floor in the middle of the little group. One of the Disciples started talking, describing a time that once was or never had been, a time and space in which the divisions we make between light and dark, death and life, and sound and silence weren't there. Don hadn't understood much of what was being said. He did remember his thoughts. "What a gas . . . here I am . . . this is really research. If only my classmates could see me now!" He had felt elated and powerful, yet underneath it all was a nagging sense of unease. "Where do I go now? What do I do?" Don felt almost hypnotized as the Disciple went on in a relentless monotone, chiming states and places that made no sense at all to Don.

"Hey, feller, watch where you're going." Don was jarred back into the reality of the campus quadrangle. Class was over, and Don was on his way to the library. The couple he bumped into glared at him and walked on.

Things hadn't been the same since that night in the Crypt. Looking back now, he realized getting into the group had been easy enough. The more difficult problem was what to do then. Don's mind once again played back over the past few months' involvement with the Necrons and how many things had changed.

The first several nights of returning to the Crypt, sitting in a small circle with some of the Disciples, listening almost hypnotically to the rendition of "The Place," smelling the funny candle, and sensing the closeness yet aloneness of the Disciples made him feel distant from his classmates, work, and even from Jenny. Whenever he tried asking the Disciples any questions, they said, "Yes, you will soon know." Within ten days, Luthor, the Disciple who was spending the most time with Don, indicated that Don was ready for entrance to the next stage. This was the first time Don was able to speak to one of the Disciples in anything but the highly ritualized monotone. While Luthor wasn't exactly warm, he did seem to be concerned about Don. More importantly, Don was struck by Luthor's commitment to the group. And he seemed to be genuinely convinced that the "vision," as the Disciples called the happenings in "The Place," could ultimately help the world. Don didn't believe the ho- cus-pocus stuff, but almost in spite of himself he felt good about Luthor and some of the other Disciples. Even a few "weird sisters" were begin- ning to take on separate personalities for Don. The next step, Luthor had told Don, was the "Oathing," the first of the more formalized initiation rituals. At the heart of the Oathing was the pledge of secrecy. The initi- ate declared upon his soul and honor that he would never reveal to any outsider, regardless of the circumstances, the rituals and secrets of the group.

As Don left the library and made his way toward his seminar, these thoughts clashed in his mind. Today it was his turn to give a preliminary report to Dr. Kincaid's class, and Don still wasn't sure how to go about it. He arrived at class a few minutes late and could see that both the class and the professor were eager for him to begin. Dr. Kincaid motioned Don to the empty seat next to him at the head of the large U-shaped table. He made a few general observations about how the class projects were pro- gressing and then said, "Well, Don, what can you tell us so far?"

" . . . and so the story is told of a place before the beginning of history or when time is no more." Don carefully described the mythology of the Disciples of Necromancy. The students hardly breathed as Don related the elaborate cosmological structure, and he could feel the tension mounting as he recounted his first initiation ritual. Even the sound of traffic on the busy street outside Lindsey Hall seemed to vanish as he described the Oathing, during which he had mixed a small amount of his own blood with that of the Disciples in a lead chalice and had pledged fidelity, solidarity, and secrecy as he drank the commingled blood.

Don described the other rites in more general terms. He talked about his fasts and the long periods of seclusion for meditation that would help him clear his mind and develop his own memory of the Place. Don de- scribed the second stage of his initiation. The Disciples had killed birds and rabbits, mixed their blood, and "read" it as it congealed. Don dis- cussed the language of the Disciples, giving examples of the wealth of words they used to describe anything having to do with death. Everyone in the room was riveted by Don's account of the strict monastic life and the elaborate social structure that regulated existence in the Crypt. Don said he expected to learn even more about the Disciples as his "spiritual education" proceeded and that he had developed several hypotheses about how the group sustained itself and how individual members achieved stability.

Don stopped talking. A couple of students asked questions about his fast and ordeal and about his reference to drug use within the Crypt. Don answered concisely and everyone looked at Dr. Kincaid. It was clear that the professor was impressed. He had a habit of fidgeting in his seat, scribbling, and sometimes looking bored. But none of that today. Rob Kincaid cleared his throat and said that this was undoubtedly the most ambitious senior paper he had ever had the pleasure of supervising. "I hope you'll think about publishing it when the research is completed, Don. I'm sure that this is the kind of thing that the university's scientific report series would scoop right up. Good job, full speed ahead, and I— or should I say we—can't wait 'til your next report on your work with the Necrons."

The hour completed, Kincaid looked around, assured himself that there were no further questions, and gathered his papers and left the room. Within a few moments, Don had the room to himself. "I wish my other classes were going this well," Don mused. The truth was that because of his involvement with this project, everything else was going to pot. "Now what am I going to do?" Don thought to himself. "It seems I'm digging myself in deeper every moment. Now I've got Dr. Kincaid talking about a publication."

Don was worried. What he didn't tell the class was that within the week he would be expected to participate in the Ritual-of-One ceremony, which would signify his full admission into the cult. This ceremony was giving Don difficulty.

The Ritual-of-One was the most elaborate and the most frightening of all the cult's mystical rites. The ceremony was based on the moment of interconnection between life and death. For it, a female Disciple would take a heavy dose of sedative medications to simulate a death-like sleep. Other members would prepare her as though she had died, washing the body and placing the comatose, white-shrouded body on a bier with candles burning at her head and feet. Cult members, after taking heavy doses of powerful hallucinogenic drugs, would then have sexual intercourse with the comatose hag.

"What am I going to do now? . . . What am I going to do?" Don had never felt so trapped before. He was frightened about what was happening at the Crypt. He was worried about the drugs the Disciples used, and he was still bothered by killing that cute rabbit the other night. Most of all, he knew he would be expected to have sex during the ceremony, and he didn't want to do it.

"What's the right thing to do? How did I ever get myself into this?" Don thought. "I wish I had someone to talk to. No, I needed someone to talk to before I ever started this project. If only Dr. Kincaid had told us how complicated participant research really can be!"

SOME INITIAL REFLECTIONS

Let us stop here for a moment, step back, and consider the situation. Don Clark is in a quandary. He feels that he is being pulled in several different directions, and there is little question that he is bothered by what is happening. Has Don done anything wrong? Or is he simply the victim of "insane" circumstances? We feel uncomfortable about the situation. To begin to understand why we are uneasy, it might be useful at this point to put ourselves in the places of several of the central characters.

First, let's try thinking about how the Disciple, Luthor, would feel if he found out that Don has deliberately misled him and is trying to force his way into the group for "impure" reasons. How would *you* feel if you discovered that the person who asks to attend church services with you on the pretense of being interested in joining is really doing a sociological study and has absolutely no interest—other than a detached, scientific one—in you, your church, or your feelings? How would you feel if one of the pledges in your sorority or fraternity were there solely to study the initiation process? Don, of course, has gone farther than expressing some interest in becoming a Necron. He has gained access to the most guarded secrets of the cult by pretending to be a true Disciple. He has himself taken an oath of secrecy and loyalty, which he has already broken by sharing his initial "scientific findings" with the class, and he may ultimately broadcast the results to a wider audience in a publication. How would you feel if you were Luthor and knew what you now know?

Now let's take a different perspective. How do you think Dr. Kincaid feels about what is going on? From the case narrative, we get the sense that he is extremely pleased with both the nature of the research and the findings that Don is producing. We do not know how much Don told him about his means of entering the "inner sanctum" of the group. Surely Dr. Kincaid must have asked that question if Don didn't report it, because assessing the method of a study is so essential. If he does know and has therefore tacitly condoned it, has he done anything wrong? Perhaps Dr. Kincaid, himself the veteran of several participant observation studies, doesn't share our discomfort. Nevertheless, we should ask whether Dr. Kincaid has been negligent in his duty as a faculty member by failing to discuss potential ethical problems with his students. Are there any standards of professional ethics by which we can assess Professor Kincaid's conduct as a sociologist overseeing the work of a student?

What about the University? If some difficulty results from the study, how would the University community feel about it? Does Don have any special responsibility to those who are not directly the subjects of his work? How would you feel if you were a member of Don's seminar class? Would you simply be interested in the Necrons, or would you be concerned about the ethics of the study?

Then there is Don's relationship with Jenny. The study has already created something of a barrier in their relationship, not just because of the time the study has required, but because it has interfered with their communication. Don seems unable to talk with Jenny about what has been happening to him. More importantly, perhaps, Don seems concerned about the Ritual-of-One. Should he consider it a neutral act committed in the name of science, or will it constitute a breach of trust with Jenny? What would Jenny think if she knew? Does she have a right to know?

Finally, Don is concerned about his own feelings. What is Don's responsibility to himself? On the one hand, he is clearly excited—even exhilarated—by his breakthrough into a world very different from his own. He is also frightened because he has set in motion forces that he isn't sure he can control. He has made his way into a group that has a different way of looking at the world, and even if he is not aware of it, he has opened himself to the risk that his new "teachers" may actually convert him. At least some change of his own values is possible, or his psyche may in some way be altered. Currently, he faces an initiation ceremony which he views as distasteful at best, one that may even constitute a violation of his own moral code. He certainly risks feeling guilty. His personal concerns may range from worrying about his grade point average because of the neglect of other courses to fear of possible physical harm should the Necrons discover that he is an impostor.

We ask you to begin your thinking about Don and his study by looking at your *feelings* about it. As you place yourself in the position of the several characters, you may have several reactions. You may admire Don's ingenuity or you may feel uncomfortable. You may feel confused or upset about the motives behind the project or even angry at the researcher. In any event, we hope that you *feel* something, because we believe that being able to feel, and being able to recognize one's feelings, is an essential part of the moral life. The very notion of conscience has as one of its components an emotional reaction to wrongdoing. Our feelings about moral issues are a manifestation of the values we have internalized. My feelings say a lot about the kind of person I am, morally and psychologically. Our feelings may make us aware of moral issues, and we think that emotion is also important in ethical analysis. But we must always probe more deeply to be sure that our immediate intuitive response really makes sense in some larger ethical framework.

Throughout this book, we ask you to look at other cases and your responses to them. We hope they are interesting enough to get you really involved with the characters. Take these cases and play with them. Identify with the investigator and put yourself in the place of others who might be affected. Observe the similarities that run through them, think about how you would feel if you were in the positions of the characters, and ask yourself how you would respond if you were a member of a committee asked to consider the appropriateness of these projects. We will not be offering authoritative solutions, and we may leave you with more questions than answers. Our most important aim is for *you* to think about these issues so that you can formulate a balanced position on the basis of which you can *act* with some confidence even as you search for yet more understanding. A study of ethics should not end in paralysis, but with a resolve to do the best we can with the insight we can achieve at the time.

For several reasons, we have chosen to present composite cases rather than present some of the well-known, hotly debated studies. One reason for not using real cases is that we could evoke factual arguments. The ethical discussion could bog down as people debated whether the researcher actually did what was alleged. Moreover, using real cases could involve us inappropriately in personalities. It is appropriate for colleagues and the public to judge the ethical quality of a researcher's work, but this book is not the proper forum.

Fictitious cases have other virtues. They make it easier for students and instructors to use their imaginations, altering the "facts" or filling in the details with several alternative scenarios and noting the difference those changes would make in the assessment. They also allow us to highlight certain issues, perhaps by exaggeration, without worrying about fairness to a real researcher.

This last point leads to a disclaimer. We do not suggest that our cases are representative of current research. We are not implying that all or even most researchers are engaged in ethically questionable activity. To the contrary, we feel that most research is conducted in a manner that few of us would find objectionable. We do attempt to illustrate a range of type and seriousness of ethical problems that researchers may face.

The cases are not necessarily typical, and some may feel that they are exaggerated. However, we do not feel that they are unrealistic. We have known social or behavioral scientists who are as naive or as cavalier or as committed to the cause of scientific truth or public benefit *at any cost* as the characters whom we present. There are Professor Kincaids who don't spend much time overseeing student projects with careful attention to ethical issues, either because they don't want to spend the time or because they honestly think that students can learn best from their mistakes. There are well-intentioned, compassionate researchers who simply neglect to ask what effects their presence and departure will have on the population they are studying. There are some who are so convinced that what they are doing will help people that they forget to ask about the rights of people to accept or reject help. And there are skilled researchers who are willing to leave ethics to someone else—to their employer, or senior researcher, or even their institution's human subjects committee.

We are asking you, then, to think with us about some very real issues. Later chapters will examine ethics in the context of different kinds of research. Before we can go any further, however, we must look at some fundamental issues, beginning with the most basic question, "What is ethics?"

II

WHAT
IS ETHICS?

2

Some Basic Ideas in Ethical Theory

In the introduction, we noted that this book is about applied ethics. Before applying ethical theory to our chosen subject, we must discuss the nature of ethics more generally. We all know what "ethics" and "morality" mean, yet we may have trouble putting our sense of these words into clear definitions. A standard dictionary definition of ethics as "a set of moral principles of values" does not satisfy us because we then ask, "what are *moral* principles or values?" If we look up "moral" in a dictionary, we will find ourselves referred to other words like "right" and "good."

WHAT IS MORALITY?

Imagine trying to explain the idea of morality to someone with no notion of such a concept. You would find it an almost impossible task, since you would have to use other words that are equally difficult to define. More importantly, we simply don't understand abstract concepts by hearing words defined.

Developmental psychologists have shown how children's capacity to comprehend abstract concepts and engage in abstract reasoning develops as they mature. A number of these researchers have been studying the moral development of children, and some of the things they have described as the early stage of it don't look much like what we would call "morality" at all.[1] Children begin to learn the meaning of "right" and "wrong" simply in terms of punishment and reward. Instructions from

---

[1]Jean Piaget (*The Moral Judgment of the Child,* trans. Marjorie Gabain [1932; reprint, New York: Free Press, 1965]) and Lawrence Kohlberg ("The Cognitive-Development Approach to Moral Education," *Phi Delta Kappan* 56 [June 1975]: 670-77) are the formative scholars in this research. Kohlberg's theory distinguishes six stages of moral development, moving from an egocentric through a societal to a universal perspective.

parents not to touch the hot stove or the vase on the hall table are perceived as basically no different from admonitions not to tell lies. All are "no-no's" that may bring down the wrath of parents. Lessons on eating with a fork and sharing with a sister or brother are perceived as being essentially in the same category. A young child may perceive the praise achieved for a good grade in spelling as no different from the praise received for telling the truth when it hurts. As we grow, we develop a more abstract concept of morality as something different from prudence (don't touch the hot stove) or etiquette (eat with your fork) or legal requirement (don't drive through a red light).

Most people develop a sense that there are some claims that go beyond simple reward and punishment and are even independent of the opinions of other people. Sometimes we conclude that an activity isn't right even if "everybody's doing it" and even if we are taunted for not "going along with the crowd." When we *do* look to others for approval, we recognize that there is a difference between approval of our manners or accomplishments and *moral* approval of our actions and intentions. It is not that moral approval is necessarily stronger or more intense, because in many cases it clearly is not. The hero's welcome of a Charles Lindbergh or John Glenn after their historic flights is certainly a "stronger" approval by any measure of public opinion than the commendation that I may receive for a simple kindness toward an invalid neighbor across the street. But I receive approval for a *morally* good act. The hero's welcome often acknowledges other kinds of values. The difference is a difference in kind, and we recognize that moral claims and moral approval are in some ways "superior." For example, we may value good grades and business success and good common sense, but ideally we don't think people should cheat in order to achieve success in their ventures; and we may commend someone *morally* for ignoring those prudential, commonsense warnings about fire when trying to save someone from a burning building.

THE LANGUAGE OF MORALITY:
VALUE AND OBLIGATION

Even if we cannot explain the concept of morality with precision, we know that the sphere of morality is somehow set apart from other dimensions of our lives and we can distinguish between moral and nonmoral uses of some of our most common words. Some are *value* words like "good." When a history professor returns a paper with the comment "Good paper—A + ," we recognize that "good" in this context is a different kind of good than when we describe the altruistic act of a saintly individual.

Another kind of moral language is the language of *obligation,* words like "should" and "ought" and "right" and "duty." The nature and tone of these words is quite different from "value" words. It may be "good" to do our "duty," but clearly we are not *obligated* to do every "good" act that is thinkable. Just as value words may be used in both moral and nonmoral statements, so too with words of obligation. Telling my children that they *should* be in bed by ten o'clock or instructing a class that papers *ought* to be turned in on Thursday are not statements of moral obligation. Choosing the *right* word or getting the *right* answer to a math problem are different uses of "right" than "morally right."

This book is concerned with *moral* value and *moral* obligation. But nonmoral values and obligations sometimes become moral concerns when they affect the lives of other people.

DIVERSITY IS THE NAME OF THE GAME

Although there may be some common elements, people experience moral obligation and moral value differently. If there is one thing that all students of ethics will agree about, it is that disagreement is at least as common as agreement. Diversity pervades the entire landscape of moral discussion. Differences exist about the definitions of basic terms, about specific moral norms, about the seriousness of morality, and about the fundamental sources of morality.

As we discuss morality with others, the first difference we may note is that we don't even use basic terminology in the same way. For example, the words "ethics" and "morality" are so common that you may never have thought about the similarities and differences in their meaning. But if you ask people the difference between the two, you hear an amazing variety of answers. Some people say that morality refers to social norms, the mores of a particular society or subculture, whereas ethics has to do with more universal norms. Think for a moment about the application of this definition in describing Don's experience with the Necrons. Using this definition, both the culture from which Don comes and the culture created by the Necrons have their own morality. Ethics, then, would embody more universal standards by which both might be judged.

Somebody else may say that morality is personal and internal, whereas ethics is more external. With this usage, Don might talk about his own inner turmoil concerning his current moral dilemma. This would be contrasted with the ethical expectations of others.

Still others define morality as the general patterns of behavior expected of everybody and ethics as specialized requirements of a particular profession, such as business ethics, medical ethics, or other professional codes. From this perspective, we would talk about Don's general *moral* behavior but about the *ethics* of his research, employing in the latter assessment the standards adopted by professional groups regarding the conduct of research.

For some the difference is more in connotations of the words than any clear definition. "Immoral" seems somehow harsher and more judgmental than the word "unethical." Then there is a common usage that identifies "morality" with sexual norms. If we read in the newspaper that someone has been arrested on a "morals" charge, we know immediately that some sexual offense is involved.

Yet another way to distinguish between these terms is one employed by ethicists. Ethicists often use the term "morality" to refer to the daily conduct of the moral life. "Ethics" would then refer to the process of thinking about morality at arm's length, theorizing about morality rather than making a concrete decision to act right now. In this sense, *Don* is engaged in *moral* decision-making. He decides and acts. *We* are involved in *ethics* as we discuss Don's case in a classroom or sit at home in an easy chair thinking about the issues raised by his study. Thoughtful reflection on the ethical level may help us make better decisions at the moral level, but it is a step removed from it.

Whether or not we adopt the ethicist's convention in the use of language, it is important to note the differences in these two levels—action and reflection. But we must also be aware of their interaction. It is, after all, moral experience that provides the subject for ethical reflection and theory, and the purpose of ethical theory is ultimately to aid decision making.

Words, of course, don't mean anything in themselves; they have meaning only because people give them meaning. But we can't individually just decide to use words in any way we want; we must recognize the conventions of our language in order to communicate with others. In fact, the use of the words "ethics" and "morality" is far from consistent, and they are often used interchangeably. We do not propose a "proper" usage, but you should be aware of the diversity of usage and the issues reflected in that diversity.

Another noteworthy difference among people is in their moral seriousness. Some people have internalized strong emotional responses to moral situations and would endure a great deal of emotional or physical pain rather than violate their "conscience." Some are much more casual about morality, viewing it as something worthy of attention but not taking it too seriously. Others even appear to pride themselves on their contempt for morality. Finally, some would categorize "morality" along with "God" as a figment of the human imagination, to be outgrown along with the belief in fairies, dragons, and sea monsters. They may perceive "morality" only as a means that some people use to control others. It will become obvious as you progress through this book that we consider moral questions serious business. It is not our purpose to make you more morally serious; that is the task of moral education, not ethical analysis. But you should know that we believe that morality is important, and we can *hope* that our readers will share our sense of urgency about ethics in research.

But equally serious and sincere individuals will differ in their views about what actions are right and wrong. The Necrons are a dramatic example of this diversity, since many of their values are exactly opposite to the values of "mainstream" America. The evidence of pluralism is all around us, as, for example, "pro choice" forces square off against the "right to life" faction and the exponents of traditional sexual norms take issue with those who support more modern sexual freedom. We can expect the same diversity when it comes to thinking about research ethics. Readers will respond differently to the questions raised by Don's study of the Necrons. Our task is not to resolve these differences, but to illuminate the issues underlying many of these diverse opinions. We want you to engage in careful thought, whether you agree with our conclusions or not.

Disagreements about morality or ethics go beyond differences in moral norms. People also disagree about where morality comes from and what makes right acts right and good acts good. Some people believe that morality is rooted in a religious tradition; morality is understood as ultimately based in the nature or will of a deity who is the source of both moral norms and the sanctions that enforce them. A secularized variation defines the justification for a moral claim as that which would be approved by an "ideal observer" who possesses some of the qualities attributed to a deity, the qualities of objectivity or impartiality and complete knowledge (omniscience).[2] For others, morality is grounded in human nature itself, discovered rationally or intuitively in individual or social experience. In one such view, the basic moral datum is that people are by nature egoistic; their only concern is for themselves. Thus ethics must begin with this assumption, though it may be possible to demonstrate that self-interest requires a commitment to the welfare of others, in order to promote a reciprocity that will benefit oneself. Others

---

[2]See the discussion of the Ideal Observer theory in John Hospers, *Human Conduct: An Introduction to the Problems of Ethics* (New York: Harcourt, Brace & World, 1961) 546-51.

would insist that human beings are basically rational and social and thus by nature recognize obligations toward others.

It is worth noting that differences of opinion about the *source* of morality do not necessarily lead to disagreements about what acts are right and wrong. The theologian who begins with God and the philosopher who begins with reason may come to precisely the same conclusion in judging whether a particular act is right or good. Likewise, people who begin with the same philosophical or theological assumptions may come to widely divergent conclusions about whether a particular act is right.

STYLES OF ETHICS

Diversity in ethics is nothing new. It has been the name of the game throughout the long and illustrious history of Western philosophical and religious thought. Even a superficial introduction to the most prominent theories is beyond our scope, and we should refer students to an introductory ethics text for that important study.[3] Instead we want to comment on some different styles of ethics. By "style" we mean the mood and tone and manner with which a person approaches the moral life. The different styles that we will describe represent different approaches at the practical level in the daily moral lives of real individuals, many of whom have never studied theoretical ethics at all and who may not even have thought very consciously about why they believe and act as they

---

[3]Several books in applied ethics begin with excellent summaries of some of the classical ethical theories. Two examples are Tom L. Beauchamp and Norman Bowie, eds., *Ethical Theory and Business,* 2nd ed. (Englewood Cliffs NJ: Prentice-Hall, 1983) 1, and Ronald Munson, *Intervention and Reflection: Basic Issues in Medical Ethics,* 2nd ed. (Belmont CA: Wadsworth, 1983) Introduction. For a more comprehensive introduction to ethical theory, we recommend William K. Frankena, *Ethics,* 2nd ed. (Englewood Cliffs NJ: Prentice-Hall, 1973); Tom L. Beauchamp, *Philosophical Ethics: An Introduction to Moral Philosophy* (New York: McGraw-Hill, 1982); Paul W. Taylor, *Principles of Ethics: An Introduction* (Belmont CA: Wadsworth, 1975); and Robert C. Solomon, *Ethics: A Brief Introduction* (New York: McGraw-Hill, 1984). Another of Solomon's books, an anthology, presents a good concise overview of ethical theory in the introductory chapter; see Robert C. Solomon, *Morality and the Good Life: An Introduction to Ethics through Classical Sources,* (New York: McGraw-Hill, 1984). Two books that provide an introduction to the long history of Christian ethics are Edward LeRoy Long, Jr., *A Survey of Christian Ethics* (New York: Oxford University Press, 1967) and his *A Survey of Recent Christian Ethics* (New York: Oxford University Press, 1982). For an introduction to Jewish ethics, we recommend M. M. Kellner, ed., *Contemporary Jewish Ethics* (New York: Sanhedrin Press, 1978) and Marvin Fox, ed., *Modern Jewish Ethics* (Columbus OH: Ohio State University Press, 1975).

do. The styles are also found at the intellectual level in different types of ethical theories.[4]

Rule Morality

Some people approach morality as a set of rules to be followed. Rules may be simple and straightforward or complex. There may be a series of rules with exceptions specified for each rule, that is, rules for when the rules apply or which rules apply when two rules come into conflict. The language of this kind of ethic is often more the language of obligation—right, wrong, duty, and ought—rather than the language of value.

To illustrate, a rule ethic might tell Don never to lie, or it might spell out exceptions, rules for breaking the rule not to lie. Perhaps he should lie only if the person with whom he is speaking has already lied to him; perhaps he can lie if the safety of another person or his country requires it, and so on.

Similar in approach but somewhat different in language is a morality based on "human rights." A proponent might contend that lying to research subjects violates their rights. This shifts the focus from the obligations of the actor and focuses on the claims of the one affected by an action. But the mood may be similar.

Rigidity and legalism may infect the morality of a rule-oriented person. It frequently has. For example, at various times and places the Christian and Jewish religious traditions have become inflexible and le-

---

[4]Describing moral practice or ethical systems in terms of the mind-set that they represent is fairly common. H. Richard Niebuhr, *The Responsible Self* (New York: Harper & Row, 1963) described certain images that portray the outlook of various thinkers. His categories of "man-the-citizen" and "man-the-maker" embody both a quality or style and an indication of the underlying assumptions about the nature of moral claims. The first focuses on "moral duty" or "moral obligation," reminding us of the way in which a citizen may define responsibility as the duty to obey the laws of his nation. This kind of ethic is frequently called "deontological," based on the Greek word for "duty." The second approach, "man-the-maker," is more concerned with the consequences of action and the ends or goals that we try to achieve in our action. This type of ethic is called "teleological," derived from the Greek word "end," in the sense of "purpose." Niebuhr's own approach he called "man-the-answerer," playing on the root "response" in the origin of the word "responsibility." For him, ethics is relational because moral agents are continually responding to one another. Critics debate about whether his approach is really distinctive or merely a variation of a teleological ethic. We acknowledge our intellectual debt to Niebuhr. The categories that we describe in the text cut the same ethical "pie" in a somewhat different way.

galistic. Such an approach can lead to "minimalism,"[5] that is, doing precisely what the rules require but no more. And such an approach can lead to a kind of self-righteousness on the part of someone who feels that he lives by all the rules and is therefore morally superior to others who don't. It was such an attitude that Mark Twain chided in saying of someone that he was a "good man, in the worst sense of that word." But not all people who understand morality primarily or exclusively as living by the rules demonstrate these characteristics, and the approach has much to commend it. There is probably something of this attitude in all of us.

Saying that someone approaches morality as a set of rules says nothing, of course, about where people get their rules. For some, the rules come from the outside, given by God or created by society or some great leader. Others think the rules are embedded deep within human nature and are discovered through introspection or known intuitively.[6] Still others believe that people adopt rules based on their observation of human experience, noting what works and what doesn't. We may see the bad results of certain behavior and decide to adopt rules prohibiting such acts as lying, stealing, or killing. Such rules seem necessary so people can live together harmoniously.[7] The rules people adopt and their reasons for adopting them may be worlds apart, but a common mood or spirit makes rule approaches to morality similar.

---

[5] William F. May uses this term unfavorably in describing an approach to responsibility that only seeks to satisfy minimal obligations rather than being genuinely committed to promoting the welfare of others. See "Code, Covenant, Contract, or Philanthropy," *Hastings Center Report* 5 (December 1975): 29-38.

[6] The eighteenth-century German philosopher Immanuel Kant believed that all statements of moral obligation were rationally derived from a single principle, which he called the Categorical Imperative. See *The Groundwork of the Metaphysics of Morals,* 3d ed., trans. H. J. Paton (New York: Harper & Row, 1964). By contrast, the British philosopher W. D. Ross believed that we recognize intuitively a number of rules, each of which represents a prima facie duty. When prima facie duties conflict, our actual duty depends on which of our prima facie duties is most compelling in those circumstances. See W. D. Ross, *The Right and the Good* (Oxford: Oxford University Press, 1930).

[7] A well-known philosophical tradition, known as "rule utilitarianism," is an example. Like other utilitarians, they hold that it is the consequences of actions that determine their morality, but they believe that we must adopt *rules* that will, if followed, produce good consequences, rather than assessing the probable consequences of a particular action. Because the ultimate justification for the rules is a judgment about consequences or "ends," rule utilitarianism is a teleological ethic. But because their decision-making process is governed by rules, rule utilitarians in their daily lives may resemble some "deontologists" more than they resemble other utilitarians.

Visceral Morality

Another approach rejects all rules and relies on a more immediate moral sense, a kind of visceral response to a situation. We might inelegantly call this a "gut-level" morality, meaning that people see a situation and simply respond intuitively and perhaps emotionally to it. Don might be advised by someone espousing such a view to " do what feels right to you." Some may describe their experience as responding to the voice of conscience, others as "doing my own thing," and someone else as listening for the command of God.

At its worst such an approach can consist of a "knee-jerk" reaction, reinforcing all our worst prejudices and predispositions and preventing us from exercising the best judgments of which we are capable in our more rational moments. Nevertheless, there can be a quality in this style of life that deserves more credit than its critics usually give it. Such an approach to morality can reflect an internalized moral seriousness in which clear moral insight arises out of a reservoir of moral wisdom.[8] But most of us should be wary of relying too easily on our immediate emotional responses to moral situations, because too often they are not our best judgments, especially in complex situations.

The Moral Cultivation of the Self

Yet another way of living the moral life is by a conscious cultivation of those qualities that characterize the "good" life in the moral sense. Among these qualities may be harmony and balance, peace and tranquility. For some, the style means less attention to the agonies of making decisions in complex situations and more concern for being "fulfilled" as a person. Much of contemporary popular psychology encourages this sort of ethic, without necessarily calling it ethics, but this kind of outlook has a long history. Its roots can be traced back to such great figures as Aristotle in ancient Greece, and examples can be found in various times and places in the world's great religions. The qualities to be cultivated vary in different traditions, but the common characteristic is the centrality of the person, the agent of morality, rather than the person's actions. In such an ethic, it would be less important to discuss what Don did among the Necrons than to know the kind of person he was, to understand his moral character.

---

[8]James M. Gustafson speaks of some individuals as "moral virtuosos," borrowing a phrase from Max Weber about "religious virtuosos." Gustafson means that some people seem gifted in moral insight as others seem born with a gift for music.

Calculation of Consequences

Another style emphasizes a more rational process of decision making involving a prediction of the probable outcomes of alternative courses of action and an assessment of these outcomes in accordance with some predetermined standards. The language of such a morality is more the language of moral value—good and bad; "right" and "duty" are secondary terms arising from the obligation to promote moral value.

Following this approach, Don would project what is likely to happen to him and to others if he were to infiltrate the Necrons, take an oath under false pretenses, or participate in the Ritual-of-One. He would choose between several alternative courses of action by deciding which will produce the best consequences.

The classic example of such an approach is utilitarianism, which has as its standard the production of the "greatest good [often defined as pleasure or happiness] for the greatest number."[9] Other similar theories might adopt different standards. They might tell us to produce the most benefit for ourselves, our race or religion, our nation, or some other group. The difference between this rational process of projecting and evaluating consequences and the equally rational process of looking for the appropriate rule to follow should be obvious. The two approaches may well arrive at the same conclusion in a given case, but the way of getting there and the personal style of the moral agent in each case is different.

Relational Ethics

Finally, there is a style of ethic in which the key element is relationships. Relational ethics makes consideration of interactions within a social network the focus of ethical thought. Both in the daily life of the practitioner and in its theoretical exposition by an ethicist, this type of ethic looks at the pattern of human relationships and asks what kind of response is appropriate in the context of these relations. If Don were to adopt such an approach as his style, he would be more concerned to understand the nature and implications of the relationships he has with

---

[9]Projecting future consequences of action is difficult enough. Knowing what will make other people happy is even harder. Hence some modern utilitarians have adopted the standard of maximizing people's *preferences* rather than their pleasure. This modification of utilitarianism has substantial practical advantages, making it easy to translate the theory into political and economic categories. But it also changes the nature of utilitarianism significantly. What will make people happy is no longer the question. The question is what they *think* will make them happy. The ethical theory thus shifts from concern for the well-being of others to respect for their autonomy, however mistaken their judgments may be.

various people—the Necrons, Jenny, his fellow students, his professors, and so on—and to think about his action as part of the continuing give and take of human interaction, as part of a system that is not static because of the ongoing actions and reactions of its members.[10]

Relational considerations will be prominent throughout this book. Indeed, we feel that each style described can shed light on our moral experience and help us make judgments about right and wrong, good and bad. In the next chapter, we will illustrate more elaborately how these diverse styles of ethics actually work. But we need to introduce a few more concepts first.

NORMATIVE AND DESCRIPTIVE ETHICS

People have always wanted to know what they ought to do, what is right and wrong, good and bad. This concern is what gave rise to the theories and styles of ethics we have been describing. Perhaps it is the sense of morality, more than anything else, that distinguishes us from "lower" animals. People have always been fascinated by differences in customs, mores, and moralities. As you recall, Don Clark's research immersed him in the life of the Necrons. He will describe and analyze it in a senior paper. Part of his account of the Necrons' way of life will surely be their "value system," their ethic. As a budding young sociologist, Don must learn to describe that system accurately, coherently, and objectively. In that capacity, he is engaged in *descriptive* ethics, that is, he is describing someone's approach to morality, without passing any moral judgment upon it.

But at the very time that he is engaged in understanding and describing the Necron ethic, his own ethic is functioning *normatively* for him. He is having to ask himself, "what *ought* I to do in this situation—what norms *should* guide *my* conduct?"

It is especially important for those engaged in social research to be conscious of the distinction between normative and descriptive ethics. Failure to maintain this awareness may lead to bad science and bad morality. Poor science may result if researchers allow their own moral views to color their description of the ethical systems of their subjects. Likewise, becoming too engrossed in descriptive ethics may undermine the

---

[10]H. Richard Niebuhr was a leading exponent of a relational approach to ethics. He introduced the term "fitting" into the vocabulary of morality. For him, the basic moral question is what action is "appropriate" in the context of these particular relationships. Another leading representative is James M. Gustafson. A concise example of the approach can be found in the first chapter of Gustafson's book *Can Ethics Be Christian?* (Chicago: University of Chicago Press, 1975).

researcher's own commitment to high moral standards, including the concern for ethics in the research process itself.

ETHICAL RELATIVISM

Don could not have been a sociology student long without noticing the variety of "moral codes" among the many populations studied by sociologists. He undoubtedly learned that an adequate description of a cultural system includes a description of a group's morality, and the morality of one group may at least appear to be in fundamental conflict with that of another.[11] As he reads sociological and anthropological accounts of different societies and cultures, he may have observed these differences with considerable scientific curiosity. But at some time he probably compared the morality of a particular group with his own sense of morality, and he has become painfully aware of differences through his association with the Necrons. At some point he must have asked himself, "Why do I think my morality is any better than theirs? Are both systems of morality equally valid?" He is beginning to grapple with the problem of ethical relativity.

The term "ethical relativism" points to the fact that what a person thinks is right and wrong is relative to the social group to which he or she belongs. Groups and even individuals do differ in their values and attitudes. But that is merely an observation about factual matters—it is a matter of *descriptive* ethics. Can we say anything normatively about these different "moralities"? Is it possible to say that one system of morality is "better" than another, that one is more "moral" than another? Can we ever make the judgment that the action of someone from a different culture is wrong, no matter what that person may think about it?

At one extreme is a position that we might call "normative ethical relativism," which would hold that whatever a society (or, in our age of pluralism, some would even say whatever any individual) sincerely believes to be right is indeed right for that society or individual. At the opposite extreme are those who recognize that societies and individuals have different moral systems, but deny that the differences in perspec-

---

[11] We say "appear" to be in fundamental conflict because there have been some efforts to show that ultimately all societies have the same fundamental values; different specific rules, it is argued, arise because of different historical or social contexts. Murder, for example, may be condemned by all societies, but societies will differ in how they define which killing constitutes "murder." Capital punishment for certain "criminals" may not be considered murder by one society; killing "outsiders" may not constitute murder for another. But even if there are some fundamental norms common to all societies, their application at the level of daily conduct certainly varies widely across cultural boundaries.

tive make any difference normatively. There *is* a right and wrong, and right is right no matter what anybody thinks about it.

Both views have some appeal. On the one hand, with our growing awareness of the diversity of human experience and a new attitude of tolerance for the pluralism that we see on every hand, we find real virtue in the increased willingness to respect the views of others even if we personally do not accept them as our own. On the other hand, we recognize that there are limits to our tolerance, and if we ask ourselves seriously what we believe about the morality of another person, we may discover that we are really "respecting their right to be wrong," rather than accepting the legitimacy of their moral views.

Let's imagine that Luthor, as a leader of the Necrons, presides over and actually wields the knife in a ritual sacrifice of one of the Disciples. The Disciple is a true volunteer who believes that he will achieve instant immortality and union with the One and that the ritual will be an occasion for a mystical experience of the highest order for all who participate in the ceremony. Or suppose that Luthor takes the life of a young child in the group with the sincere belief that it was commanded by the One to spare the child the tribulation and evil of this world. Are we prepared to accept either of these actions as morally legitimate, no matter how sincere the beliefs that motivate them?

The most tolerant among us may *excuse* Luthor because of the sincerity of his motivation, but that is different from *approving* his action. We may decide that he is sick and not responsible, or sincerely misguided and forgive his error, but almost all of us will say that his action is wrong. At least in extreme cases, we may make similar judgments in examining other societies perhaps very different from our own. Most of us are probably not as comfortable with ethical relativism as we might have thought we were before we stopped to realize the full implications. We must finally live as if we believe that there is right and wrong.[12]

---

[12]Robert Solomon quotes an interesting observation by the great French anthropologist Claude Lévi-Strauss: "When I witness certain decisions or modes of behavior in my own society, I am filled with indignation and disgust, whereas if I observe similar behavior in a so-called primitive society, I make no attempt at a value judgment. I try to understand it." Solomon then concludes, "It is important to appreciate the variety of values and the tension between various ethics, but we also have to live and live well. Realizing the relativity of ethics [between societies] does not undermine but underscores the need for ethics. Ethics is like anthropology in its attempt to appreciate the *context* of our values; it differs in the fact that we accept those values as our own, indeed, cannot even imagine ourselves without them." Solomon, *Morality and the Good Life,* 6.

However, rejecting ethical relativism as an ethical theory does not require endorsing a rigid ethical absolutism. Because morality is essentially social in nature, the social context in which it occurs does make a difference in what is morally proper in that context. The traditional Eskimo practice of leaving the elderly to die alone and heroically in the cold might be justified where scarcity makes society's sheer survival a daily concern; a similar neglect in our affluent society would be unconscionable.

The culturally conditioned expectations and sensitivities of a group make a difference in our moral evaluation of the group's conduct. Some acts may be *inherently* wrong or bad, but clearly there are many other things that are wrong or bad *because they have been so defined* by a group. There is no inherent rightness or wrongness regarding traffic regulations—speed limits or driving on the right or left. But speeding down a crowded highway on the left side of the road in the United States is a moral wrong, not simply a legal infraction, because within our system such a violation of traffic conventions endangers the lives of others. The same can be said of countless other social rules.

ETIQUETTE AND ETHICS

The norms of behavior that Don is observing among the Necrons are both moral and nonmoral. Some expectations that the group imposes upon its members would be considered moral demands by the group. Violations would bring harsh denunciations, perhaps even expulsion from the group—or worse. Revealing the secrets of the group would probably be considered a moral offense. But there are probably some practices that are more a matter of etiquette than morality. In the Necrons' inverted world, perhaps eating with a fork instead of one's hands might be bad manners.

We pointed to the difference between manners and morals in our earlier discussion of the definition of ethics. Having acknowledged the distinction, we would now warn against drawing the line between them too distinctly. Manners are devised at least in part to enhance the smooth operation of interpersonal relationships. They oil the social machinery to minimize interpersonal conflict, and that is not something of indifference to morality. Rules of etiquette are largely arbitrary, not dictated by some inherent rightness or wrongness, and we do not usually feel called upon to pass moral judgments about a system of etiquette. But within a system of etiquette, adherence to norms may sometimes take on a moral dimension, depending on the extent to which "bad manners" results in harm to others. If you believe that someone can be injured psychologically as well as physically, then you may have to ask whether rude, insulting words and deeds can cause injury that has moral significance. Do hurt feelings constitute injury? Can offensiveness result in psychological harm, and if so at what point?

Manners obviously vary considerably, not only between societies but between subcultures in a single society. The brusqueness and honesty sometimes encountered in Northern cities may be perceived by Southerners as harsh and offensive; the "politeness" of some Southerners may be perceived by visitors from the North as superficial, insincere, and dishonest. Although for the most part these are merely regional differences that have no moral significance, perhaps you can think of a scenario in which some harm could result from operating with the "wrong" etiquette at the "wrong" time even within "mainstream" America.

This concern for etiquette may be an especially important issue for field researchers doing participant observer studies. They need to be attuned to the "good manners" expected by the group they are studying. Failure to do so may create negative responses that impair their ability to carry on their study effectively; in some circumstances it might even result in psychological pain that could have moral overtones.

NARROW AND EXPANSIVE VIEWS OF ETHICS

Discussing etiquette brings us to a much more comprehensive question: how narrow or expansive is the territory of ethics? Our main point in the preceding discussion is that there are no neat boundaries to morality. There is no dotted line on the maps of our daily lives that separates moral values and obligations from other kinds of values and obligations. Morality is concerned with relationships between people and the rights and well-being of people. When discord and conflict are produced by the violation of social convention, whether by a thoughtless lack of common courtesy and consideration for others, or by a deliberate affront, there may be a moral dimension.

We see morality as a matter of gradation, not an all-or-none phenomenon. Some acts are morally worse than others, and morality shades off into a gray zone where the lines between law and morality, etiquette and morality and even aesthetics and morality may not be easily drawn. Our view of morality is expansive rather than restrictive, in marked contrast to the view of many ethicists who want to lay out clearly the terrain defined by morality.

Some ethicists insist that the domain of ethics is limited to genuine dilemmas, where duty is difficult to ascertain because of confusing and conflicting demands. Without some kind of conflict, so they would imply, there is nothing interesting to examine. By contrast, we think it important to recognize that we are constantly conducting our lives in the moral sphere, usually without even thinking about it. We go through life making moral decisions, seldom stopping long enough to attach that label to them because our morality becomes so habitual. We respond spontaneously when we recognize that a store clerk has given us too much change, either quickly calling attention to the error and returning the excess change or pocketing the extra money with the thought that it is the store's mistake, not ours. We may not ask whether the moral principle about stealing or cheating applies. We just react. But if we do stop later and think about the excess change we pocketed, we recognize that there was a moral issue there, even if only a minor one, and we must either find a way of justifying our action or acknowledge that we have done wrong. Most of our morality consists of just such patterns of action that we recognize as part of our moral character only when we are forced for some reason to think about them. Unlike those ethicists who want to limit morality to cases of serious conflict, we think it important to examine the morality of the ordinary.

Another way of limiting morality is to focus exclusively on "right" and "wrong," that is, to think only or primarily of acts that are morally mandatory or morally prohibited, with little or no attention being paid to actions that are commendable, but not obligatory. Such an approach tends to deal mostly with prohibitions of wrong actions. Encouraging positive virtuous action may receive little attention.[13]

---

[13]Bernard Gert sets for himself an ambitious goal in *The Moral Rules: A New Rational Foundation for Morality* (New York: Harper & Row, 1970). He wants to establish such a clear and unambiguous understanding of morality that "no one who reads this book will be able to act immorally without knowing that he is doing so" (ix). He develops a careful argument establishing ten "moral rules": don't kill, don't cause pain, don't disable, don't deprive of freedom of opportunity, don't deprive of pleasure, don't deceive, keep your promise, don't cheat, obey the law, and do your duty. Exceptions must be justified using the same rational procedure by which the rule was discovered.

Although adherence to these rules is all morality *requires,* Gert maintains morality also includes moral *ideals.* The moral ideals may encourage positive action corresponding to the negative rules: prevent killing, prevent the causing of pain, prevent disabling, and so on. Morality requires obeying the rules *all* the time; the ideals are optional. Gert appears to have established a clear limitation on the definition of moral *duty,* a basic morality, and has distinguished it from an advanced morality consisting of ideals, much as the Roman Catholic moral tradition distinguished between the basic morality of Natural Law and the counsels of perfection. However, the clarity that he hoped to achieve in his basic morality is undermined by his tenth rule, "Do your duty." Gert does not intend the rule to become all-encompassing, but it introduces a high degree of uncertainty. Knowing clearly the duties of even a single role is often difficult; weighing the conflicting responsibilities of multiple roles is even more problematic. Gert's goal of making it impossible to act immorally without knowing it may be laudable but unrealistic.

Our view is that morality is pervasive and comprehensive, comprised not only of prohibitions but also those affirmative good deeds that benefit others, and shading almost imperceptibly into the realm of the clearly nonmoral. Moreover, the theoretical study of morality—ethics in the technical sense described above—is as extensive as morality itself, since all the data of moral experience are appropriate data for ethical examination. Many would interpret the open-endedness that we propose as worse than merely fuzzy; they would characterize it as counterproductive. They might fear that it will diminish moral seriousness by diffusing our sense of responsibility. It is our conviction, however, that life simply does not come in neat, discrete packages, but must be seen as a whole. The analytic distinction between ethics and etiquette—and between the moral and the nonmoral generally—is important as a tool for thought, but real life is often much less clear-cut.

So far, we have introduced some of the issues in ethical theory that may help us in our task of applied ethics. In the next chapter, we will present another case and use it to develop further some of the key concepts from ethical theory.

3

Research by Correspondence: Using a Case to Describe Ethical Theory

I n the preceding chapter, we introduced some key ethical concepts. As you read the following case, keep those categories in mind and think especially about how different people with their different styles of ethics might look at it.

THE "LONELY HEARTS" STUDY

November 20, 1985

Dear Montana Rangeman:

Do you believe in fate? In something that's just meant to be? When I read your ad in the *National Globe,* my heart started beating faster and I had that old feeling of butterflies in my stomach. Why, I felt just like a girl all over again!

I, too, am lonely. I've been a widow for a few years now, and with the Good Lord's help, it's probably time to start looking for new friends. I was married for 23 years and I'm that kind of one-man woman you want to correspond with.

I am in my forties (a lady is allowed a little discretion here, ha! ha!) and look much younger. My husband's estate has left me independent and all the children are married.

I like animals and all kinds of outdoor things. I belong to a square-dance group here, although I haven't really done much since Larry, my husband, passed on.

I have enclosed a picture, like your ad requested. I hope you'll write to me. Please tell me all about yourself, what you do, and about your *background.* But mostly, tell me why you chose just this time to publish *that* ad and how you *feel* about all the mail you must be receiving.

Now, do write soon. It's not nice to keep a lady waiting.

Expectantly yours,
Alma Mae Perry

Linda Princole, assistant professor of psychology at Riverbend College, read the letter once more before she tucked it into a matching lavender envelope. She rummaged in a shoe box on a nearby bookshelf until she found a snapshot of a middle-aged woman to enclose in the envelope. She followed the instructions that the tabloid newspaper, the *National Globe,* gave for responding to personal ads, placing her dainty, feminine, lavender envelope along with the required two dollars in a business envelope and depositing it in the department's outgoing mail basket.

"Well, that's off. . . . That's the end of the 'response series,' " Linda mused to herself. It was the final personal letter—one of one hundred— to someone advertising in a "lonely-hearts" column.

Linda returned to her office and carefully stapled the "Montana Rangeman's" ad to a copy of her own letter and placed both in a coded file. She glanced briefly at the few lines of the ad:

> BIG SKIES RANCHER seeks Ms. for correspondence, friendship and possible matrimony. I own my own ranch in Montana, am 55 years old and in perfect health. I am looking for an old-fashioned one-man woman between 35 and 50. Must be a non-drinker. Please include a recent photo. Respond MCD-192.

As with the other people, she wondered how this person would feel if he were to learn who "Alma Mae Perry" really was.

Linda's glance turned toward the tall filing cabinet full of "Lonely Hearts Data," as she called the results of her study. What had begun as a rather simple project, one that would get a paper or two published in a research journal, had snowballed into an engrossing study that had won her a book contract from a well-known New York publishing house.

"And to think I started this all only because the publish-or-perish rule hit home." Linda remembered her meeting with Dr. McPhearson, the chairperson of the Psychology Department. He had told her that even though her teaching and service records were superior, the question of continuance at Riverbend would be uncertain *unless* she were able to publish something in one of the national journals. Linda had protested that all her time had been devoted to preparation for her classes, which always had an overflow of students, and to work as a volunteer feminist counselor in the Women's Center on campus. Old McPhearson hadn't batted an eyelash, but had simply quoted chapter and verse from the faculty handbook. She wondered if Alan Jacoby, who had arrived on campus the same year as Linda, had gotten the same treatment. "I'll bet the 'good ole boy' system takes care of people like Jacoby," Linda thought ruefully. He didn't publish much either, but she would bet he wasn't getting the same treatment.

Back in the fall, Linda's life had really started to pick up. All through graduate school she had purposely not dated, worried that a relationship would interfere with her career plans. But now Chet Nordstgrom, an assistant professor in the Mathematics Department, had become an important part of her life. To her surprise, Linda found that she really enjoyed spending quiet evenings with Chet. Then McPhearson had dropped his bomb, and the search for a publishing project was on.

At first Linda thought she would use her counseling clients as a ready source of data, but that proved too difficult, and she began casting for another project. The Lonely Hearts study had been a stroke of genius— or maybe it was just luck.

Linda remembered standing in line at the supermarket one evening. To pass the time while waiting, she picked up one of the tabloids often displayed around supermarket cash registers. Usually Linda ignored such junk, but a title promising a psychological profile of abstract mathematicians caught her eye. As she leafed through the newspaper, which she quickly discounted as trash, she noticed the "Find-a-Friend" column. To her amazement, here were hundreds of personal ads from people of all ages from all over the country. The advertisers were looking for friendship, companionship, and even marriage.

"Are all of these people so lonely they're willing to advertise themselves as though they're just pieces of merchandise?" Linda had thought. With growing excitement, she saw the hint of a fascinating study here. "Why don't I contact some of these people and ask them about themselves. What made them seek companionship in this way? I wonder how anybody's life could be so empty—or how they could be so shy—that they'd need the intermediary of the U.S. Mail?" Linda was so fascinated that the woman at the cash register had to shake her arm to get her attention.

"Are you all right?" the checkout woman asked, looking a little perturbed.

"Sorry," Linda replied. "I must have been dreaming. . . . " She laid the tabloid on the conveyor belt and paid for her groceries. Linda couldn't wait to get home to study the ads.

Once back at the apartment, she threw the sacks of groceries on the kitchen table and grabbed the *National Globe,* flopping into the old, overstuffed chair she had kept in her kitchen since her sophomore year of college. She read through the ads. There must have been two hundred of them. Divided by sex, the ads included descriptions of a mixture of young and old folks and referred to every kind of person and interest. She began to envision her study of the "Lonely Hearts Club," as she called the advertisements. Maybe this would interest the editors of the research journals in which she would have to publish. She began thinking about how she would draw a random sample of ads over the next few months and send each person a questionnaire and a letter explaining the nature and purpose of her study. She began thinking about the questionnaire, and she spent much of the evening refining it and beginning a letter to accompany it.

The next day she approached Professor McPhearson with her idea and a request for departmental funds to support the project. She was almost disappointed that she didn't have to talk him into liking what she was doing. He simply gave her what she asked for and requested that she report regularly on her progress with the project. Within the next week, Linda had mailed out the first wave of questionnaires. She decided how many responses she needed to collect and devised a scheme to ensure representation from all areas of the country.

Again, it was almost by accident that the shift in focus of her research had occurred. At a small dinner party with some of Chet's friends, Linda found herself describing the study and some of the data coming in. Most of the guests were from the mathematics and physics departments and found her research rather amusing. In an offhand way someone mentioned how interesting it would be to write an answer—not a real one, of course—to one of the ads. Everyone joined in the laughter as a few guests fabricated "Dear Abby" style letters and responses.

After the party, Linda was still mulling over the conversation of the evening. "You know," she said to Chet, "that really wasn't a bad idea. I mean, writing some of these people as if I were just another lonely heart. I think I just might try that as a lark." Chet really didn't know what to say, so he just grunted a reply and nothing more was said.

The next day Linda went through the discard file. From the collection of ads not used in the original study, she selected a few, advertising both for men and women, and wrote a letter to each, making up an identity built around the advertised wishes. She mailed the bundle of letters and didn't think more about it.

Within a few days she had received her first response. It was a long letter from a sixty-year-old woman living in upper New York state. She wrote that she had been very lonely since her husband's death and would do anything to leave the small town where she was living. The widow explained that her Social Security payments didn't provide enough money to travel. She said she felt stranded in the small valley where she had spent most of her life. She described her interests and told a little about her church and family. She even enclosed a recipe for chicken pot pie! She concluded her letter by saying she hoped that the nice bachelor art professor she was corresponding with would write again soon. By the end of the week Linda had received a few other letters. One man had even written twice.

Linda had been reading one of these letters as a publisher's representative came to her office door. She had invited the young man in and, without really thinking about it, she told him about the letter and her study. He seemed interested and told Linda that he would mention the study to his supervisor, who was always on the lookout for new, exciting books. "But in the meantime," he said, "let me tell you about our new introductory psychology text."

Within two days Linda had been contacted by C. Warren Mitchell, vice-president of Now Press, the parent company of the college textbook publisher whose representative had visited Linda. Mr. Mitchell explained that Now Press published many "pop" psychology and social science books and that his company might be interested in Linda's Lonely Hearts study. They would be especially interested in the second part, those "wonderful, heartfelt letters" Linda was receiving. Mr. Mitchell said he would be passing through the large city near Riverbend College in a few days and asked if they might meet. Linda was flabbergasted. What had begun as a silly little research project had just attracted the eye of one of the nation's leading "pop" psychology and sociology publishers. Linda assured Mr. Mitchell that she would gladly meet with him.

Early the next week Mr. Mitchell called Linda to make an appointment for the following day. She showed him her files and the handful of letters she had written, and Mr. Mitchell commented thoughtfully, "Linda, I think you're really sitting on something here. This is a lot more than a paper or two for the *National Psychological Review*. I've got a hunch this could be a best-seller!"

Linda didn't know how to respond. "Best-sellers just don't happen to assistant professors at small liberal arts colleges," she thought.

"Now we have a few things to think about," Mr. Mitchell continued. "First of all, you'll need many more letters and you'll have to develop a relationship with these people. . . . You know what I mean, four, five or six pairs of letters. Maybe you could even interview some of these people to see if they resemble the descriptions they gave of themselves in the letters. Well, what do you think—want a shot at it?" For the second time within just a few moments Linda found herself not knowing what to say. "By the way," Linda heard Mr. Mitchell boom, "when we publish letters and those things, we change all the names and identifying information so no one can get sore at us. Get them to write whatever you can. Yup, I've had three best-sellers in the last five years, and I've a feeling your book could make it big."

"What happens now?" Linda asked.

"Well, first you decide if you want to do it. You're shaking your head. You want to do it? Good, good. Linda, this will be a great opportunity. Next you need to write me a letter telling me exactly what you're going to do. I'll want you to write at least a hundred letters to your lonely hearts. Then if it all looks good to me, I'll have our legal guys draw up a contract."

Linda could hardly believe her ears. This was the kind of thing students in graduate school bull sessions would kick around, until someone would invariably remind them of a statistics test the following day. But here it was, and it was real: career, fame, and money. Linda assured him that the detailed letter he requested would be waiting for him when he returned to his office.

Two weeks later, true to his word, Mr. Mitchell called Linda. A contract was in the mail, he said, and he was looking forward to working with her. The book would tentatively be titled *Yours Truly, Lonely Hearts.* Linda felt excited about this turn of events. Not only was this one of the most exciting things that had ever happened to her, but she thought about how important such a book might be. "We know so very little about these people," she thought. "Now we'll know who they are and what they're like. I feel really good about doing something like this."

STYLES OF ETHICS AND THE LONELY HEARTS

Linda does not appear worried about the ethics of her research. She has been proceeding diligently and enthusiastically with her work, perhaps carried away by the excitement the project has fostered. That she does not notice any ethical concerns does not mean, of course, that there are none. Let's use her situation to continue to examine the basic components of ethical theory introduced in chapter 2 and see how some of those questions and categories may help us understand Linda and her situation. Let's look at this case study from the perspective of the five styles of ethics described earlier.

Rule Morality

First is the rule orientation to the moral life. Rules may assign duties or specify rights. Are there any rules that apply to Linda's situation? Has she broken any rules in the conduct of her research?

Her life and work have been affected by a number of rules. Some are not moral rules at all. There are institutional rules at Riverbend College governing a variety of faculty responsibilities. These rules may specify how faculty should arrange to cover absences from class. Linda is not free to take off and head out west to visit the Montana Rangeman for an interview without considering her class schedule. There are probably rules about when final examinations must be given and how soon grades must be submitted. There are rules governing promotion and tenure. Normally such rules do not involve any moral questions, though ignoring these rules to the detriment of others could become a moral issue and applying them unfairly could constitute injustice.

Other relevant rules are more clearly moral rules. One widely held moral rule is that we should not tell lies. It's a simple rule, but rule morality may be more complicated than it seems at first. Has Linda told any lies? Well, that depends. What is a lie? Does a lie consist in the inaccuracy of the statement? Or is it a lie only when the hearer is actually misled into believing something that is untrue? Can we lie by telling the truth in a misleading way? Or does the lie consist in the fact that the speaker intended to deceive, even if he or she was unsuccessful? If this case, it seems fairly clear that Linda has lied by almost any definition. She has told people with whom she corresponded things that were not true, she intended to deceive them, and apparently she has been very successful at it. Few people would argue that she has not broken a rule about lying. That does not mean, however, that she has necessarily done wrong. She might simply deny that the rule has any validity. It is more likely that she accepts the rule but maintains that her situation is an exception to the rule.

How would the rule-oriented person recognize legitimate exceptions? That might depend on how the person got the rule in the first place. If the rules have come from some authoritative source (given by some religious or secular leader, for example), then there might be no exceptions unless the exceptions were also specified by the authority. Or maybe breaking the rule against lying is necessary to fulfill the requirements of another rule that appears superior.

If rules are human creations established to give specificity to more general norms, then exceptions may be possible by appeal to the underlying norms. For example, if the reason for saying that lying is wrong is that lies violate the rights of others, exceptions might be acknowledged where it is clear that the rights of others are not violated, as when a lie is too trivial to be an offense against the rights of others or when the person lied to has no right to the truth.

The term "principle" is sometimes used in ethics to designate a more comprehensive statement of a value or obligation, with rules spelling out the implications of these principles. One principle admonishes us to avoid harming others. If the reason for not telling lies is that lying hurts people and weakens the fragile fabric of society, perhaps there are occasions when lying actually helps people and strengthens society. Clearly the way in which a person applies rules and recognizes exceptions will be influenced by the rationale behind them. But the daily practice of a rule-oriented morality centers on the rules themselves. People don't spend a lot of time worrying about the source of the rules

Rules and principles have long been an important part of ethical thought. Some appeal to rules is almost inevitable. But how legalistically are they to be used? Can rules provide all the answers to moral dilemmas, or are they guideposts as we try to wind our way through the ethical maze? Do they prescribe, or do they only illuminate the ethical terrain? Our own view is that rules are useful tools in clarifying our responsibilities. In some areas of life some rigidity may be necessary to maintain social order. But, by and large, rules should not be employed legalistically. Rules may be helpful or even adequate guides for most decisions, but there are probably exceptions to every rule. Thinking about rules may sometimes be the beginning rather than the end of the process of moral assessment.

Visceral Morality

We also described a second style of morality, which we designated as "visceral morality." Some people believe that rules and kinds of rationalistic procedures have no place at all in moral deliberation because they interfere with the personal responsibility to find moral insight inside oneself. Extreme instances in which no use of rational processes is considered legitimate are rare, but many people commonly rely on their intuitive responses on numerous occasions.

Some of you may have reacted almost instantly on reading about Linda's research. You may have felt a wrenching inside because you felt she was callous toward the people with whom she was corresponding and thought she lacked concern for their feelings. Or you may have responded with admiration for her ingenuity, cleverness, or even what you perceived to be her desire to help others understand what loneliness is all about.

This approach to morality is intuitive and spontaneous. It is is not simply emotional, but this style of moral life may involve a strong emotional component, and feeling is important in morality. How do you think you would feel if you were one of Linda's pen pals and then discovered that the person with whom you had been corresponding wasn't real? Would you feel cheated? Angry? Sad? How would you feel if the mail your widowed mother had been receiving—the letters you thought so silly at first but that seemed to give her so much enjoyment—were from someone like Linda? Our "gut level" feelings may give us a clue about morality, and they may be the place to begin ethical analysis. Emotion is often neglected or even depreciated in the study of ethics. Emotion is irrational and gets in the way of our rational processes, keeping us from making "good" decisions, we are often told. It is true that sometimes our emotions do get in the way and keep us from thinking clearly, rationally. Furthermore, our experience teaches us that our emotions do not readily subject themselves to reason. Anyone who has ever been in love or experienced irrational feelings of guilt or attempted to exercise rational control in the face of grief can testify to that.

So we do need to be alert to the blinding effect of emotion. But emotion is also an important part of the moral life. A person without the capacity for moral outrage is a person who is either morally shallow or morally blind. Ethical theory has tended to be highly rationalistic, neglecting the importance of "moral emotions" in moral deliberation and decision making. Empathy and compassion should be part of both ethical analysis and moral living, alongside abstract principles of justice.[1]

---

[1]Carol Gilligan has called attention to a potential defect in the research of moral development; see "In a Different Voice: Women's Conceptions of Self and of Morality," *Harvard Educational Review* 47 (November 1977): 481-517. She notes that women seldom achieve any higher level of moral maturity than Kohlberg's Stage Three of his six stages. At this stage, good is understood as pleasing and helping others and being approved by them. Moral judgment conforms to generally held notions, but is concerned with intention and consequences. Most women do not achieve the higher conceptions of abstract and universal morality because of their strong interpersonal perspective. Gilligan points out that some of the traits considered desirable for women—including the emotional attributes of awareness of the feelings of others, easy expression of tender feelings, and the ability to feel with and for others—are the very ones that mark them as deficient in moral development. "The infusion of feeling into their judgments keeps them from developing a more independent and abstract ethical conception in which concern for others derives from principles of justice rather than from compassion and care" (484).

But Gilligan points out that Kohlberg's theory of stages derives from studies of males that he then applied normatively to females. Gilligan does not challenge the legitimacy of Kohlberg's theory based on his research, but she does suggest that perhaps there are two different modes of moral maturity, without implying that one is superior to the other. A different kind of moral maturity might be found, she believes, by studying the moral development of females. This is a task that Gilligan has set for herself; some of her findings are described in the article mentioned above and in her book *In a Different Voice: Psychological Theory and Women's Development* (Cambridge MA: Harvard University Press, 1982). Ethical theory cannot simply be read out of empirical research on moral development. On the other hand, ethicists need to learn all they can about human nature and human moral experience. Students of ethics may benefit from considering the implications for ethical theory of both Kohlberg's research on moral development (which has a strong Kantian quality) and Gilligan's research (with its emphasis on the emotional, interpersonal, and relational).

Emotion, we should argue, though it may erupt abruptly and spontaneously, is not simply impulsive. It is a function of the kind of persons
we are, and as such is significant for ethics. To suggest that emotion has
a moral quality about it, good or bad, is to suggest that we have some
control over our emotions, that we can within limits shape the nature of
our emotional responses so that they will give us better rather than worse
"intuitions." How susceptible to *rational* control are our emotions?
That's debatable. The degree to which the academic study of ethics will
affect our emotional make-up is limited, but we believe that there is some
capacity for rational control in choosing to *cultivate* a morally healthy
emotional makeup.

In discussing "visceral morality" we have implied that our gut-level
responses are a function of the kind of persons we are. Although some
extreme exponents of this style of morality would vigorously disagree,
we believe that to the extent that immediate, intuitive moral responses
are reliable, it is because they are part of a pattern. Let us turn our attention to that pattern.

Cultivation of the Self:
The Kind of Persons We Are

If you think about your own response to Linda and her research, you
will recognize that you have brought to the encounter your own particular set of attitudes developed over the course of your life. Whether you
have deliberately cultivated certain qualities in your life or have become
what you are quite unconsciously, you have developed a set of patterns
of behavior and attitudes that constitute your character. For some people, the moral life is experienced primarily as a process of being and becoming a particular kind of person. Within religious traditions, people
may aspire to develop those attitudes or dispositions espoused or mod-
eled by great religious leaders—love, mercy, humility, compassion,
moderation, self-control, inner peace, and so on. Probably most people,
religious or not, have self-images about the kind of persons they are and
the persons they would like to become. Words like sensitive, humane,
respectful and conscientious speak more directly of the kind of person
we are than of specific acts.

As you read our account of Linda, you may have formed some
impression of her as a person. The details are too sketchy for an adequate picture of her character, but there are hints of what she is like. You
may have found her too flippant in her attitude toward her subjects. You
may even have considered her manipulative and self-centered, interested only in how her research can benefit her career. Or you may have
felt that she is the kind of person who really wants to understand and

even help people, directly or indirectly. You may have seen her as an opportunist, susceptible to the allures of fame and fortune. Or you may think that she is a hard-working, deserving person, perhaps inadequately appreciated by her colleagues and by the college administration for her devotion to her students. Now she is getting her just deserts.

If we knew Linda better, we might compare our general impression with what we see in this case. We might observe that she is treating her research subjects "just as we would expect her to," or we might conclude that this was "quite out of character." "Character" refers to those patterns of action, attitudes, and emotion that have a moral quality about them. These patterns become habitual, predisposing us to act in certain ways and making our actions relatively predictable. Treatises on ethics sometimes discuss this dimension under the terms "habits" or "virtues."

Most modern ethicists have not paid much attention to this internal dimension of morality. Instead they focus on *decisions* and *actions.* Our specific task is such that we, too, will be concerned almost exclusively with the external, with what people do or should do. Nevertheless, character is at the heart of it all, the unspoken assumption of good will and integrity out of which good conduct will arise. Thinking and writing about ethical issues in scientific research is useless if only unethical people do research. The likelihood that people will behave well depends in no small measure on the character traits or virtues that they have developed. That is why it is important for researchers personally to be concerned with their own "character development." Linda is more likely to protect the interests of her subjects, both in the conduct of her research and in the publication of her results, if her attitude is one of concern rather than of indifference or contempt for other people. The great fifth-century theologian and philosopher Augustine once stated this succinctly by saying, "Love, and then do what you will." The loving person, Augustine believed, would *want* to do loving deeds. Perhaps he assumed too naively that a person with the right motivation will always *know* what to do, but the statement highlights the importance of attitude in predisposing us to right action. It makes a difference whether Linda is caring or callous, selfish or giving, thoughtful and considerate of others or oblivious to the effects of her actions on others.

Thinking about what we mean by "attitude" can bring us to the border between character and personality. Here, even more than in some of our earlier discussions, we become aware of the gray zone between the moral and the nonmoral. When does insensitivity cease to be only a quirk of personality and become a moral issue? The inconsiderate person who cuts in line or parks a car so as to block others or plays music so loudly that the whole neighborhood is disturbed may be offensive but is probably not committing a moral offense. Does an act become a moral issue only when someone is injured? How serious must an inconvenience or verbal assault be to render it an "injury"? What is the relationship between such personality traits and moral character?

Although the style of ethic we have been discussing focuses predominantly on the person who acts rather than the action, it must necessarily pay some attention to action as well. We develop a "good" character by performing "good" acts, and a good character will predispose us to conduct ourselves properly. Thus the definition of a "good person" is linked to the definition of "good conduct." If someone defines good conduct as living by rules given by some external authority or by an internal "voice of conscience," then the good person will be the "law-abiding" person, the person who wants to live by the rules. If good conduct means devotion to the welfare of others, then the good person will be the one dedicated to avoiding harm and promoting the well-being of others. An "ethic of character," important as it is, necessarily presupposes some kind of "ethic of action."

The Ethic of Consequences

Almost any system of ethics will pay some attention to the consequences of action. Earlier we identified utilitarianism as one ethical theory in which the calculation of consequences is the essence of the moral life. Here we can almost speak of a moral "equation," because it involves a tallying and weighing of good and bad consequences. Two stages are involved in the moral assessment of consequences. First is the "factual" level, the projection or "guesstimate" of the probable consequences of each course of action. Think about the number of questions Linda might ask. What will happen to the people with whom she corresponds? How will they feel during the period of correspondence, and how will they feel several months later when the relationship ends? If she ends the relationship by simply writing no more letters, how will that make her "pen pals" feel? Would they be hurt more if she explains to them what she has been doing? Would it be more or less painful if she wrote a "Dear John" letter explaining that she has found somebody else? How likely is it that these people will see a copy of her book? Will they recognize themselves in it? How would they feel about the book, about Linda, and about themselves? What if their friends see a copy of the book and recognize them?

What will happen to Linda's own career? Will she be promoted and tenured on the basis of this work? Will she establish herself in the pop-psychology market, pursuing other studies and perhaps even discarding her academic career altogether? Or will she get burned, arousing the disapproval of her superiors at Riverbend and the contempt of "respectable" behavioral scientists who may regard her work as specious or unprofessional?

What will be the effect on Riverbend College? Will the college remain untouched by her work, or will she bring either embarrassment or acclaim to the college?

Finally, what will be the effect on her discipline? Will she make a contribution to the understanding of the human situation or will the field find itself embroiled in needless controversy because of her? Or will her work simply be ignored, condemned to the oblivion that is the destiny of so many academic labors?

It is, of course, impossible to be certain about outcomes, but if consequences are relevant for moral assessment, it is necessary to make as good an estimate as is possible. Then comes the second stage: making value judgments about consequences.

If Linda concludes that her correspondents will be sad when the relationship ends, how much *moral* weight should that carry? How should she evaluate positive or negative publicity that her study might engender? Is this consequence morally significant or morally irrelevant? If she attracts animosity from within the college, does that have any moral significance?

Many times our apparent *ethical* problems are really *factual* problems—that is, we disagree about what the facts are or about what will be the probable outcome of a particular course of action. Linda may feel her study is *good* because it will benefit everybody. It will bring her fame and fortune, bring the college some good public relations, and bring the subjects of her study some immediate gratification in having a pen pal and long-term benefits by having their plight understood. A colleague may disapprove ethically because he believes the study will not be well received, that the college will be embarrassed, and that the subjects will be injured both by the termination of fictitious relationships and by the adverse publicity they will receive with the publication of Linda's book. If Linda and her colleague agreed about what the consequences were likely to be, they might share the same view about the ethics of her research.

It is possible, however, that people may agree about the probable outcome and still disagree in their moral evaluation. The fundamental values by which consequences are judged may be different. Linda might argue that knowledge is the fundamental value; her colleague might insist that happiness is the ultimate good. Linda might, therefore, be unconcerned about the psychological pain she inflicts, because knowledge is being discovered in the process. Her critic might object to her research because it will make Linda's correspondents unhappy.

More often, differences in evaluation are disagreements about the appropriate weighting of the many consequences. We may think that both happiness and knowledge are good. But how much psychological pain is knowledge worth? Whose happiness is most important? How much is Linda's promotion worth compared to the happiness of her subjects? How shall long-range consequences be compared with immediate consequences? The concept of an ethic of consequences is simple. Its implementation can be quite complicated.

Relational Ethics

All the approaches to ethics discussed have their merits, and in our judgment none is complete in itself. They all include the theme of the effect of actions and attitudes on people, including ourselves. Morality is social in nature. Not only do moral and immoral actions affect other people; the nature of the relationships themselves is part of the moral equation. This relational dimension is most clearly evident in an analysis of the roles we occupy.

A comprehensive ethical system must recognize that people play different roles in life, and each role carries with it specific responsibilities. Different theories of ethics may treat role obligations differently, both in explaining their origins and in assessing their importance. But no thorough theory of ethics can ignore the fact that most of our lives are governed by the roles we occupy, and the application of rules or principles is always filtered through the roles that define our lives.

Linda plays a variety of roles: she is a social scientist (a researcher), a professor, an employee of a college, a friend, a colleague, and a citizen, to name a few. With each of these roles come special responsibilities. Linda has obligations to the particular students in her classes that she does not have to anyone else in the world. Her students have a right to expect her to be in class prepared to teach at the appointed time. Except in the most unusual circumstances, Linda will not even ask herself whether it would be morally better to do something else instead of teaching today. She has specific obligations to her students to fulfill. Besides her teaching, Linda has other responsibilities to the college—serving on college committees, and so on. Some of these obligations are legal and contractual; others are moral in nature. Linda has taken on certain moral obligations by virtue of the roles she has accepted. She would not have any special moral obligations to these particular students had she not accepted the role of faculty member at Riverbend. Having done so, her time is no longer entirely her own.

Linda also occupies the role of researcher, a member of a community of social and behavioral scientists. As a psychologist, Linda belongs to a community of practitioners to whom she owes duties. The public has certain expectations of these communities, expectations that have been created partly by the professional community itself, either by its codes of ethics or by its implicit norms. Linda has obligations to her research subjects and to the general public that she would not have except for the socially defined role she now inhabits. The norms that govern her research are in part determined by the community of research scholars with whom she identifies.

In addition, there are more general roles, such as citizen and friend. Some are roles which she did not consciously adopt; they were thrust upon her, yet they make their own demands of her. She did not choose to become a citizen of the United States; she was born that way. Nevertheless, she is generally expected to obey the laws of the nation. Many of her roles have open-ended responsibilities. It is difficult to specify precisely the nature and limits of some roles. What responsibilities go with the role of friend, for example? That depends partly upon the particular relationship. Linda's responsibilities to Chet are different from those to some more casual friend.

It is often easier to describe the responsibilities that arise out of relationships in terms of characteristics rather than specific behavioral norms. One quality we consider especially important is commitment.

Specific commitments may arise either by express promises or implicitly from relationships. Linda's original study of the "lonely hearts" began with a questionnaire mailed to the people who advertised in the *National Globe.* In requesting their response, Linda probably promised respondents that data for this scientific study would be handled confidentially or anonymously. Her express commitment created an obligation that did not exist previously. It might be argued that those who responded to the questionnaire implicitly made a commitment to Linda to be as honest in their responses as she was honest with them.

This use of the word "commitment" refers to clearly definable acts that can be expected. But we also speak of commitment in a more general sense as loyalty to a person or institution. Linda's relation to Chet or Don's to Jenny may include some explicit statements about the relationship, but the personal loyalty they have for each other is a quality of the relationship that is not exhausted by enumerating specific expectations.

Such commitment constitutes the texture of much of the moral life, but it is difficult to capture the content and quality of these relationships in theoretical discussions of ethics. Hence these matters are sometimes overlooked in the ethics texts and academic classrooms. Nevertheless, to determine *what* our obligations are and to understand the *source* of some obligations, we must frequently think about our commitments.

Another quality of relationships that helps us understand both the nature and source of our responsibility is *gratitude.* Unlike some ethical theorists who attempt to identify *one* ethical principle from which all other moral norms can be derived, we should not argue that gratitude is the sole source of all moral obligation. However, it would be a good candidate for such an honor. It is both an attitude and a principle for action. We ought to *feel* grateful for the benefits that others have bestowed on us, and our gratitude should result in *actions* toward others that correspond to the benefits that we have received. This "gift relationship" has interested modern sociologists, but its importance in ethics is ancient. A recent development is the use of this concept in understanding professional ethics.[2]

How does the idea of gratitude affect our analysis of Linda's situation? What duties derive from gratitude in her case? Taking the narrow view, she could claim not to have any "debts of gratitude" that would affect the ethics of her research. She doesn't "owe" her subjects anything because none of them [except the respondents to her original questionnaire] has deliberately done anything to help her with her research. Those who responded to her "love letters" were concerned for themselves; they didn't intend to help her with her research, so why should she be grateful to them? Furthermore, she might maintain that she doesn't owe anything to the college, which has unsympathetically insisted that she publish or move on, as required under the tenure system. If she owes anybody anything, it is Mr. Mitchell and Now Publishers for encouraging her.

Rational justification for so narrow a view is perhaps possible, but focusing solely on specific "gifts" and the reciprocity deriving from them ignores the basic social nature of human existence. We have all received gifts from the past, gifts that we cannot possibly repay, either because the giver is unknown or no longer accessible. How can we repay the immense debt of gratitude owed a parent or grandparent, a special neighbor or teacher, a coach or clergyman or scout leader for their formative influence on our lives? They would have us repay that debt by becoming

---

[2]Religious ethics have often been explicit in emphasizing gratitude. The concept of covenant, so fundamental in both Jewish and Christian thought, traced people's obligations to one another back to the prior gift of grace received from God. Without assuming that readers would accept his theological framework, William May has creatively employed the notion of covenant in understanding the ethical obligations of the medical profession. See William F. May, *The Physician's Covenant: Images of the Healer in Medical Ethics* (Philadelphia: Westminster Press, 1983).

good parents, faithful friends, loyal citizens, and persons concerned for others.

Gratitude, like commitment, is an inexact notion not to be pinned down to single discrete events, important as these are in identifying some causes for gratitude. The truth is that Linda has been given a great deal by many people, most of whom are anonymous. Ignoring for the moment the countless gifts from people who have made her what she is personally and focusing only on her professional role, we can point out that the specialized education that now enables her to do research depends to a great extent on "public" support. She may have attended a state university, in which case the public support through taxation is obvious. Even if she attended a private university, the cost of her education unquestionably exceeded her tuition, and that extra expense was paid by the donations of numerous individuals in endowments and annual gifts. In addition, there are the personal gifts of time and interest from her professors, who may have gone far beyond the minimal demands of their job descriptions.

On a broader scale, the fact that society permits and even encourages research is a gift. The freedom of inquiry and freedom to present findings unhampered in an open society, no matter how distasteful some conclusions might be, is likewise a gift Linda has inherited, not something she has earned.

Linda's relationship with Riverbend College is a reciprocal gift-recipient relationship in which both sides give and both receive. Although this relationship can sometimes become mechanical and legalistic, for the most part such relationships operate with an assumption of good will and commitment to a common good, both sides doing more for the other than could be legalistically required of them. Linda *is* expected to do a lot of things in connection with her faculty position, including research and publication, but she is also given a great deal of freedom in how she spends her time, as long as some appropriate balance of teaching, research, and service is maintained.

Her relationship to her students is not one-sided either. It is not that she does all the giving and they do all the taking. She needs her students and almost certainly benefits from working with them. The more eager and inquiring her students are, the more she will benefit from her association with them, but even having to prepare to teach dull students will force her to sharpen her own thinking as she tries to communicate sometimes complex ideas in ways that make sense to somebody else.

Finally, what about her research subjects? Can she really feel that she has no debt to them just because they are not intentionally helping her? One could argue that she is indebted to them in quite another way. She has profited significantly from them, having taken something from them that they did not intend; she may owe them a debt of restitution rather than a debt of gratitude.

Moreover, she can still be grateful for what she has received from her respondents whether they intended the gift or not. Some of the greatest gifts are not intentional; and even if gratitude to the "giver" is sometimes not required, gratitude is still an appropriate attitude. An especially apt illustration is the special talents that people possess. To the extent that they are transmitted by biological inheritance, it really makes no sense to thank one's parents for the gift of intelligence or physical strength or musical or artistic talent, or even good health. The quip that the best way to avoid heart disease is to choose one's parents wisely reminds us of the degree to which pure chance controls our lives. To praise our parents for providing good genes is as foolish as blaming ourselves for choosing the wrong parents. Praise and blame are inappropriate. But gratitude is not. We can be grateful for things that we receive by pure chance, and having received them we can respond by using effectively these happenstances of life. The fact that Linda was born into a family that provided an atmosphere conducive to her development, that she was born in a nation and a society that offers such immense opportunity and freedom, that she attended schools where her creativity was encouraged to develop, that somewhere along the way someone inspired her to pursue college and graduate education—all these things are gifts that she cannot claim as her moral right.

To be sure, life is not all gift. Linda has used her opportunities, and she has "earned" some rights as well. The university she attended didn't *give* her a degree. She had to work to get her current job, and she has to work to keep it. Our lives are a mixture of gift and desert. An adequate account of the nature of morality will acknowledge that the balance between gift and desert can never be calculated to the penny, and an ethical system constructed on such calculation of obligation is surely impoverished. Most of us are put off by people who attempt to give exactly what they have received, no more, no less. Such individuals, we think, fail to understand the nature of friendship or any human relationship. Ethics as gratitude redefines the terms "obligation," "duty," and "ought," which need not be viewed as legalistic, rigid, and external impositions upon us.

Thus how Linda should translate her "debt of gratitude" (or restitution) into concrete action is a matter of considerable latitude. Thinking about morality in terms of gratitude is useful, not only because it can help us identify our obligations, but because it can help us think of ethics "responsively" rather than legalistically. The Western religious tradition illustrates this concept clearly. The Jewish and Christian traditions at their best have understood morality as the joyful response to an undeserved gift from a loving God. The Ten Commandments, which describe the appropriate response to both God and fellow human beings, are rooted in this kind of responsiveness to the God of love who has given his people their very existence and identity as a people. That theme also undergirds Christian faith.

The relational nature of ethics and other basic concepts from general ethical theory discussed so far with be recurring themes in later chapters. In the next chapter, we will discuss some specific ethical components of science as a social institution.

4

The Business of Science and the Ethics of That Business

In the introduction we noted how important science is in our society. Science adds to the store of human knowledge. Knowledge, of course, is not just an accumulation of unrelated facts; it involves some understanding about relationships between those facts. There is little value in the collection of raw data for its own sake. But we value real knowledge, and we invest large sums of money and much human effort in those activities that promote new understanding. We say that knowledge is good, but what kind of "good" is it?

KNOWLEDGE AS AN INSTRUMENTAL VALUE

Knowledge is power, we often hear, and clearly one of the reasons that we value science is that knowledge allows us to control our environment and ourselves. All around us we see evidence of how life is better because of scientists. Researchers often find meaning in their work because they are helping to make our lives better. In justifying to themselves and others the inconvenience or risk involved in a research project, researchers frequently try to show that their project will *benefit* someone, that life will be better—more pleasant or less painful—because of the study. Almost any system of ethics will *encourage* service to others, even if it is not considered *mandatory*. Thus the search for knowledge may take on a moral quality if it becomes a *means* to morally good ends, that is, if it improves the quality of life. Sometimes researchers can't point to an *immediate* benefit to justify research. But they may be able to appeal to a *long-term* benefit that people in the future will enjoy because of current research. We are also painfully aware that knowledge can be used immorally to the detriment of humanity.

Social and behavioral research may not produce the same dramatic material benefit that results from some research in the physical sciences. However, the findings of such research often illuminate the human condition and thus increase our understanding, which in turn paves the way to improvement. As with the natural sciences, the payoff is seldom immediate. Usually, basic knowledge must be translated into a usable "technology"—a new drug, a new machine, a new social program—to improve the human condition. Moreover, advances are incremental, with each discovery providing the base from which to launch a new endeavor.

We don't expect *all* knowledge gained through scientific study to prove "useful" to society. But to have the benefits of some research, we must be willing to study all kinds of things, because we don't know in advance what will "pay off." Many ventures conducted even by experienced researchers lead nowhere. On the other hand, some seemingly useless research may prove useful in the future or may inspire another new idea that will eventually produce enormous benefits. Thus we support a *system* of research, convinced that the system will produce useful results along with failures or "useless" discoveries. Society in its *funding* of research, the community of scientists in *defining and evaluating areas* for investigation, and individual researchers in *deciding* what they will undertake all must make some estimate about what seems likely to produce societal benefits.

But it may be short-sighted to become focused only on the *instrumental* value of science. Science is often most useful when it seeks knowledge without concerning itself with usefulness. Many discoveries for which no application could be foreseen have turned out to be immensely useful. Thus the search for all new knowledge might be seen as good because of the possibility of even *unforeseen* future benefit to humanity.

KNOWLEDGE AS INTRINSIC VALUE

In the quest for financial support, scientists often talk about the applications of their project. But must scientists always justify their research as potentially beneficial, however remote the benefit might be? Can't scientists simply say that knowledge *itself* is good? Isn't it worthwhile simply to seek for "Truth"? We may be reluctant in our day to speak so augustly about "the Truth" with a capital "T," but the ideal of attaining knowledge for its own sake is a basic assumption of science. Knowledge is presumed to be intrinsically valuable, that is, valuable in itself and not because it can produce other "goods."

Our culture places a high value on education, knowledge, and understanding. At least in some quarters, we still uphold the ideal of the "educated man" or the "gentleman," though we now realize that we must find a less sexist language to express that ideal. We pride ourselves on being "civilized" and feel that we *ought* to maintain and promote civilization. We extol the virtues of education because we think people are "better" because of it.

But does all this have anything to do with ethics? It is easy to see how instrumental knowledge gains moral worth; it promotes human welfare. But can knowledge for its own sake become part of the moral equation? It may in some systems of ethics. Let's look at several ways in which the pursuit of knowledge as intrinsic value may have moral roots or implications.

First, the classical *utilitarian* may say that the very pursuit of knowledge is *pleasurable*. Since pleasure, happiness, or fulfillment is the good that people ought to seek, the search for knowledge becomes a moral good—for those who enjoy it. The leading spokesman for classical utilitarianism, John Stuart Mill, considered the "pleasures of the mind" superior to physical pleasures, a view captured in his famous aphorism that it is better to be "a Socrates dissatisfied than a pig satisfied."[1] Intellectuals may speak eloquently about the virtues of a life of the mind in ways that may seem far removed from the actual intentions and practices of active researchers in the sciences. But a lofty idealism undergirds science, helping it maintain its integrity as an enterprise distinct from technology.

Yet there is something disquieting about Mill's formulation. If the value of truth is only in the pleasure of its pursuit, what if it sometimes causes discomfort rather than happiness? Does the search for truth become immoral? A tortured argument that the dissatisfied Socrates is really more satisfied at some deeper level than the pig is not entirely satisfying.

An alternative that avoids Mill's problems consists of identifying truth as an *independent* human good that ought morally to be sought for itself, not just for the satisfaction that the quest provides. A group known as the *ideal utilitarians* espoused the view that truth and beauty are ideal values and that morality consists in promoting these values as well as pleasure.[2]

---

[1] Mill's statement had more to do with the humanity of Socrates than his wisdom. "It is better to be a human being dissatisfied than a pig satisfied; better to be a Socrates dissatisfied than a pig satisfied. And if the fool, or the pig, are of a different opinion, it is because they only know their side of the question. The other part of the comparison knows both sides." John Stuart Mill, *Utilitarianism*, George Sher, ed., (1861; reprint, Indianapolis: Hackett, 1979) 10.

[2] For example, G. E. Moore, *Ethics* (1912; reprint, New York: Oxford University Press, 1965).

Other ethical theories may be less explicit in showing how knowledge is good, but moral practice requires some accounting for it. If "truth"
is not given moral weight at the outset (directly as with the ideal utilitarians or indirectly as with Mill), it will be encountered elsewhere. In
some situations a moral good will conflict with the value of knowledge,
as when knowledge can be acquired at some risk of harm. Can the intention to gain knowledge offset an almost minuscule amount of harm? Will
a lot of truth make up for a small amount of "suffering"? If suffering is
"bad," even consent would not make it morally good in these circumstances, unless truth is given some moral weight. Even experimentation
on oneself that caused some "harm" would be wrong unless the search
for truth had moral status.

The issue of the value of knowledge is also implicit in decisions about
how to *allocate our resources.* Whether it is at the societal level where
funds are being distributed to promote human welfare or at the individual level as all of us decide how to spend our time and energy, we are
implicitly evaluating and ranking numerous activities. Included are those
activities that promote "ideal" values, such as truth and beauty. When
we expend resources to promote the arts or to study and teach history or
to explore frontiers in the animal kingdom or in space just because they're
there, we are implicitly deciding not to spend those resources on food
or health care or shelter for the needy of the world. Because those decisions affect the welfare of other people, we have implicitly made a
moral decision to promote truth and beauty at the expense of other human values.

THE SCIENTIFIC ETHIC

Scientific investigation is one approach to understanding the world
of things and people. Art is another. Neither is ultimately more valuable
than the other. But those who would help us understand reality from the
perspective of science must use appropriate scientific methods. The
"ethic of science" is the set of norms that define the scientific endeavor.
They are not rules dictated arbitrarily by some external authority, but an
ethos that evolved gradually and organically. The recent professional
codes of ethics embody some of these norms, but the "ethic of science"
is more like the charter or constitution that makes science possible than
like a law book that spells out the specific rules. The norms are not self-
evident or necessary. Scientific discovery might have occurred without
these norms or with different ones. Because these particular norms have
been defined by a scientific community as the best way to investigate our
world, those who would join that community and embark on that common venture will be initiated into the community ethic. This ethic de-

fines the boundaries that must be respected by those who wish recognition as part of the scientific community. Let's look at some of the expectations of the scientific ethic.

A key element of the scientific ethic is the *duty to use appropriate methods.* Floating around in popular culture is the myth of "The" Scientific Method. There is no single scientific method, but numerous "methods," each developed for examining a particular dimension of reality, and each method requires special skill in determining what observations will bring to light the "truth" the scientist seeks. But some agreement exists about appropriate procedures for a given subject, and "good science" requires choosing methods that fit the specific task.

These methods were developed because of the fundamental *duty to be objective.* Scientists must keep their personal perspectives from interfering with what they see in the world. The norm of objectivity was defined first in the natural sciences, and as the social and behavioral sciences emerged as disciplines claiming to be "scientific," they, too, adopted it.[3] According to this view, science is value-neutral, and scientists who let their own personal values color their perception are guilty of "bad science."

This view was the unquestioned standard for the social and behavioral sciences at one time, and the ideal of objectivity remains an important one for these sciences. However, the view has been qualified significantly since its earliest formulation. A number of social and behavioral scientists have argued in different ways that absolute objectivity is impossible.[4] Even if *science* is neutral, *scientists* will have values, some of which may affect their ability to be objective. Try as hard as they may, scientists can never be sure that they are seeing only what is there and not what they expect to see because of their preconceptions. Because social scientists are part of the instrument of measurement, they do not know how objective the measurement is.

---

[3]One leading exponent of this view was Max Weber. Value judgments of the researcher should not intrude into the scientific work. Science ought to study what is, not what ought to be, Weber thought. He contended that science was value-free. See Max Weber, *The Methodology of the Social Sciences,* ed. and trans. Edward A. Shils and Henry A. Finch (New York: Free Press, 1968). Another of the great sociologists early in this century held a similar view; see Emile Durkheim, *The Rules of Sociological Method,* trans. Sarah A. Solovay and John H. Mueller, ed. George E. G. Catlin (New York: Free Press, 1938).

[4]A noteworthy example is Howard S. Becker, "Whose Side Are We On?" *Social Problems* 14 (Winter, 1976): 239-47. See also Alvin W. Gouldner, "Anti-Minotaur: The Myth of a Value-Free Sociology," *Social Problems* 9 (Winter 1962): 199-213.

A branch of sociology known as the "sociology of knowledge" investigates how people's social settings determine what they perceive to be "knowledge." It is easy to see how the perceptions of people from other cultures are affected by their social definitions of reality. It is more difficult to see that in ourselves. But we are all part of a social world, and what social scientists see will be determined in part by their professional and social environments. This is one of the reasons why it is so important for the investigator to be as open and honest as possible in reporting the method of a study, so that others will have some opportunity to assess the extent to which objectivity may have been compromised.

Some critics maintain that insisting on objectivity can be a rationalization that enables researchers to avoid the moral consequences of their work, especially when they consciously or unconsciously defend the status quo. From a Marxist perspective, such "objectivity" masks the class interest of the scientist who benefits from the current class structure. To counteract this bias, some sociologists have argued that researchers should always assume the role of advocate of the less powerful whom they study.

We do not believe that scientific endeavor can never be carried on in an entirely value-free manner; even Max Weber, a classic spokesman for this principle, acknowledges that the goal is difficult to attain. Researchers must recognize that their values may influence their perceptions in ways that they do not appreciate, so that they will not presume to speak as if they have achieved some kind of absolute truth. Self-deception is one of the most serious ethical concerns in any human endeavor, because people who do not understand how their own perspectives and their own interests color what they see may be morally zealous for a cause that serves their own interests at considerable cost to others and never even recognize what is happening. But if it is impossible to eliminate bias completely, objectivity must still remain an ideal toward which to strive or much of the value of the behavioral and social sciences will be lost.

Moreover, researchers must be *honest in reporting* what they find, whether it corresponds to their own political, moral, religious, or social views or not. However, striving for objectivity in the search for knowledge does not mean that researchers have no ethical responsibility in deciding what is to be studied or about the uses to which knowledge should be put. Their first job is to seek truth and make it available. But they may also have a responsibility concerning its purpose and use.

Yet another duty imposed by the scientific ethic is the *duty to publish*. Because science's function is to add to the store of knowledge, scientists are expected to do research and publish their results for the scientific community. The duty has two roots. First, publication allows new "discoveries" to be tested by colleagues who are able to understand, evaluate, and criticize the study. This makes the scientific canon of replication possible. Going to the popular press with scientific findings that have not been properly evaluated in the scientific community may be more than a breach of etiquette. Short-circuiting the procedures of the scientific community risks publicizing erroneous claims or at least creating misunderstanding in a public not equipped to understand or assess a scientific study.

The second purpose of publication is simply to share with colleagues in a common endeavor what one has discovered. Traditionally, scientists who chose to horde a secret store of knowledge committed a cardinal sin against the scientific ethic. The ideal is still espoused, but the matter has become much more complicated. Many scientists work for national governments or private industry as employees or under contract for purposes that serve the employer and not the cause of "public" science. As science becomes increasingly the servant of technology, this traditional norm faces considerable erosion. Some social scientists must now ask whether to engage in research under contract if the results cannot be made public.[5]

The converse of "secret" research is the ambition for public attention. The ideal of a community of scientists engaged cooperatively in a quest for knowledge is in reality often undermined by competitiveness. The frenetic search for truth is often accompanied by a vicious battle within the scientific community for recognition, position, and financial support. This may be more pronounced in the natural sciences where the funding stakes may be higher, but it can be found at all levels and in all fields, from students to senior researchers and among social as well as physical scientists. The ambition to produce the "best" study may improve the quality of the work, but competition may sometimes be self-defeating. Unrestrained competition might lead someone to publish misleading information in order to gain an advantage while one's competitors are led down a wrong path. More often, striving to be the first in print may lead to publishing preliminary results too soon. Or the competition to get ahead could lead to cutting corners in the data gathering and analysis. The best and worst features of the duty to do research and

---

[5]"The Principles of Professional Responsibility" of the American Anthropological Association specifically states, "Anthropologists should not communicate findings secretly to some and withhold them from others." Likewise the American Sociological Association's Code of Ethics, in the section on cross-national research, states that sociologists "should not agree to or provide any government with secret research, secret reports, or secret debriefings."

publish may be reinforced by the promotion and tenure system of our universities.[6]

Often neglected is the duty to publish *negative* results. Data that count against one's hypothesis may be as important as results that support it, yet there is a tendency to publish only positive results. Likewise, researchers are naturally reluctant to admit errors in method or interpretation, and it is tempting to pretend that a chance discovery was part of the hypothesis in the original design. Adequate reporting of such negative material is part of the ongoing growth of the sciences. Researchers may learn as much about method and content from the mistakes and accidents of others as they do from their own mistakes and accidents.

One of the important elements in the scientific ethic is the *prohibition of distortion.* Publication presents current findings and provides a base for further investigation. Thus, results must be presented fairly and accurately; in addition, other scientists need sufficient detail about the conduct of the study to form their own judgments about its validity. Even though the data and conclusions of the research may be flawless, the researcher has an obligation to be scrupulous in reporting how the research was done. A stark fabrication (saying something occurred when in fact it did not) or a "whitewash" (glossing over an error of commission or of omission) represents a "mortal" and not a "venial" scientific "sin." Numerous factors can distort the findings, some intentional and some unintentional.

Let's begin with the most obvious distortion, *falsification of data.* Falsification may occur in obtaining data. A researcher might simply make up data, perhaps filling in missing information or inventing a whole set of data. It could mean discarding data that dispute a valued hypothesis. Such falsification contradicts the very purpose of scientific research.

More subtle distortion may occur when the researcher is responsible for recording data. Researchers must guard against "encouraging" or "discouraging" specific responses. Moreover, it is important to record *data* and not one's own *opinions.* In administering an interview schedule, for example, it is important to record what the respondent said, not what the interviewer thought the respondent meant. Participant observers should not record their own conclusions as if they were observations. Moreover, researchers must also be aware of how the personal traits of an interviewer or observer may influence the outcome.

---

[6]A splendid example of these issues in the natural sciences can be found in James D. Watson, *The Double Helix: A Personal Account of the Discovery of the Structure of DNA* (New York: Atheneum, 1968).

Procedural irregularities may also distort results. For example, interviewing only residents on the first floor of an apartment building when the research plan called for a random sampling of all floors is a shortcut that undermines a study.

Little need be said about the ethics of falsifying data. Such behavior is simply wrong, a clear violation of the research ethic. It is an affront to colleagues and a disservice to the cause of research. It makes the research useless or worse than useless. Fallacious results reported by a prominent researcher could cause an incorrect hypothesis to receive more credence than it deserves, leading other researchers on a wild goose chase and wasting valuable effort and resources. Reported by an influential scientist, it could contribute to bad public policy. If detected, it could be detrimental to the public's image of science.

Other distortions, often unintentional, may occur in the design of a study and in the analysis and presentation of results. Researchers must exercise care in designing a study to measure what they think they are measuring and in analyzing data to avoid erroneous conclusions. Improper handling of statistics, for example, may result in unfounded conclusions. A book published a number of years ago purported to teach people "how to lie with statistics."[7] Recalling Disraeli's famous dictum that there are three kinds of lies—"lies, damn lies, and statistics"—the author illustrated, often humorously, how figures can be misleading.

Of course, statistics will be meaningless if the procedure for obtaining the data was scientifically unsound. Sometimes people draw unwarranted conclusions from too small a sample. The value of data from "self-selected" participants is also limited. Caution is necessary in assessing data provided by respondents who may be inaccurate in their reporting. At best, they are reporting what they remember, which isn't necessarily what really happened. The passage of time or subconscious repression of painful experiences may affect their recall. People may be reluctant to admit to others, or even to themselves, certain negative things about themselves. Or people may express attitudes that they think they ought to feel or that they think the researcher expects rather than their true opinion or experience. One very clear example might be basing a study of alcoholism treatment solely on the self-reports of a limited number of alcoholics.

Moreover, accurate statements of fact can be colored in their presentation. Suppose a surveyor found that 1 percent of all ministers surveyed answered yes to the question, "Have you ever seriously

---

[7]Darrell Hugg, *How to Lie with Statistics* (New York: W. W. Norton, 1954).

contemplated an extramarital affair?" The surveyor who wants to make clergy look good can report that *only* 1 percent of the ministers surveyed report *ever* having seriously contemplated infidelity. If he wishes to make clergy look bad, he can state that one in every one hundred ministers has given *serious* thought to an affair. Or suppose that 51 percent of physicians responding to a survey state that they would stop at the scene of a highway accident to render aid. The surveyor can report that "*most* physicians surveyed say that they would stop to render aid," or she can report that "*almost half* of the physicians say that they would *not* stop to offer assistance at the scene of an accident. Both conclusions would be supported by the data, but there is a world of difference in the way they sound. Incidentally, it is obvious that the surveyor cannot presume to judge what these individuals *would* do, based on her data. She can only note what they *say* they would do. The respondents themselves don't know what they would really do.

Choosing proper tests in statistical analysis is absolutely essential. These tests are intended to determine that a correlation that a researcher observes was not simply a chance occurrence. Using the wrong test will yield erroneous results.

Some correlations, though valid, are meaningless. Suppose a researcher finds that the number of homicides over a given period increased at a rate parallel to the increase in the gross national product. That correlation does not mean that prosperity and murder are directly related. Perhaps both were fueled by a population boom.

Sorting out cause and effect may be problematic. A correlation between regularity of church attendance and the individual's judgment that abortion is a sin might seem to imply that religion *causes* people to consider abortion a sin. It is possible, however, that the reverse is true. People who believe abortion to be wrong may be drawn to the church for other reasons, and they may influence religious leaders to condemn abortion.

A final obligation in the ethic of science is the duty to *do one's own work.* Students may "cheat" by passing off someone else's work as their own. Even apart from classroom ethics, cheating in research is simply wrong, whether or not one gets caught. Recognizing blatant wrongdoing of this sort is easy. "Plagiarizing" another's *ideas* is more subtle and ambiguous. A Hebrew proverb advises that one of the surest ways to find a place in heaven is to give correct attribution to other people's accomplishments. The scientific ethic requires giving credit to the person who advances an idea, and this may mean crediting colleagues or mentors or fellow students for private communications in addition to published material.

Many times ideas and concepts become so well known that they seem like "community property" not needing citation. Moreover, our experience over time becomes so diverse and extensive that it is sometimes difficult to know whether an idea is our own or an idea received from another, and if from another, *which* other. Even remembering *who* years ago gave us an idea still may not make attribution easy if we can't remember *where* we read it. The opposite situation can also arise. A friend, a man given to independent and sometimes creative thinking, once remarked that "the ancients have stolen all our thoughts." With some regularity he would arrive at a new insight, only to discover that Plato or Aristotle or St. Augustine had said much the same thing long ago. Need one acknowledge these parallels when they were not the source of one's thinking? Deciding what should be cited requires a large measure of judgment that does not submit readily to a system of rules. We are usually aware of our direct or major borrowing from others. But how far should we go in acknowledging our indebtedness to others? Accuracy and fairness are the principles, but the application is sometimes perplexing.

Part of the "ethics of one's own work" applies to teachers in relation to their students. Not long ago graduate students regularly found that data obtained in their dissertation work would soon be published by their professors. In some cases, the professor would mention the student in a footnote. In others, the student would be accorded junior authorship. The practice was an accepted ritual of graduate education. The student was, in a way, paying admission fees to join the club. Without belaboring the point, we find this practice as unacceptable as other kinds of plagiarism. It is unconscionable for senior researchers or academics to exploit their positions, taking credit for work and ideas that belong to junior colleagues.

The norms we have been describing are part of the "ethic of science." They define the expectations within a system. But what is the *moral* status of the claims of that system? Is the scientist morally bound by these dictates, or are these only prudential considerations necessitated by the desire to maintain one's status and position within the scientific community? The norms clearly presuppose the ethos of Western science. This ethos is not morally *necessary*. We might conceive of another system that might be equally defensible. Just as "theft" can be wrong (indeed can even be conceived of) only where there is a concept of property, so too "plagiarism," for example, can be wrong only when ideas are considered a kind of private property. If ideas were considered "public property," if the ethos emphasized only the *common search* for truth without regard for individual credit, status, prestige, or advancement, the notion of plagiarism would be unintelligible.

Likewise, the search for human knowledge need not necessarily be an open venture with an obligation to publish. Science could be proprietary in the same way that technology is, and the trend in that direction may be gathering steam as science and technology become increasingly entangled. The ideology of an open, public science is an accident of history. We consider it a happy accident, without which scientific advance would probably have been retarded, but it is an accident not required by morality.

The abhorrence to the falsification of data or distortion in interpretation parallels the general ethical prohibition of lying. If science were considered a game, like poker, deception would be part of the game. But it is not a game. Falsification and distortion contradict the purpose of the whole endeavor. Science cannot succeed if these practices are not condemned.

Although the scientific ethic is not morally necessary, we should argue, based on our conception of the ethics of roles, that those who wear the mantle (or lab coat) of science take on the moral duty to be "good" scientists.[8] What constitutes "good science" is a technical matter. Each of the sciences has developed procedures for acquiring and sharing knowledge within that field. Those methods, far from being permanently fixed and static, are continually being refined. But the researcher cannot ignore those standards that define the arena within which further development will occur. "Good science" becomes an ethical concern for those who undertake that vocation.

---

[8]There are limits to the obligation to comply with role expectations. One way to discuss those limits is to acknowledge the possibility of conflicts between roles, including ultimately the "role" of "fellow human being." For example, some researchers in Nazi Germany may have felt that they were satisfying socially defined roles in performing their deadly experiments on human beings. Such absolute loyalty to a finite role may in religious language be called "idolatry." A term compatible with a secular humanist ethic is "crime against humanity."

III

DOWN IN THE TRENCHES: QUANDARIES IN PARTICIPANT RESEARCH

5

Studying People
Where They Are:
The Nature
of Participant Research

ew methods of social research have captured the public's imagination as much as "participant observation" or, as it is sometimes called, "participant research." Many students who contemplate a career in sociology or anthropology see themselves doing a participant study that involves observing a group with norms and customs significantly different from their own. How many of us have imagined ourselves as anthropologists studying a preliterate culture in which we were the first Westerners the people have ever seen; thoughts of windswept islands or jungles and scientists like Margaret Mead, Franz Boas, A. L. Kroeber and the other greats in anthropology flash through our minds.

In participant research, more than any other, the researcher is the method's focus. The efficacy of the research rests upon the relationship between the scientist and the people being studied. Because a relationship must exist between subject and scientist, the term of study is longer than in other kinds of research. Participant research is typically not a "one-shot" operation. Other methods may require collecting data over a relatively brief period. A survey may involve interviewing individuals for only a few minutes each. Naturally, the interviewer must establish some rapport with the respondent, but the relationship will be less intense.

The participant researcher enters the world of the subject. Using both observation and intuition, the scientist seeks to learn what the subject's life is about: its special customs, rules, sanctions, meanings and rewards. Not only are researchers bound by the ethical and moral constraints imposed on them as scientists, but there is likely to be a stronger overlay of obligations incurred because of the human relationships that are formed.

THE METHOD AND THEORY OF PARTICIPANT RESEARCH

What is participant research?[1] The answer at first appears simple. However, if we followed a field worker during the course of a study, we would likely note that the research is a blend of methods. What emerges is regular interaction with subjects, direct observation of specific events, formal and informal interviewing, some systematic counting or organizing, recording of documents, and collecting of artifacts or objects. In one sense, participant research is an extension of the "case-study method" in which a thorough study of a single case is used to represent many others. Because of its inclusiveness, the case-study method enables researchers to examine more subtle aspects of the situation—motives, folk-explanation, and interpretations not provided by statistics.

Participant observation studies offer analytic descriptions of social situations, groups, complex organizations, and social systems. The social scientist is, in fact, a little like a journalist. The journalist tries to depict an event fairly from a particular point of view. Social scientists take the process one step further by relating their observations to a larger body of abstract or theoretical material. An analytic description uses concepts, propositions, and empirical generalizations from a body of scientific theory in its analyses, organization, and reporting of data. As they collect data, social scientists try to employ thorough, systematic, unbiased reporting and classification of facts. One goal is to generate new empirical generalizations, concepts and propositions. In one sense, the primary objective of these studies is *model building:* a conceptual replication of a social system's component parts, an examination of these individual parts, and ultimately their recombination into a whole that "makes sense" to the subjects, whether they are gang members, Necrons, or Lonely Hearts.

Commentators on participant research have discussed the "latent" nature of social organization. Members of a group are often unaware of the social structures in which they live and their role in these structures. Asking participants what they are doing, therefore, is unlikely to provide adequate information for the scientist. In addition to asking questions, researchers must actually observe events. This presents several problems. First, it is physically impossible for the researcher to be in all

---

[1]An excellent discussion of the issues and problems of this method can be found in *Issues in Participant Observation: A Text and Reader,* ed. George J. McCall and J. L. Simmons. (Reading MA: Addison-Wesley, 1969).

places at all times; and, second, some important activities have probably occurred before the study begins. Researchers have been able to overcome these problems by the use of "informants," the observer's extra "eyes and ears." Informants are passive, reporting to the scientist only what they've seen and heard. To say this, of course, oversimplifies the matter, because people are rarely able to provide wholly unbiased and complete descriptions of events. Nevertheless, becoming an informant places a person in a different role from what he or she would normally play in the group. While the informant is cast in the role of substitute researcher, sometimes undergoing training to fulfill the task, respondents are always themselves. Respondents report to the researcher about their feelings, beliefs, intentions, and motives.

In turn, in their role as participant researchers, scientists take part in the activities of the group under study. This might involve taking drugs, participating in seances, dancing in native celebrations, performing illegal acts, attending meetings—in short, doing what is commonly done by the people under study. The researcher experiences in a very personal way the lives of his or her subjects. This kind of participation helps the researcher understand the data received from informants and respondents and may make the life of the group understandable in a deeper, more subjective way. As a rule, participant researchers invest much of themselves in their study. Because this is so, we believe special ethical concerns emerge from the work.

The methods and techniques of the social scientist could be as easily used by a law enforcement or government intelligence agency. Barring the use of questionable information-gathering methods such as illegal wire tapping, torture, or coercion, all groups use similar methods of data gathering and document collection. All use "informants" and "respondents," observe events first hand, and report on a situation using an accurate model of the system and its methods of operation. Additionally, a researcher's "field notes" would be a rich source of *specific* information in which subjects could be linked to illegal or questionable events. Much the same could be said about journalistic inquiry; the methods of data collection would be similar, and the final report would be a detailed account of a system, its operation, and personnel.

The intent, motive, or purpose of a scientific study is what sets it apart from other information-gathering endeavors. In the preceding discussion of analytic description, we noted that a key objective of any social-science research is to contribute to a body of theory leading to an understanding of human behavior. Researchers do so by fitting a single piece of a puzzle into the larger pattern. This is the "mission of science" as we see it.

We will examine some issues involved in participant research by analyzing fictionalized case studies that represent plausible situations. They will illustrate some of the theoretical and technical issues and processes that arise from this kind of work and will challenge us to think about ethics in the research setting. We will not attempt an exhaustive analysis of the cases, but will draw attention to a few issues that have broad application in the ethical evaluation of research. In the first case, presented in this chapter, we will ask you to think especially about the issues of privacy and deception.

GOOD PEOPLE IN FUNNY PLACES

"Damn, I wonder what took this one so long to arrive," Mike thought as he crumpled up yet another letter telling him that scholarship money was very tight this year and that schools were awarding scholarships only to students who had already achieved something in their chosen field. This was Mike's fifth "Dear John" letter. He had begun to wonder seriously whether his dreams of a higher degree in sociology would ever materialize.

After the third letter, the one from Western University, Mike began to think about doing a really grabby study, the kind that attracts instant attention and might be picked up by a publisher or by a magazine like *Psychology Today* or *Society*. As he read the message in this latest letter, he knew he didn't have a prayer unless he was able to produce something exciting. "Well, it may be too late for this year, but I'll show'em next year," he muttered, "if I don't starve before then."

Mike remembered the evening the idea for his study had come to him. He, Dave, and a couple of women friends had been together at the Nite Owl, a bar that served cheap beer and good blues-jazz music. It was Mike's Western University condolence party. Dave, who was a few years younger than Mike, was going to be staying at Clarion University for doctoral work in social psychology. Mike and Dave had met a few years earlier during some campus protests and had become good friends. Dave had just been awarded a large scholarship by the Woodralph Foundation for his master's essay, which was an exciting social-psychological study of radical black students.

"Hey, Weinstein, baby, you goin' to have to get it together and start learning about black folks, 'cause that's where it's at, man," Dave said in heavy street dialect.

Mike laughed at his friend and flicked a peanut at him. "Hell, you know I'm on the wrong side of affirmative action now. And besides, I sometimes wish I was more interested in something other than social deviants and other assorted nasty things!"

The banter between Mike and Dave Foster was easy. And then, during a break, Val, Dave's girlfriend, said: "But what will you do, Mike? Are you stopping now? Your teaching gig at Community is going to end at the end of the semester. And then what?"

It was one of those curious moments when everything seems to stand still. The music had stopped, and somehow conversations at nearby tables came to a temporary halt. Mike remembered it with an almost eerie feeling: All eyes had seemed focused on him. Dave, Val, and Marsha waited for him to speak.

"I really don't know," Mike said. "I guess I'll have to find something that will pay the rent and still keep me in the field."

No one said anything, and there was an uncomfortable silence at the table. Mike excused himself to use the rest room. As he was washing his hands, he looked at his image in the mirror. He saw a dark, hulking young man whose heavy-framed eyeglasses gave him a vague owlish look and were probably the only thing that looked "graduate school" about him. "Weinstein, you'll be twenty-seven in a few weeks," he told the image in the mirror. "If we don't get it together soon, we're gonna lose it entirely."

At that moment Mike's ruminations were interrupted by the sounds of two women talking and laughing in the adjoining women's rest room. Mike heard a word or two which tickled his interest, and he began to listen intently. Although he missed most of it, he gathered that one of the women was trying to decide whether to go home with a man she had met at the Nite Owl a few hours earlier. Mike was fascinated by the conversation. He felt like a naturalist who was in the right place and catches some facet of animal behavior that had never before been reported.

His fascination, his sense of being a voyeur, had dominated Mike's academic career. He had easily chosen sociology as a major. The discipline had opened a new world for him. People were fascinating; Mike felt kinship with everyone. Sometime late in his undergraduate career, Mike decided to concentrate on the sociology of deviant behavior. Deviance was new to him and exciting. Each book or article revealed a world of people very different from him. He even felt sometimes as if he were regarding a new species. Yet Mike really liked (or thought he did) the people he studied. He could identify with them easily. Further, he sometimes distrusted so-called "normal" society and its agents of control (such as the police) who sometimes seemed more "deviant" on occasion than the deviants themselves.

Mike sustained his interest in deviants while working on his master's. He insisted on doing field work. His master's thesis was on ghetto alcoholics. He was satisfied that he had really found his niche. But then

came the decline in funds to support graduate education. Mike knew that
it would not be possible for him to get a Ph.D. and hold down a job at the
same time. He also worried about the amount of money he owed on the
loans he had gotten for work on his undergraduate and master's degrees.

As Mike returned to his table, still mulling over the conversation he
had just overheard, he heard Dave ask, "Where've ya been, Mike? We
were afraid you'd gotten lost."

"I've just been eavesdropping," Mike replied. "It's amazing what you
can hear if you keep your ears open. Say, do you remember when I had
that argument with Peterson . . . when I was saying that Allen Funt was
probably one of the best field workers in the country and that 'Candid
Camera' was better research than a lot of what's in the journals today?"

"Sure, I remember it . . . it was right after you and I did that study of
the massage parlor downtown. That was some project."

Mike recalled that study thoughtfully and then said, "Do you remember that talk we had after we read Polsky's article on pornography
in the methods class? Polsky said that porn is a kind of societal safety-
valve that allows good people to relieve sexual tension in a way that won't
threaten society."

Dave heard the excitement in Mike's voice and said, "What're you
driving at?"

"I'm wondering if maybe we could combine Polsky's ideas about porn
with some of our massage parlor work."

Mike, Dave and the women batted the idea around for a while longer
and then the next set came on. At home that night, Mike couldn't get to
sleep. The idea seemed to stick in his mind. "This just might be the ticket
I've been looking for," he thought.

The idea went around in his head for a day or so. Then Mike decided
to try observing people using pornographic materials. He knew he'd have
to do his observations in a place that allowed him a good, private view
of what was going on. First, he went to a few art theaters in Central City,
but nothing seemed interesting.

Then Mike checked out a large "adult" bookstore, the Adult Book
Exchange. Its front windows were painted over, making it impossible to
see in from the street. The store advertised that it had a full range of adult
reading materials, marital aids, XXX-rated movies, and more than 50
"Peep Shows." On the door, a boldly lettered sign proclaimed, "You Must
Be 21 To Enter." When Mike first entered the store, his eyes were jarred
by the harsh fluorescent lights. The store clerk sat on a platform so he
could observe the entire store. On the customer side of the platform was
a display case crammed full of sexual aids, everything from artificial
sexual organs made out of latex and rubber to exotic leather and metal

implements that looked as though they had come from a medieval torture chamber. Also in the display case were 8mm pornographic movies with an explicit sex scene from the films depicted on the outside of the carton.

The front part of the store was crammed with racks of pornographic literature, arranged by subject. One section, for example, was labeled "Boobs" and had several columns of magazines featuring naked, bosomy women. Another, prominently labeled "Gay," contained magazines depicting men in homosexual activities. Other sections advertised "Swingers Publications," "Bondage and Discipline," even some sexual variations that were new to Mike. The central area contained racks of pocket books.

The "Peep Shows" were in the back of the store. These were individual cubicles with brief pornographic movies. On the door of each cubicle was a sexually explicit picture of the actors and a brief description of that film's content. To watch a movie, a customer entered the cubicle, locked the door, and deposited twenty-five cents in a coin box, activating the movie projector. A quarter, Mike learned, was good for only a few minutes' worth of the movie. He had to insert more coins if he wanted the movie to continue. Each time a quarter was inserted into the coin box, a red light over the cubicle would go on, indicating the booth was occupied, thereby assuring the customer's privacy.

After browsing for a while, he left and wandered a few doors down the street, where he found the Eros Adult Book Store. Inside, Mike discovered that the Eros was almost identical in layout to the Adult Book Exchange. Two other adult bookstores in the neighborhood were laid out in the same way. Mike was intrigued by what he was seeing. He surmised that the stores were organized similarly so that customers could find their way on their own. That way no one would be embarrassed by having to make a lot of inquiries. Given the seamy nature of the bookstores and the somewhat "deviant" character of pornography, Mike reasoned, patrons probably preferred anonymity.

Mike's idea for a study began to take shape. By clerking in one of the bookstores, he could learn about the world of pornography and its customers. Now, the problem was how to get in, how to get a job as a clerk. "I don't think the stores run ads in the 'help wanted' column of the paper. I guess you have to know someone. But who?" Mike thought. To get the job Mike finally talked to a businessman he had met during an earlier study for a sociology course—the bartender-owner of a place in the same neighborhood as the adult bookstores.

"Dobby, I'm in a bind," Mike said. "I need work, but I still need time for my studies. I know it's a helluva thing to say, but I need to work in a place where I could read and write on the job. You know, maybe like a watchman or a clerk in one of those stores [Mike tossed his head to indicate the cluster of adult bookstores down the block] around here. You know, nothing really strenuous. I don't need a lot of money, just enough for the rent and a couple of your watered-down beers," Mike said, laughing.

"Well, it ain't exactly my cup of tea, but I'll ask around for you. I see a couple 'a the guys every now and then. Maybe somebody will know something. Why don'cha stop back by in a couple 'a days." Both Dobby and Mike turned their attention to the TV set above the bar, and Mike left a short while later.

A few days later Mike stopped by Dobby's bar and ordered a beer. At the other end of the bar, Dobby was talking to a short, heavyset, middle-aged man. Mike had drunk about half of his beer when Dobby came over and said he wanted Mike to meet someone.

"Mike, this is Big Al. This is the kid I was talking about." Mike and Big Al shook hands.

"Whad are ya—a college boy?" Big Al said. "One 'a the boys, he left and I need somebody for afternoons. The work ain't hard, but ya gotta be dependable. That means ya gotta be there six days a week and ya gotta be on time. Ya make change for the peeps, ya work the register, and ya keep the place clean. I know how much money is there and I keep track a' the inventory. At the end of the week I add everthing up and deduct what's missin' from yer pay. I don't care whether you take it or some-body lifts, you still pay. Understand?" Mike nodded, and Al went on, almost nonstop. "And another thing . . . if there's any trouble you gotta handle it. Yer on yer own. I don't know nothin', ya know what I mean? I'll come settle up with ya on Saturday, like I said. Oh yeah, the pay is five bucks an hour, OK? Oh yeah, one other thing. When yer there I don't want none of yer college friends hanging around. No questions? OK, be at the Exotic tomorrow at noon and let Bernie break ya in. OK, college boy, now be a good kid and run along. Me and Dobby got something to talk about."

Mike left the bar feeling numb. Everything had happened so fast, but there he was, he was in! Mike had trouble sleeping that night. The idea of the study had really turned him on. "And here's hoping," he thought, "it'll be my ticket to grad school."

Before noon the next day Mike was at the Exotic Book Store and Adult Cinema. He was disappointed to find the door locked. In a few minutes, however, an aging, nondescript man unlocked the door. Mike approached him and held out his hand. The man looked puzzled for a moment and then said, "Oh, yeah, you're the college boy. Come on in. Yeah, my name's Bernie. I'll come on by and open up for you. Go ahead, look around a bit while I get set up."

The Exotic was almost identical to the other places Mike had been in. When he stepped up on the platform with Bernie, he noticed an elaborate system of mirrors that gave the person behind the counter a full command of the store, even a view of what was happening in the peep show cubicles. Mike noticed that from the platform he could also see out the window and up and down the street. His vantage point also gave him an excellent view of the adjacent parking lot used by the store's customers.

"You ever work a store before?" Mike heard Bernie ask. Without allowing him time to answer, Bernie continued, "Na, I guess not. Well, it's just like a candy store—'cept it don't ruin your teeth, just your eyes!" Bernie stopped to laugh at his own joke. After a moment he went on, "You just gotta sit up here and keep an eye on things. There ain't no salesmanship in this business. Either they're buying or they ain't. The only important thing, you make sure no kids come in here. You see anyone that looks under twenty-one you throw him out. Don't even mess aroun' looking at I.D.'s. You don't let nobody bother the merchandise and if somebody hangs around too long, you tell him this ain't no public library."

"You see all these mirrors, you can watch the whole joint without moving a muscle. Now if anybody gets loud or starts making trouble, or if you see any punks hangin' around in the lot outside . . . here, you see this. . . . " Bernie reached under the counter and took out a heavy length of pipe wrapped with electrician's tape. "This here is the 'Equalizer.' You look like a strong kid. You know what I mean. . . . "

Mike was glad Bernie stayed with him the first day, but he quickly discovered that the work wasn't hard and that trouble—at least the kind that might call for the 'Equalizer'—was unlikely.

During the next few weeks, Mike learned much about the porn business and the social organization of pornography consumption. No one seemed to object—or even seemed to notice—that the young man behind the counter was writing. Mike's field journal grew by leaps and bounds. He recorded detailed notes both on the store's traffic patterns and the interactional patterns of its patrons as they encountered each other in what was a potentially embarrassing, or even harmful, social setting.

The possibility of embarrassment struck Mike powerfully one day after a few months at the Exotic when someone requested that he change three one-dollar bills into quarters for use in the peeps. Mike looked down and nearly fell out of his chair when he saw the provost of his university in front of him. The official did not recognize Mike, of course, but Mike was somewhat shaken. He watched as Dr. Andrews went into a cubicle showing a gay film. Dr. Andrews then went into a second cubicle, this one showing a film about a homosexual orgy, with six men having sexual relations together.

After the provost left the store, Mike began thinking about the consumers of pornography. Short of recording their behavior on film and analyzing it, Mike was reasonably satisfied that he had a good view of their activities, but he wanted to know more about his customers personally.

He realized that interviews in the store were out of the question. In the few months he'd been working there, he'd had no conversations with any of the store's customers. They had been intent on going about their business. How could he get to these people? How could he find out how much disparity separated their public from their private lives? Mike realized he could keep detailed records on customer preferences and behavior. Then, because most customers parked in the lot adjacent to the store, Mike began identifying them by license plate numbers. He recorded the plate number on a file card and wrote a brief description of the customer whose license number it was. He also noted other details: general appearance, the presence or absence of a wedding band, the customer's demeanor and in-store behavior. Finally, Mike documented each time the person came into the store and the pornography the customer either bought or watched. Mike had soon amassed a detailed file on several dozen people.

Mike then began working out the second part of his study. He started translating license plate numbers into names and addresses. For a small fee, the state department of motor vehicles readily supplied information. Getting interviews with these people away from the store would be difficult. Mike concluded that a direct, up-front approach would almost certainly get him nowhere and might even cause trouble. Because Dave was an expert in survey instrument design, Mike decided to get his advice. While Mike didn't tell Dave whom he wanted to interview, he did say he wanted to elicit some fairly sensitive material and asked what might be the best way to go about getting it.

Dave said that a health-oriented survey is one good way to go after personal information. Studies focusing on knowledge, attitudes, and preferences also usually work well. These data could then be compared to social and demographic data and whatever else Mike might have. The combination of public, private, and attitudinal information would make for a good psychological profile, Mike realized.

Mike's first decision was to quit his job at the store before going after the interviews. He enlisted some friends to help him conduct interviews, and he decided to tell them the "private history" of each subject. Only if they were fully informed, Mike reasoned, would they be able to get the in-depth interview he needed. Finally, in designing his questionnaire Mike decided his subjects would be told that their names had been randomly drawn. Some questions would concern personal happiness, job satisfaction, and marital adjustment. A few "smoke-screen questions" about health and general symptoms would be asked and then the subject would be led into a series of probing questions about sexual preferences. A good interviewer could elicit information about how subjects obtained sexual satisfaction. After sketching out the questionnaire, Mike sat back feeling really good. This should get him the attention he needed, he thought. "Damnit, you're good, Weinstein!" Mike said to himself.[2]

GOOD PEOPLE:
A LOOK AT SOME OF THE ISSUES

Mike's involvement in this study was partly the result of his creativity and diligence and partly plain good luck. Chance conversations, the memory of studies he had read about, and one of his own research efforts converged in his mind. Then there was his good fortune in landing the job just at the right time. Without detracting from the importance of careful planning, the success of some of the best work in both the natural and social sciences involves just such a fortuitous confluence of factors.

Some social scientists choose their fields of study primarily because they want to help other people and hope that their research will promote the welfare of others. Mike may be motivated in part by the thought that someone may benefit from his work. He doesn't harbor any ill will toward the people he studies and certainly doesn't intend harm to anyone, but helping doesn't seem to be his primary motive. He has chosen sociology simply because he finds it fascinating. He is a kind of professional voyeur. He finds people fascinating and wants to learn more about them and about social behavior. He may study deviants because what he learns from them may help him to understand human behavior in general; hence he may learn from them something about the rest of society.

---

[2]This fictitious case is in some ways similar to a well-known and highly controversial study of homosexual behavior in public rest rooms in parks. See Laud Humphreys, *Tearoom Trade: Impersonal Sex in Public Places* (Chicago: Aldine, 1970).

Mike does not appear to have any qualms about the ethics of his research; as the case is presented, there isn't any indication that he even raised any serious questions about ethics. Some people might think that ethics is unimportant here because they feel, even unconsciously, that deviants have fewer rights than "normal" people. There is no evidence that Mike has that attitude. More likely, he has just never thought much about ethics at all. Mike may not have thought to pose ethical questions for himself simply because he assumes that people aren't bothered by being observed. Even applying the Golden Rule may not seem to suggest any problems for Mike. He may expect people to watch him with the same curiosity that motivates his observation of them. We need to go beyond a Golden Rule which deals only with what we would want done to us, constituted and situated as we are. We need to ask what we would want done if we were wearing the other man's shoes. We need to ask Mike to put himself in the place of those people he is studying. How would he feel if he were a respectable, middle-aged patron of the Exotic Bookstore?

Asking Mike to look at things this way challenges him to use his sociological skill and imagination to get inside another person. Such efforts may be as important to the study of ethics as they are for sociology and anthropology. This approach will not solve all our ethical questions, but it will certainly make us aware of issues we might otherwise miss. If Mike can accomplish this act of imagination, he might find himself uncomfortable as the object of scientific scrutiny. He would probably realize that his study raises several issues worth examining from an ethical perspective. In the next chapter, we will focus our attention on two of these, privacy and deception.

6

The Researcher
as Uninvited Guest:
The Issues
of Privacy and Deception

Participant research, such as that described in the preceding chapter, can be fraught with ethical problems, but we will discuss only two suggested by Mike's pornography study: privacy and deception. These issues are not unique to participant research, and we urge you to consider the implications of our discussions of Mike's study as you think about our earlier cases and those that will follow.

RESPECT FOR PRIVACY

At least in our society, most people agree that privacy is fundamental. At the level of personal relationships, we acknowledge boundaries limiting the intrusion of others. People seem to require a degree of physical and psychological space, though they may differ about its relative importance and about the areas that they define as private. Some people will talk freely to almost anyone about intimate details of their lives; others build such impenetrable walls to protect themselves that no one ever knows the real person behind those defenses, often to the detriment of the person's emotional health and well-being.

Everyone probably has some holy ground where intruders are not welcome, and we expect a certain reticence. "Spilling one's guts" or "washing dirty linen in public" can be in bad taste; perhaps it can even be "sick" or "immoral."

Part of the art of friendship is the gradual disclosure of the inner self as mutual trust develops. The process requires a willingness to know and accept the other person and the sensitivity and skill of knowing when and how far to penetrate the hidden recesses of the other person; friendship requires learning when the boundary protecting privacy has been

reached. The same is true of counseling and psychotherapeutic relationships. People will allow others to enter the inner sanctum of their lives
only if they trust them, and trust will not develop if a person feels that
another is prying without permission. The desire for privacy in one-to-
one relationships carries over into the more impersonal and sometimes
depersonalized institutional dimensions of our lives where our interactions may be fleeting contacts with strangers.

But does the *fact* that people guard their privacy have any *ethical* implications? From the fact that people desire privacy we cannot deduce
by logic alone that privacy is their right and respect for it our obligation.
But if we believe that respect for others is a basic moral requirement, then
respect for privacy is also an obligation. If people *in fact* want privacy,
how can we treat them with respect if we don't give them the psychological space to be individuals and to choose when and to whom they
will disclose themselves?

Privacy is related to personal liberty and autonomy. These concepts
include the right of people to govern their own lives, to decide what to
share with others, and to be left alone.[1] Personal liberty is woven into
the cultural fabric of Anglo-American society. *Political philosophers* may
defend this liberty in terms of the "social contract" on which our social

---

[1]Some thinkers derive the right of privacy from the right to liberty. We see
them more as integrally related and interdependent. One writer has insisted that
privacy is fundamental, more basic even than liberty or autonomy. See Arthur
L. Caplan, "On Privacy and Confidentiality in Social Science Research," in Tom
L. Beauchamp, et al., eds., *Ethical Issues in Social Science Research* (Baltimore:
The Johns Hopkins University Press, 1982) 315-25. His argument is that privacy
is a basic human need, like food, and it is a mistake to derive privacy from autonomy. "Autonomy and self-determination are concepts that can only be pred-
icated of persons. But to be a person and to remain a person, human beings require
a modicum of privacy" (320).

Identifying something as a *need,* however, does not logically make it a *right*
unless we add the moral judgment that people have a right to have their needs
met. It may be *reasonable* to base moral claims or duties on people's needs, but
it is not *logically* necessary to do so. Moreover, even acknowledging that needs
give rise to rights does not tell us how extensive those rights are or what others'
obligations are with reference to them. The rights may be essentially negative
ones, for example, requiring that we not interfere with a person's efforts to acquire food. Or they may make positive claims, meaning that we individually or
as a society have an obligation to provide food. We must still ask "How much
and what kind?" Must we provide cake, or is bread enough?

Obviously the same questions arise with privacy. If privacy is a fundamental
need that we ought to respect, how much privacy do people deserve? Just as the
claim to food may be conditioned by society's resources, so a claim to privacy
may be a function of social structure and social needs.

and political system is based or as an expression of the "Law of Nature" (and perhaps of "Nature's God"). Some *theologians* insist upon respect for individual freedom and privacy, not because people have any inherent dignity that requires respect but because they have been given such dignity by being the object of God's love irrespective of merit. The theologian may note that the Jewish and Christian concept of human creation includes human freedom. God will not override the freedom to choose evil instead of good or even to reject God. If even God respects human freedom, how much more imperative it is for human beings to respect the freedom of one another, so the theological argument might go. A very different approach might be taken by a *utilitarian* who espouses the principle of personal liberty because adopting it will make people happier. We ought to respect people's privacy, the utilitarian may tell us, because we will all be happier if we can rest assured that we will not be subjected to undue surveillance.

These different forms of ethical theory may arrive at the same principle of liberty or autonomy, though they travel different roads en route. Privacy is a correlate of freedom, and the total abolition of privacy coincides with the demise of freedom. The horror of George Orwell's novel *1984* is marked by the complete denial of any legitimate sphere of privacy. In the society dominated by Big Brother, not only have freedom of action and freedom of speech been eliminated. Even the last outpost of liberty, freedom of thought, has been overrun by the agents of the totalitarian state, the thought police. Regardless of the starting place one chooses in developing an ethic, it seems clear that a respect for privacy is an essential component if there is to be any space for human freedom.

It is easy to endorse the *concept* of privacy in principle. It is quite another matter to know when something is private and to define the scope and limits of privacy in daily life. Any patron of the Exotic Bookstore might feel that Mike violated his privacy, and that feeling deserves ethical attention. But the man's *feeling* alone does not *prove* that his privacy has been invaded. We must look more closely to see what constitutes a violation of privacy.

Defining Privacy

It is one thing to discuss what privacy means to a particular individual whom we know well. We may then decide whether John's or Sally's or Henry's personal definition is binding on us in our relationship with them. But researchers don't even have that personal information to aid them. How can we know what privacy means?

Perhaps some areas of life are simply private "by nature." The customers of the Exotic Bookstore might claim that Mike has intruded into just such an area of their lives: their sexual behavior. Our society considers sex more private than many other topics, though the increase in "R-rated" and "X-rated" movies may indicate that sex has become less private. Some critics of the sexual revolution contend that the public display of sex is destructive precisely because it demeans an area of intimacy that is nurtured by privacy.

Is it possible that some areas of life are so private by nature that any research is simply inappropriate? For example, should the well-known studies of human sexuality by Masters and Johnson not have been done? Their scientific observations and analyses have enlarged our understanding of sexual behavior and promoted the development of effective therapy for some of the sexually dysfunctional. Nevertheless, some may think that the researchers were wrong in suggesting such studies and participants were wrong in cooperating because the techniques changed an intimate personal act into a laboratory experiment.

Even though the *subject* of sex is no longer a taboo in our society, we daresay that most people still consider *their own sex lives* a private matter. Privacy is not an all-or-nothing proposition, but a matter of degree. Privacy does not mean sharing something with no one; it does mean that we are discreet in determining with whom and how to share something. Thus many people rarely discuss their own sexual activity and are highly selective in deciding with whom to share such talk.

The nature of an activity has something to do with its privacy, but surely *its location* is also a factor in determining the degree of privacy that people can reasonably expect. Mike has chosen a semipublic place for his field observations. He has not hidden under the bed in a motel room or installed hidden cameras in a private dwelling. Although the setting is not as public as an open-air market, the store is open to anyone over twenty-one. Any patron must be aware that he can be observed by anyone else in the store. Moreover, Mike (the clerk) is in clear view, acknowledged by all as one who has a right to be there to "keep an eye on things" in the store. Anyone who does not wish to risk being observed in this way should stay out of the store.

Mike might tell a disgruntled customer who discovered what he was doing, "Look, I'm just sitting here in a public place making notes about what I see. You gave up your privacy by coming into the store. If you want privacy, stay at home, or wear a mask when you come in next time."

But that may not be entirely fair. Is not the store's structure designed to provide a kind of mask? The darkened windows to prevent passersby from peering in, the arrangement of the store (including private viewing booths), and the aloofness of the clerk create an atmosphere of anonymity. However, the measure of privacy that the proprietor can provide is clearly limited. Whatever impression of privacy the setting provides is partly illusory, depending in no small measure on the assumption that customers will afford each other some protection. The banker who bumps into one of his tellers in the store can normally count on the other's not "telling stories out of school" because doing so requires the teller to reveal that he too is a patron. But if the teller happens to pride himself on being a "dirty old man," he may be delighted to share this gossip with his fellow workers. The banker may be embarrassed at seeing his employee in the Exotic, and he may be infuriated about the tongue-wagging around the bank—and he may find a way to get even. But it is far from clear that his right to privacy has been violated by his employee. The location was, at best, only semiprivate, and no oath of secrecy was exacted from customers as a condition of admission to the store.

Another factor in defining the limits of privacy may be the individual's own *intentions.* To some extent each individual's own definition determines what is private for him or her. A self-proclaimed prostitute talking about her "professional" activity on a nationally televised talk show apparently does not consider her sexual affairs private. Compare her to Dr. Andrews, the provost, who steps stealthily into Mike's store, quickly views several pornographic movies, and slips quietly back onto the street.[2]

Even when the observed behavior occurs in a public place, intentions may affect levels of privacy. A gay-rights activist engaged at a park in a demonstration calling for changes in public policy regarding homosexuals has less claim to privacy with regard to sexual preference than the homosexual couple discreetly holding hands in the same park, even though the locations are identical.

Finally, we should ask if the definition of privacy—or of the invasion of privacy—may partly depend on "the eye of the beholder." Everyone,

---

[2]Not only do *individuals* differ in their understanding of privacy. Different *societies* will also have different definitions of what is generally considered public and private. J. A. Barnes, *The Ethics of Inquiry in Social Science* (New Delhi: Oxford University Press, 1977) 16-17, illustrates the difference between Western societies by a comparison of Britain and Norway. In Great Britain, income tax returns for ordinary citizens (in contrast to public officials) are considered private and do not become part of the national archives but are destroyed after a number of years. If, however, a person is charged with drunken driving, that fact will become public knowledge through the local newspaper. In Norway, tax returns are considered more public, and lists showing the income and tax of individuals are posted in local post offices. But arrests for drunken driving, even though conviction carries a mandatory jail sentence, are reported only anonymously in the press, so that one's friends may never know.

to some degree, is a student of human behavior; looking is part of living in a social world. Nevertheless, the systematic observation conducted by a social scientist like Mike, one who is trained to use research tools to see things that others would miss, is a greater intrusion than the more casual observations of a fellow patron or the ordinary store clerk. Although Mike may observe only what anyone might see, because of his skill and organized procedure he sees more than others because he sees more deeply. Research subjects generally may not recognize how much of their lives will be open to the discerning eyes of the social or behavioral scientist whom they invite in. They may reveal far more of themselves than they realize or intend, simply because researchers know what to look for and how to interpret what they see.

So far we have been dealing with the definition of privacy. If Mike wants to know whether he is sticking his nose into a private area, he must ask himself several questions suggested above. How *public* is the bookstore, how *private* is sex itself, how *private* do the patrons believe their presence in the store is, and how *invasive* are the research techniques?

However, the discussion does not end with the definition of privacy. Even if Mike has invaded the privacy of his subjects, it is possible that it is a *justifiable* invasion. Let's assume for the moment that Mike's investigation is an incursion into private territory. What reasons might he give for violating privacy?

Justifying Intrusions

Mike might say it is permissible if he has obtained the permission of his subjects. Then it would not be an *invasion* of privacy. It might still be wrong, if there are subjects so private that they ought never to be studied, even with consent. Perhaps we should turn our backs, as it were, when faced with an "exhibitionist" intent on revealing the "unspeakable." But that question will seldom arise. Obtaining subjects' permission and making provisions to protect their privacy in handling data is usually sufficient to satisfy ethical concerns about privacy. This is because our society generally considers privacy a *right* that people can waive. Knowing how to obtain that waiver is more perplexing. We will deal with this issue in a bit more detail in the next chapter.

But even without consent, invasion of privacy might be morally justifiable because there are other "goods" besides privacy and other duties besides respecting autonomy, and sometimes these might be more important than privacy. Criminal and congressional investigations and hearings are examples that come quickly to mind. The public's "right to know" is greater than the "right to privacy" of those being investigated. Can this weighing of conflicting goods or duties apply to research? Several possible lines of reasoning can be considered.

First, Mike might argue that the reason for respecting privacy is that intrusion makes people uncomfortable. Since his research is not going to make anyone uncomfortable (his subjects don't even know their privacy is being compromised), insisting on privacy serves no useful purpose. Especially when no harm results and benefits are clear, it may seem reasonable to ignore any question of privacy. Mike may personally derive great benefit from his study—admission to graduate school and a future career. Even more telling, some *social good* might result. His project might help answer questions with implications for public policy: Does pornography contribute to rape, incest, violence, and other forms of social disruption? Or does it provide that safety valve which reduces the occurrence of crimes of sexual violence?

Another rationale for Mike's violating the privacy of his subjects might be that the *subjects themselves,* or at least the category to which they belong, may benefit from his research. If the study contributed to the development of a profile that would predict dangerous sexual deviants, early recognition might mean early therapy, and people might be saved from the worst effects of a terrible psychological disorder. Or the study might increase understanding and encourage greater tolerance for Mike's subjects.

Mike's study, of course, is unlikely to produce dramatic results, but positive consequences are conceivable. Would these considerations justify an invasion of privacy? Some would insist that the *principle* must be defended if liberty is to survive, and that people's privacy needs protection most when they are least aware of a threat, since that is when they are least able to protect it themselves. To endorse even an innocuous compromise of such an important principle for Mike's benefit or some social good would contribute to the erosion of individual liberty. Some would thus resolve the problem entirely on principle, disregarding all cost/benefit analysis.

Roles, Relationships, and Privacy

General principles about privacy become personal when we encounter the issue in our own specific roles and our relationships. My responsibility may be somewhat different if the object of concern is my friend, my spouse, my child, or my boss. An attorney will treat his or her client's privacy differently than will the district attorney. Physicians will have a different approach to their patients' privacy than will an investigative reporter on the trail of a scandal. Sometimes we find a conflict between our several roles. A supervisor who is also a friend may learn something about an employee that company policy would require him to report but that his friendship makes him want to hide. An employee's obligation to keep company secrets might conflict with his obligations as citizen. General ethical principles may define some parameters, but not all the particulars, that are conditioned by roles and relations. Specific social roles, complete with rules for their conduct, were not prescribed by the gods on some exalted Mt. Olympus. Roles and their requirements are human creations, emerging subtly from personal relations or self-consciously created by acts of deliberate definition. Neither process is ever finished, but some periods see more changes in expectations. Recently behavioral and social scientists have become more explicit about their role obligations.

The codes of ethics of these sciences reflect concern for the privacy of research subjects.[3] Setting clear policies, either in professional codes or in law, might be useful in guiding researchers. But one problem with codes, professional or legal, is that they may be too rigid to accommodate the subtle differences between situations. If rigidity is avoided, then regulations may be too vague to be enforceable or even helpful.

Respecting and Protecting Privacy

So far we have been dealing with respect for privacy. Researchers should realize that they are not welcome to enter people's private lives at will. Recognizing the boundary between public and private and negotiating a consent to enter a private area will require a sensitivity and skill not acquired simply by learning a set of rules or techniques. But concern for privacy is not limited to the acquiring of information. Respecting privacy also involves protecting it both in handling data and in publishing the results of a study. Violations of privacy can consist of either invading a private sphere to obtain information that we never make public or the unauthorized public disclosure of private information legitimately available to us. As citizen and social scientist, Mike has the capacity to commit both "sins."

Some readers may feel that Mike has been a bit cavalier about the issue of privacy in acquiring his research data. But even if this is so, this does not mean that his subjects' privacy was completely ignored. The

---

[3]The Code of Ethics of the American Sociological Association, for example, states that "research subjects are entitled to rights of privacy and dignity of treatment." With regard to cross-national research, the code provides that "research should take culturally appropriate steps . . . to avoid invasions of privacy." The basic ten principles of the American Psychological Association do not refer specifically to privacy, but seem to include that concern under Principle J, which is expressed in terms of "confidentiality." The Principles of Professional Responsibility of the American Anthropological Association refer to the "informant's right to welfare, dignity and privacy."

very fact that Mike is a social scientist may offer his subjects a kind of protection not available from other, more casual observers who populate the adult bookstore. In the first place, *as a scientist,* Mike is not really interested in the behavior of identifiable individuals. Individuals provide *examples* of behavior that typify more general human responses. Because the social scientist is concerned with social phenomena, not with the practitioner thereof, Mike is not ultimately interested in Dr. Andrews the provost, or Mr. Bigbucks the banker, or Mr. Shaw the truck driver as individuals. He looks beyond the individual to the composite picture shaped from aggregate data. Hence one might argue that subjects' privacy is protected by the presumed indifference of scientists to their individual subjects.

Second, as a social scientist, Mike almost certainly feels a professional obligation to protect the identity of his subjects. Dr. Andrews should be grateful that Mike-the-scientist was on duty the day he visited the store instead of Mike-the-college-kid. His secret is more secure this way. We do not mean, of course, that scientists do not violate the privacy of individuals, but the norms developed by the disciplines of the social and behavioral sciences themselves recognize the importance of privacy, probably for both pragmatic and ethical reasons. Behavioral and social scientists must be especially careful not to abuse their power, and we believe that most of them are responsible about this.

Problems with privacy can occur in the *handling of data.* Personal information about identifiable individuals should be protected by researchers. The principle is simple. The *how* may be more complicated. In the handling of his data, Mike must take special care that the personal information he has obtained not be allowed to fall into the hands of someone who does not need and cannot justify having the information from Mike. This may mean coding his notes so that there are no names on his note cards, in case anyone else should find and read his field notes. He may need to take special precautions about storing such information, too, especially since the material is sensitive. This problem is becoming increasingly difficult in the computer age, and some social scientists are going to great lengths to protect computer-stored information from too ready access.

The more hands that handle data, the more likely it is that someone will leak information. This raises a question about Mike's assistants who help with the follow-up interviewing. Can they be relied upon to keep private information private? Should they be trusted with the information about Phase One of the study so they can be more alert to the information Mike is after in the interviews? Or does that increase too much the likelihood that the protection of privacy will be breached, either

willfully or inadvertently? Developing techniques that protect private
data is essentially a technical matter, though it is certainly one of those
technical matters with significant ethical import. Especially when they
are handling sensitive information, researchers must exercise as much
imagination in developing systems to protect their data as they do in obtaining it.

Problems can also occur at the time of *publication.* If Mike follows
commonly accepted procedures, he may disguise the location of the study
by using some fictitious city name like "Widgetsville" and he will avoid
details or alter insignificant facts to disguise the identity of his subjects.
Dr. Andrews will become bald rather than having gray hair and Mike will
omit any reference to Mr. Bigbucks's distinctive red blazer. In spite
of these efforts, Mike may find it difficult to develop a really effective
disguise.

Considering the kinds of sensitive issues that psychologists, anthropologists, and sociologists sometimes study, it is amazing the degree of
acceptance they find. Not infrequently the anthropologist or ethnogra-
pher is more concerned with protecting a subject's privacy than the subject is. Sometimes subjects will insist that there be no disguise or will
keep a copy of the book close at hand and freely identify themselves to
anyone who is interested.[4] Notwithstanding this lack of concern for privacy on the part of some subjects, behavioral and social scientists rightly
continue to be cautious in their publications, attempting to protect the
privacy of their subjects. It is part of an implicit bargain that the profession has struck with society, not just with their individual subjects.

---

[4]J. A. Barnes refers to T. N. Madan's work among Kashmiri Pandits. He became deeply involved in the most intimate details of their lives and was thus
greatly concerned to protect the privacy of the village, even deciding not to publish some information relevant to the theme of his book. The citizens of the village, however, insisted that the identity of their village not be disguised at all.
Barnes also comments that the primary informant for William Whyte's *Street
Corner Society* acknowledged that he would be embarrassed by Whyte's description of him but insisted that he go ahead and print it, because "this is the
way it was" (Barnes, *Ethics of Inquiry,* 31-35). Sometimes the researchers can go
to great lengths to protect people who aren't interested in being protected. Carl
Klockers, *The Professional Fence* (New York: Free Press, 1974) carefully disguised his study of a professional fence to keep him from getting arrested. The
fence himself, however, was proud of the book and kept one in his store to show
to virtually anyone. By contrast, one of the most noteworthy sociological studies
a generation ago was Arthur J. Vidich and Joseph Bensman's, *Small Town in Mass
Society* (Garden City NY: Doubleday, 1960). Because the authors were well
known, it was easy to deduce which small town near their university was the
subject. Apparently many of the residents of the community were offended and
embarrassed by the book.

We have argued up to this point that privacy is an important part of human life, especially in a free society. It is not unlimited, as we have suggested by our allusions to criminal investigations. It is important that we point to one issue regarding privacy and research about which controversy continues—the possible limitation of privacy for an important social purpose. Suppose that Mike's work brings him face to face with a man whose picture he saw on the front page of the morning paper, a man wanted by local police in connection with a rape and murder. Can Mike ignore claims of privacy and call the police? Would he be wrong in *not* doing so? Suppose Mike's recognition was not based on simple observation but was deduced from information gathered in the second half of the study, where confidentiality was explicitly promised? Or suppose that Mike is called to testify in the case, not because he was responsible for the arrest but because police discover that the accused was a customer at the Exotic Bookstore? Should Mike share his in-store observations of the man with the court?

For better or worse, researchers are not automatically accorded legal immunity from producing information about their research subjects when courts deem it necessary. The *moral* question, of course, is not resolved simply by knowing what the *law* is. Many researchers insist that they would not reveal private information about their subjects even if refusing to do so led to legal penalties. But there are also good ethical arguments for recognizing that civic obligations are moral duties.

Assisting the apprehension and conviction of someone guilty of some heinous crime is perhaps a much clearer case than those less dramatic but more common occasions when the public welfare might be served in some way by ignoring privacy. Individual researchers must undoubtedly weigh a variety of factors in coming to a decision in a concrete situation: the degree of privacy involved, the seriousness of the evil to be avoided or good to be achieved, the degree of harm to the one whose privacy is at issue, and the nature of the relationship of researcher and subject.

Privacy is important but sometimes difficult to define. It is neither absolute nor insignificant. And it is not the only ethical issue that researchers must consider in their quest for new understanding of human behavior. We turn now to another, and we will return to topics closely related to privacy and its limits in subsequent chapters.

LYING AND DECEPTION

The second aspect of Mike's study that we wish to explore is deception.[5] The issue arises several times in this case. First, did Mike deceive Dobby and Big Al when seeking employment? He did not blatantly lie. What he said was true. He did need a job, he didn't need much money, and he did need to study while he worked. Nevertheless, he has declined to tell either his friend the bartender or his new employer that his *primary* purpose was *to study*—to study the customers in the store. This omission might be seen as deception. He is not "just another college kid" looking for a job, as it would appear. Likewise, Mike presents himself to his customers as "just another clerk," instead of as the sharp-eyed social scientist he really is. Is this deception? Has Mike lied to them, not by his words, but by his actions? Is there any moral difference between deceiving and lying?[6]

Even if we don't characterize these actions as "lies," Mike does seem to have deceived a number of people in this first stage by the covert nature of his research. Like Don in the first case, Mike is engaged in a study in which his subjects do not know they are research subjects. But deception can also be present even when subjects know they are being studied, since they may be misled about the nature of the research. This is evident in the second part of his study. He plans to track down certain customers from the store to gather more data. In doing so, he intends to misrepresent his purposes. He plans to tell people they have been selected *at random* in connection with a *health* survey. He will seek his subjects' consent for this survey, but it will not be an *informed* consent. The subjects are in fact to be *mis*informed. He may contend that he does not plan to *lie* to his survey subjects. There is a randomness to their selection—they are the people who randomly happened into his bookstore. And he is concerned with health, in the broadest sense of that word. Yet it is hard to argue that he does not intend to deceive them. A person

---

[5]We recommend three concise articles that present a taxonomy of research deception. See Joan E. Sieber, "Deception in Social Research I: Kinds of Deception and the Wrongs They May Involve," *IRB: A Review of Human Subjects Research* 4:9 (November, 1982): 1-5; "Deception in Social Research II: Evaluating the Potential for Harm or Wrong," *IRB: A Review of Human Subject Research* 5:1 (January/February 1983): 1-6; and "Deception in Social Research III: The Nature and Limits of Debriefing," *IRB: A Review of Human Subjects Research* 5:3 (May/June, 1983): 1-4.

[6]The most comprehensive book on lying in recent years is Sissela Bok's *Lying: Moral Choice in Public and Private Life* (New York: Pantheon Books, 1978).

can lie while telling the truth, and Mike clearly intends to mislead his respondents.

Underlying the preceding discussion is an assumption that deception is wrong. But is it? Mike might admit that he is lying and ask, "What's wrong with that? Everybody lies." At one level, we know that's true. Everyone does deceive others, at least occasionally. Yet we may be uneasy about such a flippant endorsement of lying. Why?

One of the ethical tests often offered to determine right and wrong is whether we can universalize or generalize our action. What's right for one person ought to be right for anyone else as well. To say that *everybody* lies is certainly generalizing. But that is generalizing about people's actual behavior, not about what they ought to do. Can Mike or any of us believe that it is *right* for *everybody* to lie or deceive? It certainly could not be right *all* the time. Society couldn't exist without some honesty in human relationships. But, you may say, deception might be right sometimes, depending on the circumstances.

In the first place, speaking words that are literally untrue in circumstances where no one expects to be told the truth might not even be considered a lie. Are the exaggerated claims promoted by the advertising industry "lies"? Do people really expect that buying a new toothpaste will cause a significant alteration in their social lives? Etiquette also seems to call for "lies." When we respond to the greeting "Hi, how are you today?" we can grunt "fine" in return even if we are feeling lousy— and we don't feel we've disobeyed some great moral precept in doing so.

In negotiating for a piece of real estate or new car or labor contract, does anyone expect an honest answer to the question, "How much are you willing to give?" It is clear, at least in our society, that the truth is not expected in some contexts. Some "lying" is simply part of the bargaining process. Some social scientists imply that this is the situation with at least some social and behavioral research. They would suggest that researchers need not be more open and honest with subjects than the subjects are with each other and with the researcher.[7]

But research isn't exactly like the negotiations described above, in which both parties have something to gain and are bargaining for their own advantage and where everyone expects a measure of "puffery" and "bluffing." Even in the market place where we as buyers know to beware, we will probably be upset or even outraged if the merchant has written something into a contract that we had not agreed to in the ne-

---

[7]For example, see Gerald Duane Berreman, *Hindus of the Himalayas: Ethnography and Change* 2nd ed. (Berkeley: University of California Press, 1972) xxxiv-xxxix.

gotiation process. Labor leaders do not expect an honest answer to the
question, "What's the highest wage you would consider?" but they do
expect the figures that management presents about the financial condition of the company to be accurate.

We expect people *not* to lie to us in *most* situations. Only in a context
where people are expected to tell the truth can a lie be effective. Mike
can't casually rely on the notion that everyone expects lies as a justification for his deception. People usually expect or want the truth. How
else might Mike try to justify his deception?

If Mike were to operate with a rule-oriented morality, he would look
for rules that will tell him whether he may lie to his subjects or deceive
them. Some moral philosophers and theologians would advise him that
moral rules prohibit all lies.[8] Others would acknowledge a rule against
lying but recognize exceptions to the rule or say that other rules may take
precedence.[9]

---

[8]Immanuel Kant, the prototype of this position, held a nearly absolute view.
In his essay "On the Supposed Right to Lie from Altrustic Motives," Kant argued
that because it is logically impossible to universalize the principle of lying, a lie
is always wrong, though it may be legitimate to withhold information if this can
be done without lying. See Immanuel Kant, *Critique of Practical Reason and
Other Writings in Moral Philosophy,* Lewis White Book, ed. and trans. (Chicago:
University of Chicago Press, 1949) 346-50. Elsewhere Kant presents a more qualified view. Some people who *do not deserve* the truth *cannot expect* us to tell
them the truth. In such a situation, a false statement is not a lie. See Immanuel
Kant, *Lectures on Ethics,* Louis Infield, trans. (New York: Harper & Row, 1963):
147-54.

A contemporary Catholic moral theologian deals with the same issue by relying on a traditional notion of "mental reservation." One may *never* lie, but one
need not be committed to telling "the truth, the whole truth, and nothing but the
truth" either. A true statement that misleads may be acceptable (i.e., is not a lie)
if there is additional information in one's mind that is not stated. See Bernard
Häring, *The Law of Christ: Moral Theology for Priests and Laity,* Edwin G. Kai-
ser, trans. (Westminster MD: Newman Press, 1966) 3:556-76. Rather than saying
that all lies are wrong, but that some deception is not, it seems to us more intellectually honest to say that deceit and lies are both in the same moral category
and sometimes both can be justified.

[9]For example, among W. D. Ross's *prima facie* duties is a rule not to lie. That
rule falls under the duties of faithfulness. Though a real duty, our *actual* duty
might require lying if another *prima facie* duty conflicted with this one and was
a more "stringent" duty. Ross, *The Right and the Good,* 28-29.

For Bernard Gert the rule "Don't deceive" is one of ten basic moral rules. His
moral rules are those that a rational man would publicly advocate as being universally required, but this does not mean absoluteness. Gert says that all moral
rules have exceptions. The exceptions are determined by whether a rational man
would publicly advocate not obeying the rule in this situation; see Gert, *The Moral
Rules,* 68, 90-93.

If Mike's approach to ethics were more consequentialist, he would "guesstimate" the results of lying and not lying. He might say, "If I have to tell these people the truth, I won't find out anything about them." And he might add, "And it's important that I do this research." Such statements raise both factual and value issues. His first remark purports to be a statement of fact; unless he lies he wouldn't obtain reliable information. The second is a value assertion that the study is worthwhile.

Let's look at this approach more carefully, starting with the factual question. Is it true that Mike would not learn anything if his subjects knew they were being studied and what about them was being studied? It is easy to assume that the Exotic Bookstore would quickly lose its customers and Mike would soon lose his job if he were overt about his intentions. Likewise, it may appear obvious that the subjects wouldn't respond to the "health" survey if they knew it was linked to a prior observation of their behavior in the bookstore. Perhaps that is true in Mike's case. Some research probably can't be done unless it is done covertly. Nevertheless, Mike needs to do more than simply assume in an offhand sort of way that his subjects must be deceived. The strategy must be carefully considered before deciding that that is the only way. Numerous skilled researchers have found people surprisingly open in allowing scientists into their lives when they understand the reasons for it and the protection that is afforded.[10]

The second reason that Mike might assert that he "won't find out anything" is that people's behavior changes if they know they're being watched. The term "artifact" is used to refer to the artificial behavior that results from subjects' knowing too much about a study. For example, subjects who are told that a researcher wishes to study their gestures while they converse will become self-conscious; their gestures will probably change because they are thinking about them. Eventually they may relax and begin gesturing normally again. Some artifacts may never disappear,[11] but researchers may assume too easily that deception is necessary. More thought may uncover an effective way to achieve the research goal without deception.

---

[10]Besides Klockers's study of a fence and Madan's study of the Pandits mentioned above, Iannis's experience with the Mafia and Heclo and Wildavsky's study of the British civil service are surprising examples of the openness of some institutions that one would presume to be impenetrable except by covert means.

[11]The feeling, correct or not, that one is being lied to will also create artifacts. That is, subjects who think they are being deceived may try to guess the "real" purpose of the study, and their guess, whether right or wrong, may affect their behavior.

This brings us to the second issue Mike might raise—that "it's important that I do this research." What might make the study important enough to justify deception? Some of the same considerations apply here that we discussed regarding the invasion of privacy. Who will benefit, and how much, and is the benefit worth the moral cost? Will Mike's getting admitted to graduate school justify the deception? If knowing more about the clients of pornography enabled society to protect itself against sexual deviants, would that justify the deception? If the public were to be relieved of fear by knowing that pornography reduces rather than increases the likelihood of sexual violence, would that legitimize the deception? If Mike's subjects benefited from being better understood, would that warrant deceptive practices? In an ethic of consequences, all these considerations would be valid.

A relational approach to ethics would consider both rules and consequences, but may highlight additional features of the situation. A relational ethic will inquire directly into the nature and quality of human relationships involved in our actions. Such an approach, for example, would emphasize the different roles that people play and the differences in relationships that result. Although Mike is still a student, he is functioning as a social scientist, and that role will in part define his relationships with the people he sees in the bookstore. His relationships and hence his moral responsibility are clearly different than if he were an undercover police officer assigned to the bookstore in a stakeout for a sex offender. Nowadays the role of a social scientist is accompanied by some specific ethical expectations. Informal norms have been developing for some time; some are institutionalized in codes of ethics of the various scientific groups. Federal regulations providing guidelines for research have emerged in recent years. These norms form part of the context within which ethical analysis and moral decision must occur.

Mike's relationships and hence his responsibilities include others besides his subjects. Was Mike fair to Big Al in failing to tell him his intentions? No doubt he has been a good employee—dependable, trustworthy, vigilant. Would Big Al be upset now to discover that Mike has been a covert researcher? Would he have cared at the beginning? If Mike is "found out" now, will that rupture the relationship between Big Al and Dobby, since Dobby had recommended him? Has Mike been unfaithful to Dobby by not being more forthright? Or can Mike rightly feel that he has kept faith with his old friend and his new employer by doing his job well, confident that they wouldn't really understand what this research business really meant anyway and wouldn't care as long as it didn't cause them any trouble?

A relational ethic may be more concerned with the "honesty" of a relationship than the veracity of what is said. Faithfulness in relationships may be the fundamental value. In a situation in which Mike will be misunderstood by speaking the literal truth, faithfulness might justify some forms of deception.[12]

It is difficult to imagine human relations without trust. In the absence of some underlying confidence in the honesty of others, society would be a "war of all against all," and individual relationships would be marked by suspicion and fear. Isolation and alienation would be the perennial characteristics of such a "social *dis*order." An ethic that sees human relationships as the fundamental moral category may be grounded in a theology of a God of love whose creatures need to love and to be loved or in a philosophy that begins with the empirical observation that the human animal is a social animal and moves from there to an ethic emphasizing relationships. From their different perspectives countless theologians and philosophers and counselors and psychotherapists of all stripes insist on the necessity of loving relationships as essential for human fulfillment, health, and happiness. Deep and enduring relationships require truthfulness and honesty. Lying and deception must therefore be seen as exceptional rather than normal. Yet exceptions may sometimes be warranted within a framework that affirms human community.

Relational ethics need not stop at immediate interpersonal relationships. Institutional and impersonal relationships are difficult to assess, but the ideal of human community may be the basis of a critique of social institutions or even of societies themselves. In many ways, American society may be perceived as having made significant moral advances in the past two decades. A number of "rights" movements (civil rights, women's rights, gay rights, consumers' rights, and so on) have promoted the cause of social justice. This new spirit brought a new concern for the human rights of research subjects. But these several movements are a

---

[12]The German theologian Dietrich Bonhoeffer held such a view and describes an example of "truthfulness in the situation." A child, asked by his teacher in the classroom whether his alcoholic father is a "drunk," does not lie by saying "no," Bonhoeffer argues, because the question is an inappropriate one for a child in that setting. To answer "no" is more "true" in those circumstances than a literally correct affirmative response would be. The child's loyalty to his father and the inappropriateness of the question combine to require a higher level of truth than verbal veracity. A more mature person might have found a way to maintain loyalty to the father and reproach the teacher at the same time. The best that the child can do is a simple negative response. Dietrich Bonhoeffer, *Ethics,* Eberhard Bethge, ed. (New York: Macmillan, 1965) 363-72.

mixed blessing, for the emphasis on rights and autonomy has fed an individualism and a legalism that may undermine the development of human community. The language of rights is a useful tool for a disenfranchised group making its just claims upon the majority, and the concept of "contract" is a useful device in equalizing a relationship (like management and labor or a doctor/patient relationship) that has been unequal. But there is a danger that excessive use of these categories will be detrimental to human relationships. Morality may become external and legalistic, imposed upon relationships rather than flowing from them. We may protect our rights and not worry about the "common welfare." We may live up to the letter of our contracts, but feel no need to go beyond them. There is always the danger that the "good" will crowd out the "best." The welfare of people and the quality of human relationships should be the driving forces in our quest for ethics in research.

Rules and principles, policies and procedures (including guidelines regarding privacy and deception) may be essential means for achieving our goal, but they must not become abstractions that command our allegiance for their own sake. Trite as the words may seem, peace, brotherhood, and understanding remain noble ideals, beacons that should guide us even in the sometimes mundane process of the design and execution of a research protocol.

7

How Much Do They Need to Know? The Problem of Informed Consent

Participant research sometimes requires only minimal direct contact with the observed group. Mike was almost a passive observer in his study. Don's participation with the Necrons, on the other hand, was all-consuming. Our next case falls midway between these two. This case will open up two more major issues—informed consent in this chapter and harm in the next.

TWILIGHT AT DARKWOODS MANOR

"I don't want you! I want the nice lady!" Mrs. O'Brien's querulous voice could be heard down the hall. The night duty nurse, Ms. Brownell, was close to the end of her rope with elderly Mrs. O'Brien, who refused to take her medicine and complained endlessly about her aches, pains, and other symptoms. Recently, she had also complained to her children about the treatment she'd been receiving, and Mr. Johnson, Darkwoods' administrator, had made a special trip to check on the unit. The complaints were entirely unfounded, but the incident caused the staff to add Mrs. O'Brien's name to the unwritten list of problem cases.

And now Ms. Brownell noticed that Mrs. O'Brien had spilled most of her medicine. "Damn," she swore to herself. "If things don't get better soon, I'm walking out and telling Johnson he can have his job."

"Now, Mrs. O'Brien," she decided to try once more, "if you don't take your medicine right now, I'll tell Sherry you've been a naughty girl and she won't come to see you tomorrow."

"Oh, you wouldn't do that to me! Oh, that Sherry. She makes my life here. We all love her. Oh, please, please, nurse, don't tell Sherry on me. Here, gimme the medicine. See? I really like it." Mrs. O'Brien swallowed the medicine. Her nurse knew the confused, agitated patient would soon feel the tranquilizing effects of the drug.

Mrs. O'Brien had been difficult tonight, but life had been much better at Darkwoods since Sherry McNeil had started working there as "activities coordinator." When the job had first been created, the staff saw it as a glorified orderly's position. The person hired would do "go-for" work for the nursing staff, would be an extra pair of hands when help was needed, and would keep the residents out of the professional staff's hair.

When Sherry McNeil had applied for the job, she was quickly hired. Folks didn't know much about her except that she was young, bright, outgoing, and conveyed an air of boundless energy. They knew she was "taking some courses" at the nearby university and that her work at Darkwoods was somehow related to her chosen field of study, but she never talked much about herself or her plans. Sherry had told Mr. Johnson when she interviewed with him that she was a student who needed some experience working with older people to help her in her studies; she needed some money, too, to help her through school. Mr. Johnson didn't ask any questions, but when he introduced her to some of the staff the first day he mentioned something about "field assignment" and said he hoped that what she learned here would help her in her future work.

At first, some of the staff were apprehensive about having her on the unit. She didn't seem to fit in and was overqualified for the job. Frankly, they had expected to get a semiretired person or a transient, less educated person. Despite some suspicion—even a measure of resistance at first—the staff agreed that Sherry made their jobs much easier. Her bright personality could be felt throughout the unit. The activities and groups she had organized had brought some of the more withdrawn residents out of their shells. More importantly, as nurse Brownwell learned this evening, a threat of withholding Sherry from a patient could be an effective means of control.

Sherry had worked at Darkwoods for about six months now and was beginning to have some serious questions about what she was doing. Sherry was "really" (as she liked to tell herself) a graduate student at the university. She was working towards a master's degree in social psychology. She had finished her course work and was writing her master's thesis. Her thesis was what led her to Darkwoods Manor. The essay was to be a study of how aged people adapt to nursing home life. In her course work, Sherry had read Erving Goffman, the sociologist/social psychologist. His book, *Asylums,* was about people in what he called "total institutions"—prisons, mental hospitals, and convents. Goffman's was one of the first monographs Sherry had ever really studied. She was intrigued by the ways in which inmates in these institutions were able to build a meaningful life around commonplace objects and events. She was impressed by the way Goffman could build a powerful, firsthand account out of simple observations.

In *Asylum* Goffman had chosen as his research role a mental ward's "activities director." The choice was deliberate and effective. As activities director, he had maximum access to *both* the staff and inmates at the hospital. From the patients' point of view, Goffman wasn't fully part of the professional staff and, as a result, he didn't seem as distant or threatening as physicians, nurses, or even aides. From the point of view of the professional staff, he was a quasi colleague. As *Asylum* showed, Goffman effectively penetrated the "underlife of the institution." His observations captured the inmates' experiences as they moved from everyday society into the asylum and out again. Sherry hoped to replicate the study on a smaller scale in a nursing home. She knew she related well with older people and had thought seriously about a career in gerontology.

When Sherry first thought about her study, she knew that "going native" would be impossible. Similarly, she felt uncomfortable arriving at an institution and simply saying she wanted to do a study. She doubted that the authorities would admit her. Even if they did, she was uneasy because residents and others would worry about what she was thinking about them.

"And so, here I am, 'social activities director' at Darkwoods Manor," Sherry thought. Much like Goffman, she had decided her role worked well. It allowed her to talk to both residents and staff. Residents willingly discussed their experiences in the home and their lives before coming to Darkwoods, hoping that activities reflecting their interests would be organized. Her relationships with the staff developed with equal ease. She was invited to weekly staff meetings and case conferences. These gave her a very different picture of the residents, whose situations were discussed privately by the staff during such sessions.

When Sherry arrived, no one paid too much attention to her. The oldtimers on the staff who remembered those who had occupied a similar position under the former administrator recalled that they did little more than rearrange magazines and chauffeur residents into town to movies and the drugstore. Sherry quickly proved she was not like others they had known. One of the first things she did was set up a table-games group. For prizes, she convinced local retailers to donate cigarettes and toiletries. As might be expected, the games were a great success. Residents looked forward to game nights. The day after game nights was a time for displaying and trading prizes on the unit.

Through the games, Sherry drew some interesting conclusions about the unit's social life. She learned that life at Darkwoods was intensely person-oriented. The residents were more concerned about *who* did something than about *what* was done. This became clear when Sherry took a week's vacation. Before her trip, she carefully set up the week's game night with one of the orderlies substituting for her. She arranged for prizes and made sure that the room and refreshments would be set up. Signs were posted and invitations extended. When she returned from vacation, Sherry heard the games had gone poorly. Residents complained that the evening "was different—not as nice," that the person calling the bingo numbers "didn't know how to do it right." Residents said they were glad Sherry was back so things would work again. Staff members reported hearing many similar comments. They noted, too, that, on days following game nights, morale in the unit was usually high: residents were active, their spirits were good, and everyone seemed to get along well. The day after the games at which Sherry didn't preside, they said, people seemed depressed and quarrelsome. These observations told Sherry much about how the residents perceived the world.

Her other work at Darkwoods supported Sherry's game-night observations. As she began to win the confidence of the professional staff, Sherry requested permission to review the social service intake records of Darkwoods residents. Sherry did this mostly for her study, hoping to determine whether preretirement life influenced behavior in a nursing home. Her ostensible reason for examining the records, the one she offered the staff and administration, was that she could learn from the records what kinds of activities would be best received by the residents. She did discover a number of things that helped her work as activities director. For example, she found that there were a number of retired professional people living in the unit. Among them were a physician and two university professors. Sherry concluded that "current affairs discussion groups" led by these three residents might make an exciting addition to the unit's activities. When two of the professionals had expressed hesitancy about leading the groups, Sherry had offered to spend time helping them prepare for the day's topic. Like the other activities she had organized, the discussions were an instant success. Not only did they draw large numbers of residents, but folks who previously showed little interest in group activities participated actively, even volunteering to set up rooms for the gathering and to run down additional material for the group to consider. Life at Darkwoods was much more pleasant when Sherry was on the unit. You could easily tell where she was by the hubbub of excitement surrounding her, the sound of laughter and banter.

For her part, Sherry was generally pleased with her study. It was far from a monumental study, but she felt good about it. Not only had she chosen a research role that gave her access to everything that occurred on the unit, but she had also won the confidence of both staff and residents. She had maintained detailed notes on all aspects of the unit's operation: who talked to whom and how often, how several patients were overmedicated by the night shift nurses. Because she had also gained access to medical records ("so she could understand and serve the residents better"), she was able to document claimed physician visits to the units that had never occurred, visits paid for by Medicare. Sherry discovered it was easy to get at all the information she wanted. After people got to know her, no one attempted to keep anything from her. On the contrary, she felt nearly all the staff went out of their way to show her how things "really worked."

She had made little notes while she was on the unit, and then later she had transcribed and elaborated on them in her research journal. She had penetrated the social life at Darkwoods Manor. She had interviewed each staff member, many of the consulting professionals, and every resident on her unit. Sherry knew the work was drawing to a close. She had the data she needed, and now she needed to start writing. Staying at Darkwoods would provide little more useful information, and the long hours she spent at the nursing home would interfere with getting the thesis written. Nevertheless, she had some concerns about leaving. Over the past months, she had developed several close relationship with residents. Sherry realized she had become very important to many at Darkwoods, and she felt bad about leaving. She knew she made a difference in many people's lives, and she wondered what would happen when she announced she was going away forever.

As she developed closer relationships during the past couple of months, Sherry made several references on the unit about how important her experience was in helping her with her degree, but she did not yet tell anybody that it was the basis of her master's thesis. Now that she was beginning to think about leaving, she wondered if she should offer more explanation and thank people for all the help they had been in her project. She wondered, too, whether she should have told people initially that she was at the home to do a study. At least then the people would have realized she would be at Darkwoods for only a short while. She wondered whether she would have learned as much if she had fully explained what she wanted when she began. And would she feel as bad as she did now? She wondered what Goffman had done. What had he told the patients he befriended at St. Elizabeth's Hospital? How had he felt when some poor old people told him he was the only family they had and added, "Please don't go away"?

ETHICS AT DARKWOODS MANOR:
THE CONCEPT OF INFORMED CONSENT

Sherry McNeil's case presents a typical participant research situation. As an active participant in the daily life of the nursing home community, she gathered information from personal observation, from the reports of others, and from written records. The issues of privacy and deception discussed in the last chapter are raised again, though in somewhat different form.

Sherry's subject matter is less private than Mike's, and the institution is much more open than the society of the Necrons. However, several people have shared their lives with Sherry, some in deeply personal ways, and as activities director she has gained access to some private records. If deception is present, it is deception more by omission of information than misinformation. Sherry has stated that that her presence at the nursing home has a connection with her school work, though she has not explicitly said that her experience is the basis of a master's thesis. Closely related to the issues of privacy and deception is another major concept in the ethics of research, informed consent.

The modern concept of informed consent began as an ethical and legal requirement governing physicians and researchers in the area of medical treatment and research. The atrocious medical experiments of the Nazi era led to principles governing research. It was not just that those experiments were dangerous, harmful, or fatal; a major objection at the Nuremberg trials was the absence of the victims' consent.

One of the terms that emerged to refer to participants in scientific research, perhaps the most common generic term, is "human subjects." It suggests a nice verbal play, because subjects are actors rather than merely the recipients of action. Human subjects are not merely "objects" of research. Unfortunately, our language is far from unambiguous, and the term "subject" is also used to describe those ruled by a monarch, as contrasted with "citizens" who share in the governing process.

The set of principles that emerged assumes that people have a right to control their own bodies, to decide what treatments they will accept and whether to subject themselves to an experiment's stress, danger, or inconvenience. To consent, people need adequate information, hence the doctrine of *informed consent.* This means the voluntary consent of a competent individual who has sufficient information to make a rational decision.

Informed consent was subsequently imported from medicine into social and behavioral research. The concept has been recognized by the professional organizations of behavioral and social scientists[1] and has been codified in regulations governing research using federal funds.[2] Debate continues, however, about the extent to which the biomedical model of informed consent can apply to the practice of social and behavioral research. Research that may cause some harm to the subjects may parallel the medical model. Even if there is no harm, doing research without consent might be wrong. If the research involves an intrusion into the privacy of another's life, the moral requirement of consent may seem reasonable, since it is possible to be wronged without being harmed. One way to look at this question is to use one of the great German philosopher Immanuel Kant's formulations of what he called the "categorical imperative." He said that we should always treat people as ends in themselves and not as means only. The word "only" is most significant because Kant acknowledged that we all must use others as means, but they should always remain ends as well. Would studying people with-

---

[1]The revised code of the American Sociological Association provides that "research should take culturally appropriate steps to secure informed consent and to avoid invasions of privacy." The ethical principles of the American Psychological Association state that "ethical practice requires the investigator to inform the participant of all features of the research that reasonably might be expected to influence willingness to participate." Both of these codes uphold high ideals of privacy, autonomy, and honesty, but they also seem to recognize some of the ambiguities involved. The statement in the sociology code is a "should" statement rather than a "must" statement, indicating it is an ideal and not a rule; it is further qualified by the phase "culturally appropriate." Later, however, the code provides that "where risk or harm is anticipated, full informed consent must be obtained," expressed as a rule and not an ideal.

Likewise, the psychologists' ideal of informing participants is qualified by the comment that "failure to make full disclosure gives added emphasis to the investigator's responsibility to protect the welfare and dignity of the research participant." Moreover, "openness and honesty are essential characteristics of the relationship between investigator and research participant." If deception is necessary, the investigator is then required to restore the quality of the relationship by debriefing.

The Principles of Professional Responsibility of the American Anthropological Association do not use the term "informed consent," but they do include two statements that address the issue: "The aims of the investigator should be communicated as well as possible to the informant"; and "The anticipated consequences of research should be communicated as fully as possible to the individuals and groups likely to be affected."

[2]See the *Federal Register* 46:16 (26 January 1981): 8366-92.

out their permission constitute treating them "as a means only"?[3] Although some people may think so, we are not convinced that *all* study of people without their consent would necessarily violate this principle, as long as they are not treated disrespectfully. For example, if the researcher is only observing public behavior, the requirement of informed consent seems less valid. The concept may acquire a life of its own, exceeding what can be justified by those arguments which created it.

Must we adopt the principle that all research requires informed consent? Let's imagine an undergraduate sociology student wishing to correlate style and color of dress with age, race, and sex. Seating himself on a busy downtown bus stop bench, he makes note, perhaps employing some method of random selection, on the apparent age, race, and sex of the people who pass. Making notes about what these individuals are wearing and later analyzing this data, he could make some statistical correlations. The study may seem frivolous, perhaps a waste of time. Probably we wouldn't want any of our tax money spent to support the

---

[3]Unlike many writers who cite Kant's phrase but never explain what would constitute using another as a "means only," Gerald Dworkin attempts to clarify the Kantian concept in a very thoughtful essay. We use someone as a means *only,* he says, when we know they cannot share our purposes. The criminal can share our purposes that the law be enforced even though he would prefer not to go to prison. Hence, incarcerating him is not using him as a means only. Dworkin then uses this analysis to examine several types of social research. In looking at one case not unlike our account of Don and the Necrons (the case he cites involves covert research among a "spaceship cult"), he asserts that the group studied by researchers (who appeared to be converts, true believers, and loyal friends) "could not" accept the covert nature of the research. The minimal test of whether people were being used as means only is the acceptability of the research by the group after it was completed. See Gerald Dworkin, "Must Subjects Be Objects," in Tom L. Beauchamp, et al., eds., *Ethical Issues in Social Science Research* (Baltimore: Johns Hopkins University Press, 1982) 246-51.

We agree with Dworkin's conclusion about the case he cites. It corresponds to our own judgment about Don. But his definition of "persons as ends" does not seem adequate to establish his argument. He begins by saying that a person is not used "as a means only" if he *could* rationally share our purpose. We see no reason why the Necrons (or the spaceship cult that he cites) could not share our "scientific" purpose as readily as the criminal could share our purpose in enforcing the law. Dworkin in fact seems to redefine the test part way through his argument, subtly shifting from "could" to "would." The "minimal test," he says in discussing the spaceship people, is the acceptability to the participants after the research is over. The test has now shifted from a test of reason (it could be reasonable for the persons affected to share our purpose) to an empirical test (they would in fact share our purpose). But if this latter is the test, then many a prisoner must be let go, because criminals would not *in fact* share our purpose, however much reason might tell them that they should.

project. But can there be any moral objection on the grounds that the student failed to obtained the informed consent of those he observed? If the purpose of informed consent is to protect autonomy and privacy and permit people to choose to avoid risk of injury, why would consent be necessary in this case? The observation is public and risk-free. The sociology student is simply doing what anybody could do. A market researcher advising a clothing manufacturer, a writer or drama student studying human behavior for her next novel or performance, or an elderly widow whose chief entertainment is watching people are all entitled to sit on that bench and watch people go by. Does the role "social scientist" preclude such public observation? We think not.

But what about Sherry? Does she need the informed consent of the nursing home population? The nursing home isn't a public place like a downtown street. And she is able to observe things that may not be seen by the ordinary visitor who comes to see a friend or relative who lives in the home. Certainly the average passerby who walked in and started "nosing around" would be invited to leave rather quickly. On the other hand, much of what Sherry is observing could be seen by any employee and even by many of the residents in the nursing home, and she is legitimately on the staff with a reason to see confidential records.

We see nothing *inherently* wrong with social or behavioral scientists observing anything that a person legitimately located in their position could observe, as long as they are unobtrusive and respect the physical and psychological space of the other person. If it is wrong, it is because the *role* of researcher *in our society* has created special obligations.

Everyone we meet forms some impressions of us. As a result of talking with people at a party, we could find ourselves depicted as a character in a novel or short story, mentioned anonymously as an illustration in a minister's sermon, criticized or praised by acquaintances in a gossip session, or evaluated for a promotion. We are all "behavioral scientists" in some sense, and to some degree we all work out "theories" about what makes another person or group "tick." Is social or behavioral observation in public permissible for everyone except those trained in it?

What if Sherry had been employed at the nursing home *before* going back to school and found she could use some of her recollections in doing

a "retrospective" study based on her experience?[4] Would this be ethically objectionable because of the lack of informed consent? Is it the use
to which observations are put rather than the observations themselves
that require consent?

Some people contend that full prior informed consent should be required for all social and behavioral research. Important as informed consent is for some research, we are not convinced that it applies to *all*
research. Its applicability depends on the values from which the principle derived—respect for privacy and autonomy and the avoidance of
harm to subjects. As long as there is respect for privacy and appropriate
efforts to avoid harm, consent does not seem to us to be morally required
for the observation of truly public behavior or public records.

We prefer that researchers be left to negotiate relationships with subjects that fit their context. We hope that flexibility can continue. Only if
researchers fail to act responsibly should rigid rules be adopted to prevent the abuse of discretion.[5]

The more private or risky the area of research, the more important
informed consent becomes. For example, the very personal nature of
Don's relationships with the Necrons, the secrecy surrounding the group,
and the harm they might perceive resulting from Don's public disclo-
sures lead us to conclude that Don was clearly wrong in not seeking any
kind of consent from the Disciples. Moreover, good ethics often correspond to good science. Don's method is also suspect scientifically, since
those who will read Don's report will not know how to assess the response of Don's subjects to him. Did they see through him and string him
along? Did Don's recounting of his fabricated story actually change the

---

[4]The classic case of this is Bruno Bettelheim's study based on his experiences in a Nazi concentration camp. Originally published in the *Journal of Ab-
normal and Social Psychology* in 1943, his observations were later expanded in
his book *The Informed Heart* (New York: Free Press, 1960). In the same vein,
theologian Langdon Gilkey drew some conclusions about human nature and
hence about ethics from his observations as a Japanese prisoner during World
War II. See Langdon Gilkey, *Shantung Compound: The Story of Men and Women
under Pressure* (New York: Harper and Row, 1966).

[5]Strict rules allowing no discretion succeed in prohibiting all evil by prohibiting much that is not wrong as well. Ancient rabbis spoke of "building a fence
around the law." *Avoth* 1:1. By adopting and adhering to rules that established
an outer boundary clearly beyond the absolute requirements of Jewish law, the
faithful could avoid even coming close to an infraction of the law. Such an approach upholds high standards, but risks becoming legalistic. Perhaps we need
to build such a fence by requiring that all research, however innocuous, be pre-
ceded by informed consent. But if we are "building a fence" to prevent abuse,
let's at least call it by its proper name.

group, reinforcing its beliefs or leading it in a new direction? We don't know and can't know. If we knew that the Necrons knew what Don was about, we could at least speculate about how that knowledge influenced them. Finally, pure pragmatism may also reinforce the ethical principle, since it is often easier to be honest than to keep up a facade, under constant fear of being exposed as a researcher in disguise.

But especially in participant research the question of consent is often the problem of how and when. How might Sherry have obtained the informed consent of her subjects?

Who Must Consent?

Sherry's first question might be, "Who are my subjects?" Her topic was the adjustment of the elderly to nursing home life. But Sherry will have to observe numerous other people who interact with the residents. Who would need to give consent? The residents? The staff? The families and visitors who come to the home occasionally? What about those people whom Sherry will never even meet because they *never* come to visit? She will hear about these families since both patients and staff complain about them because they never visit. Are they also subjects? In a participant study, it is sometimes difficult to know just how wide to spread the net of "subjects."

An expansive concept of informed consent might require at least the consent of the regular staff and residents of the home. How does one obtain "group" consent? Can Mr. Johnson, as the chief administrator of the facility, consent for the entire group? He's the one who hires employees and admits residents and manages the whole operation. Can he also grant consent for research? The anthropologist faces this kind of question in dealing with tribal groups. If the "political" authority of the group is lodged in the chief, can the chief give consent for the anthropologist to study the tribe? Does consent require individual consent of each subject? What if "that's not the way things are done" in a particular institution or society? Must researchers impose their own norms regarding consent on a "foreign" institution or society?

Coercion and Consent

If Sherry wants the consent of all her subjects, how might she go about it? Mr. Johnson could bring her out onto the floor where she would work and announce, "I'd like to introduce Ms. Sherry McNeil. She is going to be working as our new activities coordinator and will be doing some observations for her research project at Deadwood College. I'm glad she's here and I'm sure none of you will mind having her look over your shoulder from time to time." Would the subsequent cooperation of the staff mean that they had implicitly agreed to participate in Sherry's study?

Mr. Johnson wouldn't seem to be inviting a *voluntary* decision to co-operate; at least some of the staff might perceive his statement as pressure or coercion, though he made no overt threat to discipline or fire the uncooperative. Even if he had invited people to let him or Sherry know if they didn't want to be observed for research purposes, some employees still might have felt that their jobs depended upon their cooperation. The same might have been true of residents in the home if Mr. Johnson approached them. They might fear that their care or even their continued residence there might be jeopardized by refusing to cooperate. Being sure that consent is free, voluntary consent is especially difficult in some kinds of institutional settings. Research involving employees is sometimes problematic. Psychology departments frequently maintain research subject pools consisting of students currently enrolled in classes; care is required if the impression or reality of coercion is to be avoided.

If Sherry felt it inappropriate to use Mr. Johnson's authority to obtain consent, she could approach each individual whom she will observe, explaining her purpose in being there. Unless she invokes Mr. Johnson's name to increase cooperation, any consent she obtained from staff would probably be voluntary. It is not so clear with the patients, however, who might still feel compelled to comply in order to enjoy her favor as activities director. What if someone refused? In studying an institution, it may not be feasible to sort out a population into those to be observed and those to be ignored. Can one person veto the whole project? Perhaps Sherry can't help noticing some individuals. Would she comply with their refusal to consent by not *recording* her observations of them?

Or could Sherry decide not to request consent at the beginning, proceed with her observations, and later request permission to use her observations as part of a research project, discarding her notes on those who objected. This may partly satisfy the informed consent requirement. The subject may exercise autonomy in restricting the *use* of observations. But it cannot prevent the observation itself, which has already occurred. Nevertheless, variations on this theme, with the use of debriefing techniques, are sometimes used in studies where investigators feel that consent is important but would affect the behavior to be studied if sought in advance. Debriefing is used frequently in laboratory studies where subjects consented to participate without being *fully* informed. It has also been used where a situation is staged to study spontaneous behavior, for example to see if people in a hurry will stop to provide directions or come to the aid of a person thought to be in distress.

Competence and Consent

But if Sherry wants to obtain explicit consent, either prospectively or even retrospectively, her efforts may be confounded by the incompetence of some of the patients at Darkwoods. Some of them have been declared legally incompetent to take care of themselves and their affairs. Others have never been the subject of such a legal proceeding, yet everyone knows that they are incompetent. They came to the home of their own "free will," which may mean nothing more than that they didn't object when the family brought them there. They would have been declared legally incompetent if the family had ever found it necessary to seek such a legal ruling. Mr. McIntosh in Room 245, for example, doesn't know where he is. He usually doesn't recognize his family when they visit, and even when he is most cogent, he can't carry on a conversation for five minutes without repeating himself several times. Any consent from him would be meaningless. His family makes medical and other decisions for him, which seems morally unobjectionable; they are, presumably, making decisions that are for his benefit. Sherry's work, unlike the medical treatment he receives, cannot benefit Mr. McIntosh. On the other hand, there doesn't seem to be a risk of harm either. Can Mr. McIntosh's family legitimately give proxy consent?[6]

Even more problematic is Mrs. O'Brien, who causes the night nurse so much trouble. Is she competent? It's hard to know. Sometimes she seems bright and alert, yet other days she seems off in her own world, making little sense to anyone. Some days she just seems drugged into oblivion. Would consent obtained on one of her better days be enough?

Information and Consent

Besides being *voluntary* and competently given, fully informed consent must also be based on adequate *information. How much* would Sherry need to tell her subjects to have *informed* consent? Saying, as she did, that she was "trying to get some experience" isn't much information. Is it enough to say that she is doing a paper on nursing homes and

---

[6]Normally, in making medical decisions for an incompetent patient, the family or guardian is legally obligated to act in the person's "best interest." This could cause problems unless the family could see that Sherry's research offers some advantage to Mr. McIntosh. An alternative principle from legal medicine is available for deciding for the incompetent. Especially in end-of-life decisions, courts have frequently employed the notion of "substituted judgment" in place of the "best interest" test. This means deciding as you think the person would decide if able, even if that is contrary to the person's best interest. Using this test for Sherry's study, a family's proxy decision would mean deciding if Mr. McIntosh *would* consent if he were able.

that she will be using some of her observations at Darkwoods as part of the paper? Or should she be more specific about the nature and purpose of the study, the methods she will be using, any hypotheses she may be testing, and any ideas she may have about possible publication? Debate continues about how much information is necessary for consent to be informed. Much depends upon the specific context, the nature of the research, and its risks.

In some research situations, the scientist can and perhaps should provide detailed information at the outset of the research. In other cases, as in some participant research, disclosure can best occur over a period of time. In low-risk, nonintrusive research, perhaps formal consent should not be required at all.

A personal word may be helpful at this point. One of the authors of this book has done several participant studies of skid rows, ghetto alcoholics, criminals, and deviants. In each study I represented myself as someone "planning to write a book" about my experiences in the particular setting. At first I was surprised that subjects didn't react with hostility to this news. To the contrary, they seemed pleased that someone was interested enough in them and their problems to want to write a book. Frequently this created a more open atmosphere that actually enhanced my freedom of inquiry and movement. There are scientific and ethical advantages for researchers in disclosing who they are and what their purposes are in the course of their study. A sense of timing is one thing that separates the seasoned from the inexperienced researcher.

Sherry began simply by telling Mr. Johnson that she needed some experiences to help her in her studies. Perhaps she should have been more open with him, but it is difficult to imagine her giving each resident of the nursing home a detailed account of her research plan, certainly not at the beginning of her study. But as relationships with the residents and staff developed, she might have found it possible to talk more and more about what she was doing, what she would do with the data she was gathering, and how it might help others to understand the elderly better.

Gaining consent, where appropriate, is not a simple skill that can be learned just by reading books. It does not mean simply getting someone to sign a piece of paper. In fact, informed consent is not a *form* at all, but a *process* of informing people and securing their agreement. Even where consent forms are appropriate, they are merely evidence of the process, not the consent itself. The danger of mechanizing and bureaucratizing and hence thwarting human relationships accompanies the doctrine of informed consent. Ethically sensitive investigators will develop the skill of tailoring the consent process to fit the context, maintaining the integrity of human relationships and fulfilling the purposes for which the doctrine was designed.

Consent and Deception

The letter, if not the spirit of informed consent, would seem to prohibit deception. Informed consent is clearly lacking when a person does not know that he or she is the subject of research. But people may be misled about their role in an experiment or about the purpose of the study, in which case the consent is not fully informed. Deception is employed extensively in some categories of social and behavioral research,[7] since it is often important to have naive subjects. This is especially so in studies of conformity and studies of helping behavior. Researchers could, of course, ask people how much they are influenced by others or whether they would stop to render aid, but none of us really knows how we are influenced or what we would do in some future situation. Even asking people to play roles and respond to simulated situations often will not provide reliable data, because the actors know the situation is not real or because they play a role rather than being themselves.

If Linda wants to know how "lonely hearts" would respond to a "pen pal," the surest way to find out is to correspond with them. If a researcher wanted to find what kind of letters a contributor to a religious TV program would receive, the easiest technique would be to send in some contributions and see what comes back. Feigning deafness may be the most reliable way to observe how a hearing aid salesperson treats hearing-disabled customers.

It may be that some research simply can't be done without deception. Perhaps the research shouldn't be done. On the other hand, we have suggested that informed consent may not be morally required for all research. But sometimes consent is compatible with deception. Research subjects might agree to be deceived. One good example of this might be the pool of subjects maintained by a psychology department. All those in the pool might be told at the outset that some of them will be participating in experiments involving deception and some will not, and they

---

[7]Lawrence Stricker, "The True Deceiver," *Psychological Bulletin* 68 (1967): 13-20, studied four psychology journals for the year 1964. He found that some categories of research reported in those journals hardly used deception at all. But 81.2 percent of conformity studies, 72.2 percent of cognitive-dissonance and balance-theory studies, and 50 percent of decision-making studies employed deception. Larry Campbell (*Experimental Methodology,* 3rd ed. [Boston: Allyn and Bacon, 1985]) has summarized the results of several studies of seven journals in which the occurrence of deception ranged from 3.1 percent to 62.9 percent.

will not know until afterwards whether the study involved deception. By agreeing to partcipate as part of the pool, they are agreeing to be deceived.

This closely parallels a procedure for many medical studies, especially drug studies, where one control group is given a placebo. All participants know that some will receive a real drug and some an inert pill, but in a double-blind study neither the researcher nor the subject knows who is getting the real drug and who is getting the placebo. This procedure enables the researcher to determine which effects are really caused by the drug and which result from the psychological expectations accompanying taking a pill. The subject explicitly consents to being deceived. It is interesting to note, however, that the research about placebos that now makes the use of such double-blind procedures essential had to be done without fully informed consent; that is, the subjects in many of those early experiments did not know that the purpose of the research was to determine placebo effect.

Since a significant amount of research does seem to require deception, would it be possible to argue for an "implied" consent to be deceived? To refer again to the medical field, one of the standard legal tests for informed consent in medical treatment is the question, "What would the reasonable patient *want to know* about this treatment?" This is a difficult concept, but both law and philosophy rely heavily, each in its own way, on what reasonable people would think. Applying this principle to social science research, one philosopher proclaims confidentially that a "reasonable person would *not* want to be lied to."[8] But how do law and philosophy know what a "reasonable person" thinks? There is a real problem in locating the mythical "reasonable person."[9] Some studies of

---

[8] Ruth Macklin, "The Problem of Adequate Disclosure in Social Science Research," in Beauchamp, et al., eds., *Ethical Issues in Social Science Research*, 212.

[9] A. P. Herbert drew a portrait of the "reasonable man" as a composite from a number of legal cases. "He is an ideal, a standard, the embodiment of all those qualities which we demand of a good citizen. . . . He is one who invariably looks where he is going, and is careful to examine the immediate foreground before he executes a leap or a bound; who neither star gazes nor is lost in meditation when approaching trapdoors or the margin of a dock; . . . who never mounts a moving omnibus and does not alight from any car while the train is in motion . . . and will inform himself of the history and habits of a dog before administering a caress; . . . who never drives his ball until those in front of him have definitely vacated the putting green that is his own objective; who never from one year's end to another makes excessive demands upon his wife, his neighbors, his servants, his ox or his ass; . . . who never swears, gambles or loses his temper; who uses nothing except in moderation, and even while he flogs his child is meditating only on the golden mean." Quoted in *Prosser and Keeton on the Law of Torts*, W. Page Keeton, ed. (St. Paul MN: West Publishing, 1984) 174-75.

research subjects indicate that the subjects in laboratory research expect to be deceived, and indeed that those who expect to be deceived maintain their interest and perform better than those who do not.[10] But both philosophy and law tend to reject empirical studies as a basis for knowing what "reasonable" people would want. If real people, ordinary people, are seldom "reasonable" people, then the concept of a reasonable person may become such an abstraction that it can provide little guidance for the moral life, being only the reflected image of an ethicist's or judge's personal definition of what is reasonable. If the purpose of informed consent is to eliminate or minimize invasion of privacy, interference with autonomy, and risk of harm, then knowing how people view their privacy and autonomy and how they define harm seems relevant to the task of ethics. An "ordinary" person standard might be preferable.

Not enough investigation has yet been done to speak with confidence, but there is some evidence that subjects may be less stringent in their demands than scientists, ethicists, and lawyers are. If the studies are at all accurate, many people do not object to being deceived for the cause of science, even when they are embarrassed or learn something unpleasant about themselves in the process, if they perceive the study as being for a good cause.[11] More and better research regarding people's

---

[10]J. H. Resnick and T. Schwartz ("Ethical Standards as Independent Variables in Psychological Research," *American Psychologist* 28 [1973]: 134-39) report that fully informing their subjects killed their interest in participating in an experiment; their uninformed subjects remained enthusiastic and performed as expected. Likewise, S. S. Smith and D. Richardson ("Amelioration of Deception and Harm in Psychological Research: The Important Role of Debriefing," *Journal of Personality and Social Psychology* 44 [1983]: 1075-82) reported subjects who were part of deception experiments enjoyed the experience more and felt they benefited more than did subjects in other kinds of experiments.

[11]Mary Sissons's study in Paddington Station involved deception, as she would stop passengers and ask for directions to Hyde Park. Her object was to determine if social class was a factor in the willingness of people to take time to give a stranger directions. She informed her subjects of her purpose afterwards. Only one of eighty participants reacted negatively to her action. See Mary Sissons, "The Psychology of Social Class"; this intriguing but little-known study is discussed and cited in J. A. Barnes, *The Ethics of Inquiry in Social Sciences* (New Delhi: Oxford University Press, 1977) 13. T. M. Epstein, P. Suedfeld, and S. J. Silverstein ("The Experimental Contact: Subjects' Expectations of and Reaction to Some Behavior of Experimenters," *American Psychologist* 28 [1977]: 212-21) report that students do not expect to be told the purpose of an experiment and do not find deception inappropriate. Stanley Milgram ("Subject Reaction in Social Psychology: The Neglected Ethical Factor," *Hastings Center Report* 7:5 [October, 1977]: 19-23), though he did not ask his subjects specifically how they felt about his deception, did do a follow-up study of his subjects and found that only 1.3 percent regretted having participated.

attitudes toward such issues is needed, especially since questions have been raised about the quality of some of this research.[12]

However, simply assuming without qualification that reasonable people "don't want to be lied to" seems too facile. We may genuinely want to be lied to in some circumstances. If emptying a burning theater without causing a stampede requires a lie about the reason for the evacuation, we don't want to be told the truth. We accept the necessity of our government's deceiving its citizens in order to thwart a genuine enemy, either in protecting national security or achieving military objectives in time of war. We may be willing to be deceived by undercover police officers, unless we are the ones engaged in criminal activities.

Do people mind being deceived by researchers? It's an important question. But even if *most* people might give "implied consent" to deception for purposes of scientific progress, some people would probably object strenuously. Can those people have veto power over all deceptive research, since the researcher can't know in advance who will object?

Informed Consent and Harm

One of the pillars on which informed consent was originally built is the prevention of injury. If there is risk in a research project, informed consent becomes a central concern. Our society allows some very risky undertakings. People can drive race cars, attempt to jump the Grand Canyon on a motorcycle, play football, or ride bucking broncos in rodeos. But we want participants to evaluate risks and decide that the activity is worth it. Informed consent procedures assure that people are aware of research risks and autonomously decide that the potential benefits are worth the risks.

Requiring informed consent is expected to reduce harmful research for two reasons. First, because potential subjects are presumed to be even more concerned for their own welfare than others would be, they are unlikely to participate in research that they are told has significant risks. Second, the potential subject may be aware of risks that the researcher does not see. The subject may define something as harmful that the researcher had considered harmless. Or perhaps a particular subject is

---

[12]Donald P. Warwick ("Types of Harm in Social Research," in Beauchamp, et al., eds., *Ethical Issues in Social Science Research,* 102-103) notes that researchers who deceive subjects on the grounds that their statements cannot be relied upon to express their true attitudes are then trusted to report accurately about their feelings about deception. Most of the studies of subject attitudes are tag-ons to the original research and are poorer in design, Warwick maintains. Most would not pass scientific muster if they were proposed as free standing research projects.

susceptible to a hazard not common to the general population, and the researcher might not perceive this idiosyncratic risk. Thus insisting upon informed consent may reduce the risk of harm to subjects. Moreover, requiring informed consent may make researchers more careful in their own analysis of the likelihood of harm and the benefits that may be balanced against that risk.

Potential for harm is something researchers must examine before they even start approaching potential subjects to ask for their participation. We will examine the issue of harm more fully in the next chapter.

8

Can Social Research Hurt?
The Question of Harm

Avoiding unnecessary harm to others is a fundamental precept in virtually every ethical system, whether based on divine command, social custom, utilitarian calculations of consequences, or concern for human rights. This chapter is concerned with the potential for harm in social and behavioral research, using Darkwoods Manor to illustrate the issues.

Sherry began her work at Darkwoods Manor with little thought that someone might be hurt. She did not intend even to cause discomfort, let alone harm. Sherry's project seems harmless enough. In fact, most social and behavioral research is harmless. Someone has remarked that the greatest risk in much research is boredom. But there are some risks that are not apparent on the surface. Let's think about what harms might result from Sherry's study. Then we will have to ask how *likely* they are and how *serious* they are.

HARM TO SUBJECTS

First, there is the potential harm to her research subjects. What might ensue from *public disclosure* of information Sherry gathers? Personal information about the nursing home's residents could be damaging if shared with the wrong people. This might occur because of careless talk or because of the "wrong" people reading her thesis. Reports of negative family and staff attitudes toward some of the residents could cause *social injury,* rupturing relationships between patients and their families or between patients and the staff. Even if *individuals* do not suffer social harm, a whole *group* might. The conclusions of Sherry's study might reinforce negative stereotypes about older people, contrary to her own intentions.

If Sherry reported that one of the nurses invented blood pressure readings for the chart instead of actually taking them, that nurse might suffer *economic damage;* she might lose her job if Mr. Johnson saw the report. A reference to a physician's claiming Medicare payments for visits he never made might lead to an investigation and prosecution for Medicare fraud and abuse. The doctor could suffer *legal damage.* Does this "damage" constitute "harm"? The nurse and the doctor would perceive these results as injurious to their interests. Any harm they might suffer by the imposition of appropriate sanctions would seem justified, since they have violated both a private and a public trust. But the "punishment must fit the crime." Our society protects even criminals from excessive "harm," for example, by prohibiting the use of excessive force in arresting and restraining them.

Less dramatically, some residents or staff might suffer hurt feelings, a kind of *psychological harm,* in finding themselves described in ways they consider unflattering. Some might be angry that things they had shared with Sherry within a trusting relationship are now shared with all who read her thesis.

Sometimes harm may occur directly in a study, and not just because of subsequent public revelations. Though not evident in Sherry's work, some experiments in psychology and social psychology may traumatize participants by subjecting them to extreme stress.[1] Even psychological discomfort should not be casually dismissed as insignificant.

Physical harm to research subjects and its extreme—death—may seem unlikely in social and behavioral research, but it is not impossible. In a study of criminal behavior, a researcher might inadvertently disclose the disloyalty of a gang member. It is not unthinkable that the leader might have the traitor "eliminated."

How can harm be avoided or minimized? Sherry can reduce the likelihood of harm resulting from public disclosure in several ways. First, she can be careful about what she says and where and to whom she says it. Second, in her written report she can use fictitious names and change irrelevant identifying facts. These conventional devices, though important, are far from foolproof. If the subject population itself ever sees the published study, people may well recognize themselves and others through the disguises, and anyone who knows Sherry can probably figure out which nursing home she is describing. Sherry herself could write

---

[1] One study of stress involved telling a group of army recruits on a DC-3 that the plane was losing power and would crash-land. The recruits were asked to record their feelings on a survey instrument. Only after landing safely were they told that the induced stress was an experiment. M. Berkun, et al., "Experimental Studies of Psychological Stress in Man," *Psychological Monographs: General and Applied* 76:15 (1962): 1-39.

under a pseudonym, but that is difficult if she is trying to earn a degree or establish herself in the field.

Remember that anyone occupying Sherry's staff position could have made the same observations that she did and could be just as guilty as Sherry in making careless remarks. Of course, no one should harm others. Sherry's role as social scientist, however, places a different burden on her than she would bear simply as activities director. Her special role heightens her responsibility to avoid harming her subjects. Even if her "respondents" and "informants" are unaware of their role in her study, Sherry knows how much they are helping her; lack of concern for their well-being would be ungrateful. Especially in participant studies, the personal relationships that are basic to the method give rise to special interpersonal obligations. Sherry's subjects have placed a lot of trust in her, and this calls for loyalty in return.

Often participant observers develop strong sympathetic ties with the people they study. But even if the researcher does not share the views or values of his or her subjects and even if the researcher's final report differs from the subjects' understanding of themselves, we feel the researcher still has some obligation to insure that their view is at least presented. Reciprocity between investigator and respondent seems to call for such a commitment. Some social scientists have suggested that "undesirable" groups deserve to have their advocates just as even guilty criminals deserve an attorney. However, the view that such special obligations arise out of the research relationship is not universally held. Some researchers maintain that this approach developed while anthropologists were studying largely powerless people who were unable to protect themselves. This norm would not apply, they argue, to "bad" groups, which deserve no protection, nor to groups which have the power to defend themselves.[2] Indeed, those who take this perspective might insist that investigators should prevent harm that might be perpetrated *by*

---

[2]Jack D. Douglas argues that the model of the investigative reporter is as valid for social sciences as the traditional participant observer model. See his *Investigative Social Research* (Beverly Hills CA: Sage, 1976). He argues that the model of spies, counterspies, police, tax collectors, and investigative journalists can be appropriate for social science, in keeping with a "conflict" conception of society. Similarly, John F. Galliher, "The Protection of Human Subjects: A Re-Examination of the Professional Code of Ethics," *The American Sociologist* 8 (1973): 93-100, argues that some groups do not deserve the standard protections. He mentions the American Nazi Party and the Ku Klux Klan as possible examples, and he even suggests that it may not be necessary to secure the cooperation of the Pentagon before undertaking a study of that organization.

their subjects. If researchers have a duty to use science to promote human welfare, could exposing evil be a basic professional duty?

This is a plausible position for social and behavioral science. It is, after all, naive to believe that science can be entirely value-neutral or value-free. Yet we have serious reservations about this approach. Resolving this question involves one's view of science and one's view of political philosophy. Central to the issue is the definition of social roles in a free society. We do not find undercover police work morally objectionable if carefully controlled. Investigative reporting has its place, too, again with appropriate procedures and limits. Social and behavioral science performs a different function, and it would detract from that purpose if it became either an arm of the police or an arm of "the revolution." The social mandate for the sciences at this time is to gain knowledge, and the quality of scientific work and hence its service to society would be undermined if researchers *as* scientists made political goals their primary purpose. Moreover, police or spies should not pose as scientists in order to accomplish their work, since this would be detrimental to science and ultimately to the society that science serves.

We would not, however, eliminate completely researchers' advocacy for research subjects or their efforts to contribute to the solution of social problems. Rather, our contention is that researchers must *first* strive to be as objective and as fair in their scientific work as possible and be careful to distinguish between personal values and scientific knowledge.[3]

The researcher, though not primarily an agent of social change or social control, might be thrust into situations where role obligations conflict. Should Sherry report Dr. Waters for defrauding Medicare by claiming visits he never made? Is he a research subject who deserves protection? What is her civic duty? What is her duty to herself? Should she risk her job and her research project, since Mr. Johnson may not like whistleblowing?

Sherry might even discover that Dr. Waters has given a lethal dose of a painkilling drug to several of the nursing home patients. Even if she

---

[3]We do not reject the "political" role completely, but the presumption should be that researchers will advocate *for* their subjects if they *advocate* at all. Anthropologists sometimes become negotiators for tribal peoples who are being forced into the larger modern world. The issue even interests the popular press; see Sharon Begley, et al., "The New Activist Anthropologists," *Newsweek* 105:4 (28 January 1985): 66-67. On rare occasions, if some significant social good is at stake, researchers might find it necessary to act contrary to their subjects' interests.

personally approves of euthanasia in some circumstances, she must acknowledge that the doctor's act was illegal. Should Sherry report these crimes? Should investigators report all crimes of which they are aware? If so, all efforts to study the world of crime from the inside would be impossible, since stool pigeons can't expect to get very far working with criminals. How should researchers weigh their obligations to their subjects against their obligations to protect others?

Many of our moral dilemmas involve this sort of conflict of obligations or values. Most, fortunately, are not nearly so dramatic. Take, for example, a nurse who occasionally fabricates blood pressure readings because she has too much else to do. There may be no immediate harm. There is, of course, a risk that a serious treatable disease may go undetected and untreated. Even if no one suffers harm, the practice is dangerous and unethical as defined by the profession. What should Sherry do? Should she speak to the nurse and advise her to change her practice, threatening her with exposure if she doesn't? Should she report the nurse to her superior? Should she simply ignore it as not being really that important and not her business? Does she have any more or less responsibility to do something because she is a researcher than if she were only activities director?

This kind of problem is not uncommon in participant research. Especially in working with "deviants" or in anthropological work in other cultures, the participant observer may be called upon to condone or even participate in acts that conflict with the researcher's own norms or are even illegal in the society where the subculture is located. The anthropologist in a primitive society might observe euthanasia for the elderly, or harsh punishment for what seems to the outsider a minor offense. In our own society, a participant observer may be able to identify drug dealers, con artists, police officers who accept bribes, welfare cheaters, or students who buy or sell term papers. What should researchers do? A range of responses is possible: reporting offenses to the proper authorities, urging subjects not to perform an illegal or immoral act, simply stating objections, remaining silent (does silence give consent?), openly condoning, and actively participating in the action. Overt participation research may pose fewer ethical problems for the researcher than covert observation, since the subjects will not necessarily expect the researcher to condone all their activities or participate in them. Often the investigator can appropriately refrain from stating a judgment, or can state a moral view without being judgmental.

We do not believe that there is a "cookbook" answer to this question. Some of the examples above seem so harmful to others and are so clearly in violation of public morality that most of us would probably feel we couldn't just stand by and do nothing to prevent them. We can't police the world, we might say to ourselves. Yet faced with a concrete opportunity to prevent a *significant* injury at little risk or inconvenience to ourselves, we may feel that our obligation to others requires preventing injury. An assessment of the degree of the moral or legal infraction, a short-term and long-run estimate of the effect that an intervention will have in reducing the illegal or immoral activity, and the nature of the investigator's relationship with the group will all figure into the researcher's decision.

But doesn't intervening to prevent harm conflict with the role of the participant observer? Isn't the goal of this type of research simply to see what happens in a group rather than affecting the group? In some forms of participant research, it is clear that the observer cannot and should not avoid being an active participant who makes a difference in what happens. Sherry, in her role as activities director, necessarily effects changes, and her personal relationships with the residents might require that she become their advocate with the nurses, doctors, and staff, protecting them from harm if need be. It may be part of the reciprocity involved in the relationship.

But suppose Sherry had assumed a different role. Imagine that, as a follow-up study in a different nursing home, she receives permission to be an entirely passive observer, not interacting with the community at all. Among other things, this might help her assess the extent to which her own interactions changed the environment at Darkwoods. What if she is just watching, sitting silently in the corner of a patient's room, when suddenly the patient slumps over in her chair with a heart attack? Should Sherry abandon her defined role as passive observer? Should she call for a nurse? Should she begin CPR herself? If she is a certified instructor in CPR and recognizes that the attendant doing resuscitation is doing it wrong, should she intervene? Any of these acts might interfere with the research procedure, perhaps invalidating her findings. She has not caused the harm. If she remains passive, what will happen is exactly what would happen in her absence. She will be able to see how the nursing home really works. Yet it seems obvious to us that, in this grave situation, the well-being of a person overrides the importance of the research. It is much less obvious that Sherry should abandon her passive role if all she observes is a nurse talking to a patient harshly or treating the patient as "just a body" while rendering nursing care. Sherry's intervention in this instance would probably have no lasting effect, and she would compromise any long-term benefits that might result from her study. None of us can be responsible for preventing every harm.

Besides the potential for harm *during* a study and harm *resulting* from "publication," the *termination* of a study can have adverse effects. Sherry's presence at Darkwoods seems to have been positive: life is better for residents and staff alike. Now, however, she is going to leave, and pain will result from her departure. Such is life, we say. Were she a regular employee, we couldn't blame her for taking a better offer elsewhere. But she took the job knowing that her stay would be short-lived. Knowing that, should she have avoided developing those deep personal relationships that added so much to her understanding but that will also be painful to sever—painful to her and painful to the Darkwoods community? Perhaps the benefits of those relationships will outweigh any pain. Again we offer no easy answers, but these are issues to which any researcher should be sensitive.

In addition to the personal distress that Sherry's departure may bring, the institution may suffer because of her tenure as activities director. Possibly her example has given Mr. Johnson a new vision of what an activities coordinator can do. More likely, he will be unable to find anyone as qualified as Sherry for the same pay, and he may not be willing or able to increase the salary enough to bring in another Sherry. After Sherry leaves, Darkwoods will probably return to "normal," except now everyone will be less satisfied with the normal. Expectations may have been raised only to be dashed. The resulting disillusionment may make matters worse than they were before her arrival. Can Sherry be held responsible if this occurs? Would she be less responsible if she had been more open about her purposes at the beginning?

HARM TO NONSUBJECTS

Most discussion about harm in social and behavioral research focuses on harm to the subjects. But others can be harmed. Sometimes third parties far removed from the scene of the research or innocent bystanders can be injured in some way. Society as a whole would suffer if deception in research were to erode trust in the basic truthfulness of others or if too many studies of "helping behavior" made people less likely to help in situations they mistook for research situations. An instance of this occurred on the campus of a state university when students made no effort to stop a murder or capture the murderer because witnesses thought it was "just another behavioral experiment," a fake assault to study people's responses to an apparent crisis. Likewise, if research into basic social institutions undermined confidence in those institutions, society as a whole could suffer.[4]

Thoughtlessness by social and behavioral scientists may do a disservice to colleagues and the cause of research generally by making scientific investigation more difficult. Two possibilities are worth mentioning. If researchers' procedures destroy people's faith in their integrity or compassion or make people wary, future research may be jeopardized. Public skepticism about social and behavioral research may reduce the number of willing subjects, diminish even further the resources allocated for such research, and increase pressure for more regulation. Second, excessive use of deception may cause problems. Even if subjects do not resent having been deceived, the *quality* of research may suffer. If subjects have previously been deceived, they may try to outguess the researcher, looking for the "real" purpose of the experiment rather than responding naively, as they need to do if the study is to discover anything about human nature.[5] Although we would not anticipate any of these adverse effects from Sherry's research, the question of possible harm to the "profession" should be considered thoughtfully. The risks may be cumulative, involving the whole profession rather than isolated individual researchers. One of the threats in this regard may be the proliferation of survey research. With so many people conducting surveys, some people are becoming too impatient even to hear what the purpose of another survey is. We return to this problem in our next chapter.

Finally, harm to researchers themselves is possible. About the only harm that seems likely to afflict Sherry is the sadness and perhaps guilt she will feel in leaving people for whom she has come to care a great deal.

---

[4]One illustration was the research on the jury system in Wichita, Kansas. With judges' permission but without the jury's knowledge, researchers tape-recorded jury deliberations for analysis. Entirely apart from questions of the secrecy of the recording and the possibility that future juries would be inhibited for fear that they were being recorded, some critics were concerned that too much knowledge about the jury system may undermine confidence in the system itself, without our having a better alternative. Churchill's quip that democracy is "the worst form of government except all those other forms that have been tried from time to time" reminds us that imperfect systems that work are better than ideal ones that don't. Are there perhaps some areas of the political system that are sacred and should be exempted from scientific scrutiny?

[5]One investigator reports that excessive use of deception has made it difficult for him to carry on his research. Almost all his student subjects have been lied to by other researchers, and they believe that he, too, is lying. Philip Bonacich, "Deceiving Subjects: The Pollution of Our Environment," *American Sociologist* 5 (February 1970): 45.

Mike and Linda might also come to be genuinely concerned about some of the people they meet and might experience some anguish on their behalf. These potential "harms" are pretty much part of everyday living in relationships with others and probably carry little ethical weight. Mike is a bit more at risk of being injured if one of the customers at the Exotic suspects what he is doing and becomes resentful. The patron could even become violent. Don is the one in the greatest danger of suffering harm himself. He is already torn emotionally. The conflict between his personal moral code and his life with the Necrons is precipitating a crisis. His own personal safety may be endangered if the group discovers that he is an impostor.

You may object to considering harm to the investigator in the *ethical* assessment of the research. Researchers have the right as autonomous individuals to place themselves at risk if they choose, you might argue, pointing to some of the heroes of medical science who performed their dangerous experiments upon themselves. We would agree, within limits at least, that researchers have *the right* to risk themselves if they choose, just as we allow people to do all kinds of crazy things. But that does not make it *right* for them to do so. In assessing the potential for harm as an ethical factor in research, we would insist that harm to researchers is part of the moral equation.

Researchers ought to consider carefully all the effects of their actions: the effects on subjects, on bystanders, on society at large, on colleagues, and on themselves. Thus one important part of ethical evaluation is imagining potential outcomes and estimating their likelihood. A second factor is assessing the *degree* of potential harm. Difficult as this assessment is in medical research, it is even more problematic in social research. There is no calculus for measuring social or psychological harm. Mistakes in predicting and assessing harm will undoubtedly occur. All it is reasonable to expect of moral agents is that they make their best judgments with the information they are able to obtain. In research, people can make a moral mistake by irresponsibly underestimating the likelihood or the severity of harm and proceeding with too risky a project. But being too cautious is also possible. Ignorance may also be harmful, and our society has assigned scientists the task of gaining knowledge. Burdening researchers with needless worries that paralyze them and prevent useful research is also a moral mistake.

Moreover, risking injury is not always wrong. The potential benefits may justify some risks. Informed consent procedures allow the subjects to authorize reasonable risks, but this does not relieve researchers of the responsibility of ensuring that risks are "reasonable." Scientists should not unduly endanger their subjects even if the subjects are willing to accept such risks.

Because participant observers establish significant relationships with their subjects, entering their lives to see things as they do and feel what they feel, they should and usually do develop a commitment to avoid harming them. This issue, as well as privacy, deception, and informed consent, is important in other kinds of research as well. Moreover, some of the issues that we will discuss in subsequent chapters will also apply to participant research.

IV

ASKING QUESTIONS AND COUNTING ANSWERS: ETHICAL CONCERNS IN SURVEY RESEARCH

9

A Student Survey:
Another Look at Some Issues

A study using questionnaires or structured interviews is the most common kind of social research. The image of the mild-mannered, bespectacled poll-taker, wearing an earth-toned suit and Hush Puppies—looking like Clark Kent—is familiar to us all. We can also imagine a scientist wearing a starched white lab coat asking the respondent a battery of intimate questions. In fact, we are all touched by social science surveys. There are, for example, surveys we *must* participate in; by refusing to answer questions about ourselves and our households during a United States census, we violate federal law and are liable to fines or other penalties. The census, once a way of justly apportioning representation in Congress, has recently become a mechanism for learning about the people of our nation. The 1980 census included questions about marriages and divorces, number of bathrooms in the household, and, if the respondent was female, the number of live children and still births she had had. We assume that this information assists governmental agencies in helping those in need, but we cannot fail to notice how far from its original purpose the census has come.

Surveys have other effects that we all directly feel. Our conversation frequently refers to recent public opinion polls in which we learn not only who is likely to be our next president, member of Congress, or senator, but how people feel about current issues. These polls appear day after day; their results can be uncannily accurate in their predictive value. Some, like the Gallup and Harris polls, have become so well known that they are household words. Because sampling and analytic techniques have become so sophisticated, a small number of respondents can produce reliable results. In these cases, many people may be willing or even honored to be part of a survey, because they *know* that their responses will make a difference—if not in the way policies are formulated, at least in the knowledge that is gained from the study. Every "vote" counts big in such surveys. Many social science surveys are used by government

regulatory agencies in establishing policies that directly affect us. So
much for the *fact* of surveys. This kind of information gathering is an important part of our modern world. Those who have chosen a career in
the social and behavioral sciences are likely to be both consumers and
producers of these studies. Are there any ethical concerns that might interest us as we contemplate survey research?

The case we are about to describe may seem familiar to you. Many
undergraduate students enrolled in methods courses are expected to
compose a questionnaire and administer it to a sample of respondents
and analyze its data as one of their course requirements. Students are
usually free to explore their own interests in such surveys that range from
studies of cheating to church attendance or attitudes about drug use on
campus.[1]

<h2 style="text-align:center">"PARDON ME . . .
WOULD YOU MIND
ANSWERING A FEW QUESTIONS?"</h2>

Mary Hall, an undergraduate nursing student at Gemsdale State College, needed a research project for Nursing 304, Foundations of Nursing
Research. She decided to study attitudes about suicide and the famil-
iarity of respondents with suicide. Her questions included items to determine whether respondents had ever contemplated suicide or had
known anyone who had attempted suicide. Other questions elicited information on respondents' ethical and value determinations on suicide.
For example, would the respondent attempt to prevent a suicide and what
factors (age, location, method of attempt, and so forth) would influence
the decision? Some questions were interesting and provocative, asking
respondents to examine their values. The questionnaire was to be ad-
ministered anonymously, so there was little likelihood of disclosure or
harm occurring. Nevertheless, some questions might force the respondents to recall painful or unpleasant memories.

Mary wanted to survey the full range of university and professional
students, testing the hypothesis that different kinds of students would
respond to the questionnaire in different ways. The problem became how
to get a large enough sample to respond. When she randomly distributed
the questionnaire through student mailboxes, she got a low rate of return. With the approval of her faculty advisor, Mary decided to button-
hole students and convince them to complete the questionnaire.

---

[1]An excellent book on survey research is Morris Rosenberg, *The Logic of Survey Analysis* (New York: Basic Books, 1968). Another useful source is Leslie Kish,
Survey Sampling (New York: John Wiley & Sons, 1965).

Mary found this a formidable task. Except for medical students, it was easy to get students to *begin* the questionnaire. Many, however, refused to finish it, claiming they were displeased or upset with some of the questions, or saying they couldn't spend any more time. This was frustrating for Mary, who had to discard the partially completed questionnaire and begin again. Mary was also disturbed by students who responded in a strongly negative way either to the study or to one or more of its questions.

Mary was most dismayed by the response of medical students. When she visited nursing student lounges, she was always able to find a few people to complete the instrument. When Mary went to the medical students' lounge, she felt unwelcome. She did, however, leave several questionnaires with students who promised to complete them so they could be picked up the next day. When Mary returned, she found that none of the students had done what they had promised. On her way out of the lounge she discovered the small stack of questionnaires in a trash can. Mary was heartbroken and felt as if her fellow students had betrayed her!

ETHICS AND SURVEY RESEARCH

Let's look at survey research in general and this case in particular. Asking people to complete a simple, anonymous questionnaire seems innocuous enough. Although some of the questions might seem distasteful or even disturbing, answering the questionnaire shouldn't have caused anyone real harm. Are there any ethical problems here?

Some of the ethical issues Mary should consider are not not very different from those we have been looking at in other types of research. Let's look first at those issues—privacy, deception and informed consent, and harm—and then move on to raise some other questions.

Harm

Of all research, the survey seems least likely to cause harm. But already we have touched upon the possibilities of emotional pain that Mary's survey might cause. It is the kind of pain that the respondents might experience in daily life by reading magazine articles that revive painful memories or by conversations that arouse strong feelings.

Does the commonness of these emotions mean that Mary need not be concerned about that possibility? That people frequently receive painful injections at the doctor's office does not justify needle-happy researchers running around randomly sticking needles in people's arms. If pain is a possibility in Mary's survey, she needs to think about that as she plans her study.

Those with a close friend who attempted suicide or individuals who have attempted suicide themselves *might* experience painful memories. Mary won't know who these people are in advance. But if she did, should she avoid asking them to participate to spare them pain? She would do so at considerable cost to her study, since those are some of the most important people for her study. Yet surveying this group may dredge up long-buried memories in those most vulnerable to pain. The likelihood of this happening is considerably increased if the survey used an interview method and the interviews were conducted by a "professional" who really knew how to pick up clues and probe more deeply the respondent's experience with suicide. Should a researcher do this, even with consent, especially if the benefits are modest?

Would recalling these memories really be harmful? Does short-term emotional pain constitute harm? Might it even be therapeutic? Suppressed grief might be released as a result of Mary's survey, and the individual may begin for the first time to cope realistically with a demon buried deep inside. This may seem unlikely, but how can we know? It is, incidentally, more likely that therapeutic results could occur if a skilled professional were conducting an interview schedule. There is always the possibility that therapy could get in the way of scientific investigation. But all of this sounds very speculative. How could Mary even begin to assess realistically the *degree* of even the *risk* of harm? The illustration may at least demonstrate that the question of harm is not so simple as we might expect, even in survey research.

Another kind of potential harm involves educating respondents about some potentially dangerous activity that they might then attempt. Suppose Mary had asked persons who had attempted suicide about the means they had used, listing a number of alternative methods. It is not inconceivable that a respondent might be thus introduced to a method he had never thought of before, which he might subsequently use to harm himself.

A more likely example might be a drug abuse survey. A survey about drug use among early adolescents might inquire about whether respondents had ever experimented with any of a list of substances. Imagine that one youngster had not known that one of these substances—for example, airplane glue—could be used to get high. Because of the survey question, he began to sniff glue, with resulting brain damage. Is the surveyor at all responsible for the injury? The question is certainly worth pondering.

Finally, as we discussed earlier, there is the issue of *preventing* harm. Mary has assured her respondents that the survey is anonymous. As she began actively soliciting responses personally, the anonymity may have been compromised, but at least most of the survey forms have been handled in an anonymous fashion; that is, they have been collected in such a way that even Mary doesn't know the source of the data.

What if she received one questionnaire in which the respondent indicated that suicide was being seriously considered at that moment? Because of the section on personal data (age, race, sex, degree program) in the questionnaire and Mary's knowledge about when and where the form was returned, let's say she could be almost certain of the individual's identity. Does she have a right, or even a responsibility, to intervene, despite her promise of anonymity?

She might argue that she ought to keep her promise. She wouldn't be *causing* a suicide if that resulted. Moreover, she might argue that she does not have a really personal relationship that might demand her intervention, since she is only engaged in survey research. No one would blame her for not intervening, since no one will ever know she had the information. If she is the least suspicious by nature, she may even wonder if someone is playing a game with her, testing to see if she can be enticed to violate her promise of confidentiality.

On the other hand, this may be someone's cry for help, a way of asking Mary to intervene. Mary might look for subtle clues. Had the person said in the survey that he or she would attempt to prevent the suicide of another? A positive response might be a signal that the person would welcome an intervention in this case. Even without clues, Mary may feel she should intervene. Even if she accepts the moral right of a competent person to commit suicide, she does not have adequate information to judge the competence of this individual.

Can Mary morally act contrary to her promise? We would argue that the keeping of promises, though an important part of human relationships, is no more an absolute than other ethical rules we have discussed. Rules provide a framework for human relationships and responsibility. The purpose of the promise, Mary might say, was to protect her respondents. It now appears that protecting this person requires violating that promise. The welfare of the individual supersedes the promise that was made to protect that welfare.

Privacy

Concern for privacy lies behind the promise of anonymity. The principle of privacy protects people from personal matters being revealed publicly. It also means freedom from intrusion into private areas. Requiring informed consent is a way to protect privacy. Does Mary's research infringe on privacy? Because it is conducted anonymously, the public revelation of private material seems highly unlikely. But does the *process* of the survey invade privacy?

Let's look first at the *content* of her study, distinguishing between two types of privacy: *behavioral* and *psychological.* Mary is not observing the current behavior of her subjects, and she is not primarily interested in hearing about past behavior. She wants to know about her subjects' feelings and attitudes on suicide. This raises the issue of psychological privacy. For many people, suicide may seem like a remote topic, of some interest perhaps for rap sessions; but it is not something that has touched them personally. For others, suicide may be very personal indeed, either because someone quite close to them has attempted suicide or because they have seriously considered suicide themselves. A surveyor's questions may touch a raw nerve for these individuals. They may see it as a kind of psychological assault. The moralistic attitude toward suicide not uncommon in our society may make people ashamed to admit that they or a member of their family has attempted or even contemplated suicide. Other people may simply consider suicide a taboo, a subject unmentionable in polite conversation. Mary's questionnaire may seem inappropriate or embarrassing to some potential respondents.

It seems easy to say, of course, that they don't have to participate. Unlike covert participant research where people can be studied without ever knowing it, survey research requires the cooperation of the respondents in answering questions. And they can simply refuse, as Mary experienced, much to her dismay. But the movement into a private area may be subtle. Even if Mary didn't set out to be sneaky, her questionnaire may begin benignly enough and then progress almost imperceptibly into increasingly sensitive areas. Some respondents may feel afterwards that Mary has penetrated more deeply into their private lives than they had intended when they agreed to participate in the study. Others may not feel that way at all. Some might even be grateful that they learned something about themselves from thinking about her questions. But in any case Mary should consider that many people may find the survey quite personal as she decides how to frame her questions and how to approach potential respondents.

But concern for privacy may not be limited to the content of the survey instrument. It may also include the *place* and *manner* in which the poll is conducted. Poll-takers are everywhere. They may be especially common on a college campus, but they are on the streets or in public buildings. A person who isn't interested in participating in these surveys can normally brush off a poll-taker in a public place with as much ease as one can most religious groups distributing literature or a street corner flower vendor. Sometimes, however, pollsters may be more persistent, perhaps inappropriately so.

We also receive questionnaires in the mail from a variety of sources. We frequently comment on the mountain of paper that passes through our mailboxes, and sometimes we probably all wish that we weren't on so many computerized mailing lists. Through the mails countless organizations enter our homes to plead for our contributions, for our business, or for information about us. Undoubtedly some people are more distressed by this than others. Most of us have become accustomed to the ritual of discarding at least half of our mail with hardly a glance, including surveys.

Then there is the telephone survey or the door-to-door survey. For some of us, at least, these efforts may seem to intrude into private *time* and *space* more seriously than other forms. What one perceives as "junk phone calls" may be handled with less equanimity than "junk mail."

This point struck home with special force recently for one of the authors. Let me share the incident with you. One evening while working at home on the section on privacy, I received two telephone calls within half an hour asking for participation in surveys. One was for a local hospital. The other was from a firm in New Jersey. Both sounded like market research and were therefore greeted with even less enthusiasm by a professor than a "purely scientific" survey might have received, and probably not all telephone subscribers would even share this deference for scientific research. Having one's privacy—or was it merely solitude?—interrupted by these phone calls while writing about privacy was especially ironic.

Surveys have become so common that we can expect calls of this nature with some regularity, in addition to even more calls from insurance sales representatives or lawn care services or roofing contractors who have something to sell. Such calls are doubly annoying if they come during dinner or if the phone awakens the children who were taking a nap. The frequency of such calls may generate hostility in even the most mild-mannered individuals. Both interruptions alluded to above were unwelcome, but it was the second caller who was accorded the less pleasant admonition to "leave people alone." The practice may be irritating, but is it unethical? Posed in its most emphatic form, the answer to the question is almost certainly "no."

Is it *immoral* to use a publicly available phone directory to seek customers or survey respondents? Immoral? The word sounds too harsh. Unethical? The tone of that word seems somehow less severe, but it also sounds too strong. If ethics and morality are concerned only with actions that are *clearly* prohibited or mandated, this issue seems to fall outside the realm of morality. But morality may also be conceived as including acts that are encouraged though not required or discouraged though not forbidden. Within this framework, morality can include the good, the better, and the best, and may range from the almost trivial to very weighty matters. Viewed in this way, even these minor intrusions into the privacy of another's home may have a moral dimension that deserves attention. Although the interruption caused by those phone calls is not a matter of grave ethical concern, neither is it entirely frivolous.

We think researchers should be expected to satisfy themselves that the survey they propose has some worth that warrants bothering people, and people being surveyed have a right to have some information about the survey.

Informed Consent and Deception

Informed consent may not seem to be a major issue in survey research. Consent seems implied if a person responds. People can refuse to participate simply by declining to put pencil to paper or by refusing to answer an interviewer's questions. Does answering the surveyors' questions, then, imply informed consent? A mechanical application of rigid rules about informed consent without regard to the differences between various kinds of research does not seem appropriate. The list of informational items often deemed necessary for some research, especially medical research, does not seem applicable to survey research. Some research requires explanations about the procedures and purposes, an analysis of risks and benefits, a statement of available alternatives (in the case of therapeutic research), an offer to answer questions, and a statement that the participant can withdraw at any time. Providing a detailed explanation of these items in requesting participation in a survey would seem a little silly. But embodied in these topics is a spirit of informed consent that involves respect for the privacy, autonomy, and well-being of human beings who may become research subjects, and this spirit can pervade even survey research. Without providing a lecture on the techniques of survey research, the investigator can explain the topic being researched, why it is being examined, and for whom. This information seems essential if people are consciously to assess whether they think the survey is worth their time or is too personal or too painful for them.

Feeling that a particular research project is significant probably increases people's willingness to consent. Mary's difficulty in part is that the students she wants to survey realize that these student surveys don't lead anywhere. New policies and improvements in life are unlikely to result. Nor is it even likely that the research will ever be published. While Mary struggles with her survey, countless other students in psychology, sociology, nursing, and so on are conducting similar surveys. Course credit will be the only tangible result of any of them. Students may tire of participating in "practice research" that doesn't do anything. Perhaps this partly explains the medical students' unwillingness to help Mary. They, too, have been surveyed to death about every course they've taken—sometimes, it seems, even every session they've attended. The response rate in course evaluations may not be spectacular, but many do respond, hoping their efforts might make a difference in their education or at least in that of the next generation of students. But Mary's survey won't change anything. Why should they waste their time?

Moreover, Mary's survey isn't likely to make any real contribution to human knowledge. Even major advances in the social and behavioral sciences may leave many people unimpressed. For some, it's all academic hogwash, ivory tower stuff, with no value in the real world. But no one will even notice Mary's work. Only her instructor or, at most, her classmates will even read the report of her survey.

How can Mary justify butting into people's lives with her survey, and how can she legitimately "sell" her survey to her potential respondents? Mary is really asking people to cooperate with the *system* of scientific study, which will have its successes and its failures. Training students is part of that system. If there are to be continuing advances, a new generation of researchers must be educated, and they will learn the craft only by doing it. Mary is learning some skills in constructing, conducting, and analyzing data from survey research. The benefit of her work is not the *results* of the survey but the *educational benefit* that she will derive. What she learns from doing this study may enable her to conduct more productive research in the future. Mary will learn from her subjects as medical students learn from their patients. The first patients may not benefit from the medical students' ministrations, but future patients will. Using this analogy, Mary might be able to persuade at least a few medical students to complete her questionnaire.

We might even argue that fellow students ought to help Mary by participating as part of a "community of scholars" committed to a common venture. We frankly doubt that many of our readers will accept that argument, but that may be more because of our changing social institutions than the idea itself. Although we still frequently talk about an "academic community" and emphasize the "oneness" implied in the term *uni*versity, the sheer size of mass higher education has done a great deal to attenuate that ideal of community. Mary seemed disappointed that some students had "betrayed" her. She may not have felt a great affinity with her fellow students, but she must have felt some sense of common purpose, and the relationship took on a new dimension when students promised to complete the questionnaires and return them the next day. Apparently the medical students who discarded the forms did not take the relationship as seriously as Mary did, and didn't construe their remarks about "filling them out later" as being any kind of binding promise. They would probably be surprised that Mary felt betrayed.

If the medical students don't take their relationship with Mary seriously, how much less will most respondents who lack even the link of attending the same university feel toward a surveyor. Unlike participant research, the surveyor does not establish a strong tie with the respondents. This will reduce the respondents' sense of obligation to the researcher; there is also the danger that the surveyor will be more casual about obligations to the respondent. But the relationship is not symmetrical. The subjects are basically giving their time and something of themselves to Mary without any immediate gain for themselves. They may feel some more general obligation to others, to science, to society, but they have no particular reason to feel obligation to Mary individually. She is just another surveyor. But for Mary, these are *her* respondents whom she has *chosen* to survey (even if the choice was dictated by scientific rather than personal considerations). They are helping *her* even if their primary intent is to help others, or even if they are participating because they simply lack the initiative to refuse. A sense of moral obligation may be more important in survey research than in participant observation simply because the nature of the relationship in the latter may make the researcher *want* to protect the participants; in survey research, where the absence of a personal relationship may lower the "personal" commitment to the well-being of a respondent, the "professional" responsibility of acting for one's client's interest *on principle* may become more important.

How much of a "hard sell" is legitimate in persuading people who are disinclined to participate? If Mary had a lot of money, she could pay people to respond to her survey. As long as the amount was commensurate with the value of the respondents' time, there does not seem to us to be a problem with people being paid to participate in a scientific study. Too much money could interfere with a person's *effective* autonomy. Though it can be argued that no amount of money compels people to act against their will, it is widely held that payment for participation can be excessive, becoming too persuasive even if not coercive.

What about other means of persuasion? Would training interviewers to use sales techniques or motivational psychology to overcome resistance violate the autonomy of the potential respondent? The telephone interviewers described earlier went through a brief identification process and immediately launched into the questionnaire without pausing to ask whether it was okay to proceed. The procedure may be effective.

Probably many people find themselves answering the questions without ever consciously deciding whether to participate or not. Others may find the method more offensive than the phone call itself, and may hang up precisely for that reason. This raises both ethical and technical questions. Ethically, is it right to "entrap" people into responding to a survey by never offering a chance for refusal? Technically, is the procedure counterproductive, discouraging some people from responding because they resent the interviewer's approach? Does this skew the sample? Stated crassly, does scientific accuracy require surveyors to report that their samples consisted of people too gullible or too weak-willed to resist a high-pressure polltaker?

Mary may find that many purely personal factors can influence her ability to get responses: her dress, her demeanor, her accent, even her ethnic or racial background may influence some potential respondents. To what extent is it legitimate to manipulate these factors in seeking respondents? Can she justify pleading, cajoling, flirting, or playing on guilt feelings in order to secure responses? Is this an ethical issue?

Dwelling on the positive is a key to salesmanship, whether selling a dishwasher or a survey. But is Mary also obligated to mention *negative* features as well? Can she say, "May I take a minute of your time?" when she knows the survey will require at least fifteen minutes? What about warning participants of the risk of unpleasant emotions? "This survey may make some individuals uncomfortable." Is such a statement required for obtaining the "informed consent" of respondents? Does Mary need to *tell* her respondents that they are free to withdraw at any time?

We are not convinced that elaborate informed consent procedures are required for Mary's survey research. When one student is buttonholing other students on campus, it is clear that respondents can simply decline to answer any questions or stop whenever they wish. Mary's experience bears that out. It is a different matter if the surveyor is the professor who is requesting a class to fill out a questionnaire. Without assurances from the instructor, students may not know what would happen if they declined to participate.

Whatever the ethical requirements, it may be prudent for Mary to provide more information—prudent because it may increase her response rate. The prudential question has to do with technique rather than values. As Mary started noticing that people would begin but not complete her questionnaire, she might have asked whether providing more information at the beginning might lead to more completed surveys. At least those who started would be more likely to finish. Some studies of informed consent for medical procedures show that people are more likely to undergo unpleasant or risky diagnostic or therapeutic procedures when they have been given more rather than less information. Those studies are far from conclusive, and they may be unique to the therapeutic setting, where more understanding of potential benefits is the dominant influence. But they may also testify to the desire to feel in control.

A number of fascinating psychological studies demonstrate the importance of feeling in control. One experiment was designed to test whether noise interfered with concentration on mental tasks. After some baseline testing, noise was introduced as a variable. One group of participants was told that they could stop the noise temporarily by pushing a button. The other group was not given that control. The group given control over the noise chose not to exercise it; nevertheless, not only did they outperform the other group, they even did better with the noise than they had without it. Another study attempted to address directly the effects of informed consent. It grew out of another study of the effects of noise. Earlier studies demonstrated significant aftereffects of environmental noise. Then strict informed-consent procedures were introduced. Participants were informed that they could withdraw at any time. The aftereffects disappeared. Repeated studies by the investigator confirmed that informed consent altered the effects that were being measured. The noise studies suggest that informed consent increases participants' tolerance for discomfort or distraction.[2] Giving people more information about a survey may make them more tolerant, more willing to accept the inconvenience it entails.

It is also possible that providing more information in some cases of survey research may, by the power of suggestion, create placebo effects. Perhaps the suggestion that the survey "may prove painful to some individuals" might increase the probability that some will feel distress that they otherwise would not have experienced. This brings us back to our discussion of *deception* in an earlier chapter. Informed consent may produce artifacts, and this might apply to survey research as well as to

---

[2]G. T. Gardner, "Effects of Federal Human Subjects Regulations on Data Obtained in Environmental Stressor Research," *Journal of Personality and Social Psychology* 36 (1978): 628-34. It is probably not surprising that the interest taken in the subjects of research by providing the information required for informed consent might affect the subjects' attitudes and tolerance. The famous Hawthorne effect, discovered in productivity studies many years ago, demonstrates that people respond positively to interest shown in their welfare. In that classic study, it did not matter what changes the researchers made in the workplace. Any change increased productivity, presumably because the changes were perceived as indicating that the employers were interested in the well-being of the workers.

other forms of investigation. The case of Mike's "health" survey of pornography consumers is a case in point. If Mike had sought informed consent for his survey, he might not have had any respondents. It is also possible that the informed-consent procedure might have changed the answers to the survey instrument. The latter is perhaps the more serious problem scientifically; misinformation is worse than no information.

Can deception of respondents in survey research ever be justified? To what extent is *informed* consent necessary in survey research? We have asked more questions than we are prepared to answer. It does seem to us that more research about public opinion regarding informed consent is necessary as we move toward a social consensus regarding that matter. If the goal of consent is to protect privacy and autonomy and to minimize harm, it seems important to know how those who might be affected perceive their own privacy and autonomy and how they would define harm.

This chapter began by depicting a simple, straightforward example of survey research. Mary's study is not really controversial. It will not attract public attention, and there is nothing about it that will elicit cries of moral outrage. "What kind of ethical issues can there be in something so common?" you may have asked yourself at the outset. We hope we have shown that even ordinary survey research can be more complex ethically than meets the eye. We gave free rein to our imagination to identify potential problems. If Mary uses good common sense in the way she approaches people about a potentially sensitive subject, if she does not presume that her study will yield more than its method makes possible, and if she is honest and careful about what she's doing, she is not likely to do anything wrong.

Mary's case is useful as a reminder that most social research is fairly ordinary, perhaps even mundane. Likewise, most ethical issues are not especially dramatic. Nevertheless, the ethical seriousness with which we approach these commonplace issues may be the test of the ethics of any profession.

In the next chapter, we will look at experimental research, which may have more far-reaching consequences than those examples that we have considered so far. Because scientists engaged in experimental research may be altering the conditions in which people act in order to understand human behavior better, experimentation may offer both more promise and more peril than the other types of research we've discussed so far.

V

THE WORLD
IS THEIR
LABORATORY:
ISSUES IN SOCIAL
AND BEHAVIORAL
EXPERIMENTATION

10

Engineering the Social World

For many observers, "the experiment" represents the best in scientific method. From the study of *theory*—statements about how phenomena occur and are related—*hypotheses* are derived. These educated guesses or "trial solutions" are then tested against empirical data. After much careful testing, hypotheses become part of the body of theory that will structure and direct future inquiries.[1]

From their inception, the social and behavioral disciplines attempted to emulate the scientific model developed in the natural sciences. Indeed, the prestigious social/behavioral journals, those in which there is much competition for limited space, are most likely to publish work derived from some aspect of theory

Most experiments occur when the researcher is on hand to observe change. Careful, accurate *description* of change is one part of the experimental method. But an *explanation* of how and why this change occurs is the scientist's goal. What the researcher wants to find are patterns that transcend individual subjects. The researcher attempts to alter or manipulate environmental components so that these patterns, and the theory behind them, will be revealed.

Social and behavioral scientists perform two kinds of experiments: natural experiments and contrived ones. In the *natural experiment,* researchers study a situation that they had no part in creating. Some change has occurred, positive or negative: a new program has been instituted, a new expressway has been built through a older neighborhood, or a natural disaster has occurred. The researcher examines the effects of the change. In doing so, the researcher may choose two groups. The one in which the change has happened is designated the "experimental" group;

---

[1] A standard book on experimental research is Donald T. Campbell and Julian C. Stanley, *Experimental and Quasi-Experimental Designs for Research* (Chicago: Rand McNally & Company, 1963). For a current leading text on experimentation in psychology, see Larry B. Christensen, *Experimental Methodology,* 3rd edition (Boston: Allyn and Bacon, 1985).

a similar group where no change has occurred becomes the "control" group. Sometimes, the researcher has no direct contact with the groups under study. Certain phenomena, indicators, are then compared between the two groups. These phenomena are the "social facts"; they are comparable to the "things" in the physical world that the natural sciences study. It is important to remember that researchers do not react or intervene in this research; they are only observers.

A natural experiment may not involve any ethical concerns at all. For example, the famous French sociologist Emile Durkheim based his classic work on suicide on publicly available statistical data. Durkheim applied certain theories to these prerecorded data. Although the subject of suicide is usually distressing, the data collection aspect of his research does not seem to raise any ethical issues.

In a variation of the natural experiment, researchers are present to observe a change that they have no responsibility for causing. For example, some communities have enacted legislation making it illegal to possess handguns. Those who violate the law may receive stiff criminal penalties. Researchers interested in some aspect of the problem—for instance, perceptions of public safety—might conduct interviews before and after implementation of the law. They are bound by ethical constraints in collecting the data, analyzing them, and publishing the results, but they are not responsible for any of the changes that may occur.

We will focus on *contrived experiments.* In this kind of experiment, the researcher *intentionally* manipulates the environment to assess subjects' responses to change. The range of manipulation is limited only by the researcher's imagination, resources, and (of course) ethics. A great deal of the research conducted by psychologists consists of such experimentation. In studies of conformity, behavioral scientists may experiment to see how much a person's perceptions are influenced by the opinions of others. In some of the classic studies of this type, students were asked to tell which of several lines seemed longer. All but one of the students were confederates of the researcher. The researcher found that a large number of students would overcome their clear sense experience to report observations identical to that of the rest of the group, even though these observations were mistaken.[2] Studies of aggression often use simulated situations to examine the factors that increase and decrease the likelihood of aggressive behavior. Much of this research is

---

[2]The seminal work in this area was Solomon E. Asch, "Studies of Independence and Submission to Group Pressure," *Psychological Monographs: General and Applied,* 70:9 (1956) 416.

done in a laboratory where the researcher can maintain maximum control over variables.

Some contrived experiments are "social" experiments. A scientist, using the existing body of theory and data, hypothesizes that making a particular social change will bring about other predictable changes. For example, a social scientist might conclude, after a study of intergroup conflict and the attitudes surrounding it, that people *learn* antagonistic attitudes and learn them at an early age. Further, a study of the literature on antagonism suggests that racism is "institutionalized." This means that social institutions support racial segregation and assure that equal opportunities are withheld from minorities. This, in turn, ensures that a minority will maintain its inferior position. After considering the problem, the scientist decides to experiment. He or she proposes that children in one community be transported from their neighborhood to neighborhoods across town to achieve racial balance in their classrooms. In another similar community, no such "busing" will occur. The educational and psychological development of the children in each community will be carefully studied. Other institutions in both communities will be examined to determine whether busing changes racist attitudes and alters patterns of institutionalized racism. The social scientist's plan is so well-formulated and the arguments so persuasive that others judge the experiment worth doing. Not only does the scientist persuade two communities to participate in the study; the experiment results in "busing" becoming the "law of the land." This is, of course, a whimsical rendition of our nation's "experiment" with busing to achieve a social goal. The results of that experiment are still being debated.

Our intention is not to argue the merits of this or any other experiment. We do wish to point out that experimental research— whether it is an attempt to alter a community's attitudes or one to see how quickly rumor spreads and what impact it has—poses thorny ethical problems. The cases and discussion in this section will raise some of these features for your consideration.

As you read, keep in mind that bias is a great danger in experimental research. Researchers do more than explore, more than chart unknown territory. They are likely to favor certain interpretations of a theoretical perspective and may be wedded to a particular hypothesis. If so, vigilance is required to safeguard each aspect of the project from bias, however subtle. Medical science has developed sophisticated techniques such as "double blind" designs to combat bias. The social and behavioral sciences may perfect techniques to eliminate bias, but for the time being the individual researcher must diligently guard the integrity of each project.

When social or behavioral experiments are linked to public policy, diligence in applying technical skill to the design and execution of an experiment becomes ethically even more important. As you read our cases, ask yourself whether the projects are likely to deliver what is promised. Are the biases of the researchers likely to distort their perceptions and interpretations of the data they receive? Will their personal values affect what they see? Will the studies, in other words, provide a sound scientific base of information from which social policy may build? The next case will force us to think about the social costs and benefits of a community experiment.

"OPERATION ANTICIPATE": SOCIAL RESEARCH AND SOCIAL CONTROL

"We've got it! We've got it! This is the biggest piece of research out of Washington this year!" All work stopped in the "boiler room," the large secretarial pool at Datatronics, Inc., as Allen Price yelled excitedly. Everyone at Datatronics, from the president of the company to the kid who worked in the mail room, knew the importance of winning this contract. Everyone jumped up to congratulate Allen, who, along with Pam McKenzie, Datatronics's systems expert, had written the successful proposal.

The past few days had been difficult for Pam and Allen. The outcome of the "orals," the name given the second stage of the contract-awarding process, had been uncertain. Allen had made the opening ten-minute presentation, highlighting the proposal's salient points and establishing the capabilities of Datatronics's staff and consultants. He then spent forty minutes answering questions about whether Datatronics could actually deliver on its promises. Pam handled the important ten-minute summation. Allen remembered her self-assured restatement of the key issues and how the panel had listened intently to her closing argument.

In truth this was a big contract and an unusual one. The RFP (Request for Proposals) invited bids from social science consulting firms with "outstanding qualifications" in research about urban minority lifestyles. While Datatronics had an impressive record in the field, the size of the contract—almost two and one-half million dollars over a two-year period—had attracted the notice of every large consulting firm and even some university and consortium research outfits.

What made it unusual was its diverse fiscal origin. The RFP had come out of the Department of Health, Education, and Welfare (the federal agency that later became the Department of Health and Human Services); the actual offer was made by the National Institute of Mental Health. Other arms of government were also involved. Money came from the Department of Justice, the DEA (Drug Enforcement Administration, now an independent division of the FBI), and the LEAA (Law Enforcement Assistance Administration, disbanded in 1982). The FBI and even the State Department's CIA planned to review leading proposals. Representatives of all these agencies were at the orals.

"Well, we've got it—now what do we do with it?" Pam McKenzie said the following day at a top-level staff meeting.

"Mac (as Pam's good friends called her), I'll bet the day you die and go to heaven you'll be asking God how he evaluates his angels' performance in both the immediate and intermediate run," Allen said. Everyone laughed as Pam affected a look of benign tolerance that people reserve for a child who attempts to lecture adults on the meaning of life.

"Seriously, though," Pam went on, "we've got a meeting with D'Anglis the day after tomorrow. You remember how he cracked the whip on the last piece we did for that shop." Some of the jubilation left the group as they contemplated the work they would have to produce in the next forty-eight hours to get Pam and Allen ready for their meeting. Dr. Charles D'Anglis, the NIMH contract officer, was well known for holding contractors to the absolute letter of their specifications, and if the contractor even implied it could do something, D'Anglis assumed the statement was a promise. Often he even refused to accept work that did not encompass the "new" understanding. While D'Anglis could be a pain, he was also a godsend. A flexible project officer might encourage staff to expand work so that it became unmanageable. Having D'Anglis, who would dot every "i" and cross every "t" on "Project Anticipate," as the study had already been dubbed, assured that Allen and Pam would do what had to be done in the most expeditious and cost-effective way.

"OK, OK, gang," Pam said. "Let's see if we can parcel this out. Roy, I want you to work on specifics for getting the data on the criminal justice population. Mike, you work on the attitudes and authority structures portion. Nancy, your job is zeroing in on the emergency room data. And you, Allen, my fine colleague, will get those urban field stations together. Any questions?"

Everyone left but Pam and Allen. They kept their seats at each end of the long, polished mahogany conference table. "Well, Mac, looks like we've got a tiger by the tail. This is the single largest contract we've ever won and, all things considered, the most difficult. This isn't the usual nickel-and-dime research piece, you know. This, Mac, is the real McCoy. Operation Anticipate has a lot of heavy money and political biggies behind it. I hope we didn't bite off more than we can chew."

Pam was quiet for a moment. She nibbled the end of her pen and looked out the window toward the Watergate complex, which could be seen outside the Datatronics suite. "I don't know, Babe. There are a couple of really big questions in my mind. For starters, why us? Why not a really big firm or, even more likely, one of the university outfits? Second, why NIMH? The work on urban life-styles hasn't really interested them for years now. And third, why all the hush-hush? It just doesn't add up."

"Well, add or multiply, it still means a lot of work for us. Hell, Mac, you've been in this business as long as I have, and both us know how screwy the feds can be when they've got real bucks to burn!"

"I don't know, Al. You're probably right, but I'll feel an awful lot better after we get D'Anglis's write-off."

The meeting with D'Anglis was cancelled; another appointment at the same time next week was made. Pam and Allen were told that the Institute wanted a senior corporate officer from Datatronics at the meeting. While Pam and Allen thought they knew a lot about dealing with the feds, they hadn't anticipated this turn of events. All they could do was wait for the meeting and get their research plans in order.

The second meeting occurred on schedule. Not only was D'Anglis there, but key figures from several other agencies were present as well. D'Anglis quickly yielded his leadership to a Mr. Nelson, who was with the Department of Justice's LEAA.

"First of all," Mr. Nelson began, "let's get straight why we're here, or more to the point, why you're here. Datatronics was chosen for two reasons: Number one, you proved to us—to all of us—that you could do the work. You've got the in-house brains, and what's lacking in the shop you know how to get hold of. That's for the record. Now, number two—and this like everything else is gonna be off the record—is that the big outfits are too big, too open. We wanted a firm that can do the work and not be watched by the press like Rendex Corporation and U.S. University Foundation were last year. We wanted a group that everyone didn't already know about. This project is important, and it needs to be done quietly."

Pam, Allen, and Fritz Simmons, the executive vice-president of Datatronics, exchanged looks. "Well, here it comes now," Pam thought.

As the senior officer in the group, Fritz cleared his throat and asked: "Ah, what exactly are you driving at, Mr. Nelson? We more than met the specifications of the RFP in our proposal."

"No, Fritz, your proposal's fine. We just want to hone some of the methods a bit more. As a matter of fact, we're going to help you a lot. For instance, your criminal justice section was probably the weakest part of your proposal. Well, I can guarantee that you'll have no trouble at all getting into the incarcerated population, and we'll be able to identify some of the people running around on the street and tell you how to get hold of 'em.

"Now, Fritz, we know you have authority to speak for your company, so I am making this offer to you. You can bail out now and not do the work for us. I'll guarantee that all the monies, including personnel costs, that your firm spent to write this proposal will be returned to you. No hard feelings. If you want to keep the contract, what I'll—or rather what we all—want is your word that none of what's been said or will be said will leave this room. And that you'll do the work to the best of your ability with the clear understanding that you're working for us on a special project, one that has important ramifications for the internal security of our country.

"Let's lay our cards right out on the table, Fritz. We want to know what's happening on the street, and we want to know who's making it happen—that's priority one. You call it 'emerging life-styles,' 'patterns of interaction' or whatever (here with a nod to Pam and Allen) you professors call that stuff. We call it 'potentially disruptive and dangerous.' Knowing what's happening and what it all means makes it a lot easier on everyone.

"And that gets into the second part of the project. We like to call that part 'stress and disorder management.' Now, a couple 'a years ago that meant lots of men and lots of armor. Well, we've come a ways from there. Some of our people in R & D [Research and Development] tell us that we can go a lot further using and manipulating the psychological environment the subject operates in. That way not as many heads get broken."

Fritz Simmons waited until Mike Nelson finished. He studied his pipe for a moment and said, "Let's see if I've got this. The work isn't radically different from what we agreed to. You still want those ongoing accounts of social happenings and changes in social organization. Now you want names and faces as well. Second, and this is somewhat different from what we'd anticipated, it sounds like we're talking about some kind of psych experiments on selected members of these communities. My intuition tells me these will be on people who've already come to your attention and either might be in prison or have been locked up in the past. What are we talking about here, Mike? Drugs, gasses, chemicals?"

"Fritz," Nelson said expansively, "you haven't changed at all. You had one of the best minds in the OSS (Office of Special Services, the precursor to the CIA), and you were always able to put things together. No, we're not talking drugs and those things. That'll never fly. Our psych boys have told us that if we manipulate things like lights, colors, kinds of uniforms, personal body armor, even body movements—if we're able to get the right combination of these 'symbolic markers'—then so much fear will be induced in our subjects we'll have no trouble handling any disturbance. In a nutshell, Fritz, we want you at Datatronics to do the actual work for us, run the psych experiments with our guys there observing.

"And one other thing, Fritz. We go back a long way. I know you'll do a good job, just the we way want it done. This is just the first of these. You help us out, and who knows what it'll mean in the future, if you know what I mean."

The room was deathly quiet; all eyes were riveted on Fritz Simmons. Fritz turned, looked at Pam and Allen for a moment, and began. "Yes, Mike, we do go back a long way. When was it—in '43?—that we first met in the OSS? Looking around the room, I recognize other faces. We've all, or most of us, been through these things. On behalf of Datatronics, I can say that we'll do the work and you'll be pleased with it. And in my own shop, if people have trouble with it, they can seriously reconsider their continued involvement with the company. I think we all understand each other. When will you be forwarding the work specs?"

During the next few months, Project Anticipate moved quickly. Teams of Datatronics technicians were dispatched to several prisons to perform the "symbolic marker" experiments. Prisoners were not told the real reason for the research and were paid a nominal amount for their cooperation. Similar things happened in the community. People were contacted by their parole and probation officers and "invited" to volunteer for a research study; they, too, were not told the specific nature of the research, but were paid a small amount for their participation.

In addition, Datatronics offered special services to certain groups of welfare recipients: social and economic counseling, special advocates, and other support. The recipients were not told that they were getting help as part of a study to learn whether people could be more tightly bound into the official authority structures by increasing their level of dependence.

Finally, Datatronics established several urban life-style field stations. Black sociologists and anthropologists were hired to staff them. They weren't informed of the reason for the research or who was paying for it. They were directed to maintain detailed records about all aspects of social life in the ghetto area where they worked. These records were then reviewed by the Datatronics staff who supervised the field station personnel.

Meanwhile, Datatronics fed all data to participating agencies. Files were maintained on some of the respondents. Agencies were already making plans to put the findings to use. What at first had seemed to be a scientific data collection effort was rapidly being transformed into a project of control.

QUESTIONS ABOUT "OPERATION ANTICIPATE"

The fictional research project described here may seem implausible. By its very design, the study ensures that the privacy of some citizens will be invaded for the purposes of scientific investigation *and* possible police control. Major portions of the study involve deception and ignore both the letter and the spirit of informed consent. Subjects aren't told the nature and purpose of the behavioral and social experiments, and many of those under observation do not know they are being watched. The study may serve the larger society in ways that some subjects might consider injurious to their interests. Surely, you may be thinking, the U.S. government would not use social and behavioral scientists for "domestic spying" and for improving techniques of police control; and surely respectable social and behavioral scientists would not cooperate with a research effort that was so blatantly committed to such manipulation.

Probably the project would not be approved and funded right now in the form described, but it is not as implausible as it may appear. Many of the elements have been the subject of research projects in the past. In the proper climate, such as in the wake of riots in areas like Watts a generation ago or times of serious fears about the internal security of the nation, such a study is far from unthinkable. Even if exaggerated, the case points to ethical dilemmas that occur regularly in the design and execution of behavioral and social research.

Contract Research

"Research for hire," or contract research, is especially vulnerable to some of these problems. Contract research differs from research funded by grants in two important ways.

First, contract research intends to serve some interest or need defined by the contract agency. Even if the contract is for basic research, the nature and purpose of that research is defined for the scientist. The scientist becomes less independent and more immersed in the purposes of the organization providing funding. This loss of autonomy is even greater if the scientist is a direct employee of an agency. Moreover, since the purpose of much contract research is to meet some immediate need, contract research and the scientists who perform it are often oriented to a service commitment. Many researchers like to feel "useful" in solving social problems. This inclination may further erode independence, since it is usually someone else who defines what problem needs solving. This loss of autonomy is not necessarily bad, but it may lead to the neglect of important basic research that no funding agency sees as important to it. More important, becoming accustomed to marching to somebody else's drumbeat may encourage leaving ethics to others as well.

This is particularly so because of a second characteristic of contract research. Not only is there less autonomy in defining one's research task in contract research. The contract agency is also extensively involved in overseeing the conduct of the research. A proposal for a contract may be much less specific than for a grant because many of the details are worked out as the project progresses. The scientist doing contract research may rely more on the agency to determine the morality as well as the procedures than would be the case in other forms of research. Operation Anticipate is much more feasible as contract research than it would be as a grant proposal.

Ethics, Politics, and Research

Because research costs money and because the largest single source of funding is the United States government, the direction of scientific research will be profoundly influenced by what the government considers important. This political "control" of research could mean that scientific advance is sacrificed for short-term technological gain, but not necessarily. Moreover, someone has to decide that a research area or a specific project is worth supporting. The research community does have a voice in the political process and is well represented in the bureaucracy that is finally responsible for government grants and contracts.

Even beyond the issue of funding, research may have "political" ramifications. A public announcement of some research findings may reduce or intensify prejudices, increase or decrease sympathy for a disadvantaged group, or arouse public sentiment regarding some "social problem." A study of intelligence that reports a genetic superiority or inferiority of a racial or ethnic group may have profound effects on the whole group even though only a small portion were part of the study. These issues have an ethical dimension, but they are more far-reaching and more difficult to contain within the framework of a tidy ethical system than are the individualized relationships of researchers and their research subjects.[3]

---

[3]The author of one of the leading texts in social research methodology draws a definite line between ethics and politics, while acknowledging that they are often intertwined. "Ethics" deals more with the *methods* employed, "politics" with the *content* and *use* to which research is put. He also distinguishes the two by the absence of agreement on "political" issues comparable to the development of ethical norms that may even be expressed in an ethical code. The distinction employs a very narrow use of the word "ethics," implying a codified set of professional standards. See Earl R. Babbie, *The Practice of Social Research*, 2nd ed. (Belmont CA: Wadsworth Publishing, 1979) 71.

We consider this categorization unfortunate because some might infer that

Operation Anticipate involves just such political issues. Should *scientific* studies that have social control as their primary purpose be conducted? We need to ask some specific questions about that shortly, but for the moment let us deal with the issue in a more general way.

The classic case of this in American social/behavioral science was Project Camelot. This major project was funded by the Department of the Army to develop procedures to assess the potential for internal war in foreign nations and to determine what actions might reduce the likelihood of such civil war. When the project was brought to light, considerable controversy erupted about the legitimacy of research that was interpreted by critics as being part of an antirevolutionary, counterinsurgency program of the U.S. Army. The project was cancelled after about six months, largely because of a conflict between the Department of Defense and the Department of State. The social/behavioral science community was significantly divided on the question of Camelot. Many were appalled by what they perceived as the attempt to "co-opt" scientists into a counterinsurgency effort in Chile. Others, taking the opposite view, were critical of the project's termination, claiming that it had offered some hope of saving human lives (including potentially the lives of American soldiers) by preventing war. Some also complained that the new policy, introduced in response to Camelot, requiring State Department approval for all international research, constituted government censorship of academic research.[4]

No doubt, studying the conditions that lead to revolution would be a fascinating *scientific* endeavor, particularly for sociologists who are interested in social change. Considering science as a value-free enter-

---

"politics" is amoral and hence exempt from ethical scrutiny. Though the research professions may not be able to provide guidelines for resolving these issues, we believe that individual researchers should still consider these to be ethical problems—that is, that there is a right and wrong or better and worse position. Because political decisions or public perceptions affect the well-being of individual persons, politics is inherently an ethical issue. Racism, for example, is a moral issue, not just a matter of political power. However, we agree that the issues that Babbie defines as "political" often involve value conflicts that are deeper, more complex, and less susceptible to rational resolution in a particular political climate than some other ethical issues.

[4]The most comprehensive treatment of Project Camelot is Irving Louis Horowitz's *The Rise and Fall of Project Camelot* (Cambridge MA: MIT Press, 1967). See also his earlier article, "The Life and Death of Project Camelot," *Transaction* 3 (November-December 1965): 3-7, 44-47. Another useful source is Gideon Sjoberg, "Project Camelot: Selected Reactions and Personal Reflections," *Ethics, Politics, and Social Research*, ed. Gideon Sjoberg (Cambridge MA: Schenkman, 1967) 141-61.

prise, the subject seems entirely appropriate for research. Similarly, Pam and Allen may have been quite excited about a scientific examination of conditions that lead to social disruption. Seldom do researchers get to examine such a large slice of the life of a community in a single study.

But even if science can be value-neutral, scientists probably cannot. Those who *use* the scientific knowledge are not neutral. What would be the effects of a Project Camelot or an Operation Anticipate? There are several possibilities. First, a study could simply be completed, using enormous energy and resources, be presented as a multivolume report, and be put on a shelf to gather dust. That has been known to happen.

Or the study might demonstrate a connection between certain social conditions (such as social inequalities) and social unrest, violence, and revolution. Governments and other social agencies might be inspired to alter those conditions by some economic redistribution. Whether one would describe these actions as "remedying social injustice" or as "implementing the Robin Hood Principle" (robbing the rich to give to the poor) might depend on whether one was a peasant or welfare recipient whose life was improved or a landowner or stockholder whose property was "expropriated" by nationalization or taxation. Or the study could emphasize that revolution is most likely to occur when there are rising expectations, and governments could increase deprivation to prevent expectations from rising.

A third possibility is that revolutionaries might read the study. One of the troubles (or benefits) with "open" science is that the information can be used by people with radically different values. In this case, revolutionaries might use the concepts and conclusions to promote the revolutionary cause.

Given the nature of funding in the real Project Camelot and the fictional Operation Anticipate, one plausible outcome is the use of the new understanding of social unrest and revolutionary potential to put down insurrection without any effort to improve social conditions.

Given these possible applications, what is the appropriate role for social scientists? To what extent should their ethical/political views influence their decision to undertake a piece of research or to publish the findings? Put another way, how responsible are scientists for the *uses* of their findings?

Grave concern for the uses of science first surfaced in the natural sciences, where the potential for destructiveness is enormous. Americans readily condemn the Nazi scientists who devised efficient means for exterminating Europe's Jews and other "undesirables." The facade of the "neutrality of science" is no defense, we said. But what about the scientific work behind the atomic bomb? Leo Szilard represented one group of nuclear scientists who urged that the atomic bomb developed in the Manhattan Project *not* be used in the war against Japan. Other scientists believe nuclear weapons are morally necessary to maintain peace through a balance of power. Either way, it is hard for the scientist involved to avoid the issue. The same could be said for research that might lead to weapons of biological warfare or chemical warfare. However scientists may resolve their own moral questions, we do not believe they can ignore them.

But what about research that is less "earth-shaking" than nuclear weapons? A study in criminology might find that certain criminals are incorrigible. A report of this finding could, in some political climates, be used to support capital punishment. How should social scientists opposed to capital punishment on moral grounds deal with this? They could *refuse to participate* in a study that they feared might be "misused." That presumes, of course, that they are able to predict both the conclusions of the study (that some criminals are incorrigible) and the uses of the study (in the debate about capital punishment).

A second alternative would be for the researcher to *refuse to publish* the results of the work. Some would argue that research topics can be chosen freely, but that one ought never to suppress the results of research that one undertakes. The duty to publish, they would argue, does not permit discretion in publishing only results that one "likes." On the other hand, declining to publish results that will almost certainly be misused may sometimes seem to be an exercise of professional responsibility.

A third alternative is to complete the work, publish the results, and *then argue publicly* against its use to justify capital punishment. In choosing this alternative, the scientist could identify himself or herself as a scientist opposed to capital punishment. Or the researcher could set aside that role and argue only as a private citizen. Each alternative has strengths and weaknesses. Acknowledging one's social role has the advantage of recognizing that people bear some responsibility for the effects of actions performed within their professional role. But the danger is the "speaking-as-a-scientist" fallacy, the mistaken "generalization of expertise." Being an expert in one area does not make one automatically an expert in other areas. Being a good scientist does not make one a "moral" expert. Social policy needs to be determined on the basis of value (moral) considerations using the best available factual (scientific) information. Scientists *as* scientists can provide the latter; they may not necessarily be helpful with the former.

But if researchers divorce their professional role from their civic role, as the Weberian ethic of value-free science would insist, it is easy for the scientist to deny any responsibility for the uses of research. The scientist may say, "I am in the business of being a scientist. I pose hypotheses, collect and analyze data, and develop social theories. People can use this in any way they choose. If it is misused, I'm not responsible." Comedian Tom Lehrer illustrates the logical extreme of this view in his musical satire on American space program hero Wernher von Braun. Referring to von Braun's earlier work in developing the V-2 rockets used against England by Germany late in World War II, Lehrer caricatures von Braun as "apolitical," having him say, "Once the rockets are up, who cares where they come down—that's not my department."[5]

Probably most scientists today accept a degree of responsibility for the use of their work. Their ethical and political views will almost certainly influence their assessment of more controversial research, like Camelot or Operation Anticipate. Many social and behavioral scientists would probably be inclined to favor direct measures to promote the well-being of the lower classes and the economically and socially disenfranchised. They would be distressed to see their work result in stricter control over a minority population rather than an improvement of economic and social conditions. Operation Anticipate would make many researchers uneasy because of its possible adverse effects on the subject population. Even with goals stated euphemistically as "promoting social order," "reducing domestic violence," and "minimizing the need for police *force*," many would suspect that the measures would seem less benign to the group affected.

But as loyal citizens many American social and behavioral scientists readily cooperated in efforts to improve the morale of our armed forces during World War II, and work with the military to improve defense capabilities has continued. When "national security" is believed threatened from without or within, ethical limits on research may seem much less important.

We would expect a public outcry if Operation Anticipate were to be implemented now. But the reaction may be more a function of perceptions about "security" than any principled critique. The blatant use of social and behavioral scientists as domestic spies under the guise of doing research is unlikely, here and now. Some professional associations have

---

[5]Tom Lehrer, "Wernher von Braun," *That Was the Year That Was,* Reprise Records, 1965.

clearly declared it unethical.[6] Employing scientists for political control was much more prevalent during Hitler's Third Reich and is perhaps not unknown in some Communist countries today. However, if people perceived a serious threat to national security or the social order, something like Operation Anticipate is not inconceivable.

We are concerned that researchers maintain a degree of independence; failure to do so may ultimately be destructive even to the task of science itself. A danger of the links forged in contract and grant research is that scientists might become so tied to the organization's administrative control that they become subservient to government control. Scientists should not surrender their consciences to any funding agency. On the other hand, they should also recognize that they do not have a corner on moral wisdom and that moral discourse is an ongoing community endeavor.

Much of this chapter has been concerned with general political issues involving research. The next chapter will examine some more specific ethical issues in Operation Anticipate.

---

[6]The Principles of Professional Responsibility of the American Anthropological Association states, "Anthropologists should avoid even the appearance of engaging in clandestine research by fully and freely disclosing the aims and sponsorship of all research." The earlier Statement on Problems of Anthropological Research and Ethics, which is still in force, says, "Except in the event of a declaration of war by the Congress, academic institutions should not undertake activities or accept contracts in anthropology that are not related to their normal functions of teaching, research, and public service. They should not lend themselves to clandestine activities."

The Code of Ethics of the American Sociological Association states, "Sociologists must not knowingly use their research roles as covers to obtain information for other than sociological research purposes."

11

Being Fair Is Complicated

Experimental research may raise many of the same issues that we encountered in other types of research. One significant difference for a contrived experiment like Operation Anticipate is that the conditions that give rise to the ethical issues are the creations of the experimenters. Let's look at some of those issues in Operation Anticipate, with a special focus on the question of justice.

ETHICS AND EXPERIMENTATION

The Social Service Experiment

Part of Datatronics's study consists of providing special services to certain individuals to see how they respond to those services. We need to distinguish scientific experimentation from the "social experiments" that go on all the time as taxes are decreased to encourage consumer spending, farm subsidies are restructured, and school-lunch, student-loan, and welfare programs altered. This tinkering with the economy and social institutions is not experimentation in the scientific sense.

The recipients of special services in Operation Anticipate are part of a carefully controlled experiment. Although they do not realize it, the only reason they are receiving these services is to see if this will bind them so closely to an authority structure that they will not precipitate or participate in social disruption in volatile times. The effects of these changes are being carefully monitored and evaluated. Presumably the study will assess what "incentives" will *best* accomplish the goal.

It would seem that the experiment is designed to learn how to make people less autonomous and make them *enjoy* being less autonomous.[1] Is that unethical? How important is autonomy? Clearly it has been an important part of the American tradition, but the value is culturally con-

---

[1] The concept of autonomy is a difficult one. For one useful discussion, see Gerald Dworkin, "Autonomy and Behavior Control," *Hasting Center Report* 6 (February 1976): 23-28.

ditioned. People who are starving may well be prepared to trade autonomy for food. Some level of confidence in survival seems a precondition for genuine autonomy.

Operation Anticipate may show that it is possible to "sedate" people, and the project may improve the techniques for doing so. Unlike much research, this project has the potential for changing people, perhaps permanently. What if it kills initiative and makes people content to live on the dole? Is that wrong if it achieves a greater good by preventing a domestic uprising? Would the reverse be acceptable, that is, would it right to try to foster initiative and autonomy in people who prefer to be passive and dependent? Would that be a kind of "cultural imperialism"?

The most serious ethical problem for these participants may be that the study is of limited duration. The special services they receive are not permanent. When the study ends, they will be back where they started, except they may have lost some of their independence, some of their self-esteem (when they realize that they sold out), and some of their social position (because their community may now define them as defectors). They may suffer some disillusionment with "the system" when they realize that they have been used and tossed aside. If they have come to enjoy a better life during the experiment, they may find their old life much more "painful" when they return. The effects of discontinuance need to be considered any time a social experiment provides benefits that are destined to be terminated.

The Psychological "Symbolic Marker" Experiments

The other group of experiments in Operation Anticipate is a set of laboratory experiments designed to examine psychological mechanisms that influence acquiescence to authority. The subjects know they are part of an experiment and are being paid to participate. They are not told either before or after exactly *what* the researchers are looking for, let alone *why*. They might be less willing to participate if they knew the reason for the experiments.

Many laboratory and other psychological experiments are entirely innocuous. Some, however, involve potential unpleasantness. Painful stimuli, especially electrical shock, are not uncommon; drugs are sometimes used to test psychological responses to certain physiological conditions. In addition, psychological stress or distress is frequently part of the laboratory experiment. An experiment may be contrived to make subjects believe that they are about to die, or are responsible for some serious injury to another, or are the only ones who can save another individual from serious harm. The emotional stress of such situations can

be quite intense. Since the "psych" experiments in Operation Anticipate are designed to identify factors that will create sufficient fear to
thwart social disruption, they will likely stimulate such fear in the research participants. The experiment likely must include an element of
"pain."

Conceivably some pain, especially psychological pain, may be more
lasting, continuing after the termination of the experiments. Nightmares
or spontaneous moments of terror induced by memories of the experiments might plague participants long after their conclusion, though
careful debriefing often reduces the aftereffects of many psychological
experiments. Though perhaps remote, the risk of more serious, permanent physical harm—say from equipment malfunction—is not impossible. Physical injury resulting from emotional distress is not
unthinkable; a susceptible patient might have a heart attack or a seizure
as a result of a stressful experiment. Speculating about potential harm is
easy. However, there is little documented evidence of physical or psychological harm from social and behavioral experiments. Rather than
merely speculating about the potential for harm, it seems important to
know whether people really experience pain in experiments and whether
injury really does occur. Researchers need to be extremely careful not to
cause real harm, but they should not be burdened with protecting against
imaginary ones.

If an experiment involves physical pain or emotional distress or risk
of permanent injury, many potential subjects may not wish to participate. Subjects in Operation Anticipate's psychological experiments
might also be unwilling to participate if the knowledge gained can potentially be used against them. Would it be fair not to warn them of the
intended use?

JUSTICE AND RESEARCH

To talk about fairness is to raise the question of justice. Justice is like
motherhood. Who can object to justice? But defining justice is no easy
matter. It means giving people their due, but people have radically different ideas about what is due to different individuals and groups. Justice often involves a balancing of competing claims. As distributive
justice, which is concerned with the distribution of a society's "goods,"
it means balancing what is "due" to one person with what is "due" to
another. Generosity to one person can be an injustice to another who has
a claim on what is given. Moreover, the claims of justice cannot simply
be dismissed by pointing to other good consequences of an act.

Difficult as justice is to achieve, it is a minimal standard of morality,
not the ideal. It asks no more of us than that we give others what they

deserve. Many ethical theories appeal to us to do more than justice, to act with compassion, benevolence, and love, doing for people things that they could not claim as their due. Our emphasis on gratitude as a basic moral category points beyond justice, since most of us have received far more than we could claim that we deserve.

The question of justice can be approached at several levels. We will begin by looking at the research subjects in Operation Anticipate who may be treated unjustly.

Research and Special Populations

Some groups are especially vulnerable. For example, was it fair to use prisoners and parolees in Operation Anticipate? Clearly prisoners have lost *some* rights, especially the right of free movement, because of their crimes. Have they also lost the right to refuse to participate in research? Although some people might argue that participation in research is one way criminals can pay their debt to society, there is strong sentiment that prisoners should not be conscripted for research studies. It is probably even more important to secure their consent than that of subjects "on the outside." But how can we be sure the consent is genuine? Most adult prisoners are *competent* to make decisions and can be given enough information to make an *informed* choice. But can they make a *voluntary* decision to participate? Suppose you were in prison or had recently been released on parole. How comfortable would you feel in declining to participate in Datatronics's study, especially when "asked" to do so by your prison warden or parole officer? Would you feel free to refuse, even if you were told you could? Many people have argued that the criminal justice system by nature is too coercive, that giving genuine consent is impossible, and prisoners should not even be asked to participate in any research.

But is prison research coercive? Some people, including some very vocal prisoners, have argued that *denying* prisoners the opportunity to participate in research is unfair; it deprives them of one of the few free choices they can make. Deciding what is just can often be very difficult indeed!

Prisoners are not the only populations that can feel undue pressure to cooperate. A whole ghetto community may feel coerced to cooperate with the white authority structure that is sending its representatives into the community. Likewise, students in the "human subjects pools" created by psychology departments might feel coerced into participating.[2] Members of the armed forces may not feel that they have any choice but to *volunteer* for research when it is suggested to them. Social and behavioral scientists need to be careful in ensuring that their subjects are not unduly pressured, especially when conditions make coercion easy. They also need to be aware that "undue" persuasion may vary from person to person. An amount of money insignificant for the average middle-class citizen may be a very powerful inducement to an impoverished person, and a benefit that most people take for granted could be almost irresistible to someone who did not already enjoy it.

The specific procedures of Operation Anticipate seem to run roughshod over the normal constraints of autonomy, privacy, and informed consent. In the interest of "insuring domestic tranquility," some individuals or groups appear to have been defined as "the enemy" who do not deserve the usual ethical "niceties." The "enemy" model does not fit our standard approach to research. If it is morally acceptable within the framework of scientific research, then we will need to develop a special ethic for antagonistic research, as there is special courtroom recognition of the "hostile witness." We are not prepared to accept an "antagonist" model, but those who would accept it should develop clear guidelines that would delineate restraints like those that set limits in the conduct of war and law enforcement.

Research and the Community

Next is the question of justice at the community level. Is it fair for the agents of the majority to subject a minority community to intense scrutiny such as Project Anticipate entails? Even without the issue of social control, we might rightly ask whether it is fair for a group with power to impose themselves on a powerless group to satisfy their own curiosity? Do communities have an integrity that ought to be respected, like the limits of privacy for individuals? The question might apply equally to anthropological studies in primitive cultures and to studies of subcultures within Western society. Is it fair to use the Western scientific ethic

---

[2]The few studies to date about these subjects' perceptions may allay some of the anxiety on this matter. Even though a large number of students—as many as half—consider the offer of extra credit points for participation in a subject pool to be coercive, almost all the students find the experience worthwhile and do not object to being offered extra credit, even though they do consider it coercive. See G. K. Leak, "Student Perception of Coercion and Value from Participation in Psychological Research," *Teaching of Psychology* 8 (1981): 147-49. See also B. K. Britton, "Aspects of Participation as a Subject in Psychology Experiments," *Teaching of Psychology* 6 (1979): 195-98.

(including its commitment to the value of scientific knowledge) to justify imposing on people who do not share that ethic? Is that cultural imperialism?

One test of our sense of fairness is to put ourselves in the other person's shoes. Would we feel that we were being treated unfairly if Operation Anticipate were operating in our neighborhoods? Better yet, try to imagine that you were a member of a minority group already feeling the brunt of discrimination. Would you feel that this special surveillance was doubly unfair, adding insult to injury?

We do not mean to imply that research subjects are completely powerless to resist the efforts of researchers. They often have far more control than discussions of research ethics imply. Their ability to divert or sabotage a research project should not be underestimated. However, the fact remains that researchers frequently do exercise considerable authority, especially as in Operation Anticipate when the subjects are unaware of the nature of the researchers' presence in their community.

Operation Anticipate, which seems to subject a whole community to the scrutiny of researchers, may seem unfair because it seems founded on the assumption that the entire ghetto community is "the enemy." The specter of black/white conflicts and race riots has been an undertone of the preceding discussion. This image itself may be racist because the ghetto community has its own set of internal conflicts, just as the rest of society has. The "troublemakers" may cause as much trouble for their own community as they do for the rest of society.

Thus, to ask about the obligation of the researcher to the community he or she is studying is to ask about the welfare of that *whole* community. This raises two important questions, which, we hasten to add, we cannot even pretend to be able to answer.

First, to be responsible to the community, should Datatronics report observations about social conditions and recommendations for rectifying social injustices which they may unearth in their research, even if they are not asked to do so? Can they, in other words, simply do what they were "hired" to do and be done with it, or do they have some obligation to become, if not an advocate for the community they study, at least a medium through which its concerns and needs are communicated?

Second, should individual researchers take any direct initiative in improving the life of the community? For example, what if the sociologists operating the field stations are horrified by the life of the inner city— the threat of violence, the prevalence of drugs, the corruption of the cops on the beat, the drain on the already limited resources of the poor by illegal gambling, con games, and protection rackets? Further, what if these sociologists can identify underworld figures (and the police officers whom they bribe) who are committing crimes against ghetto residents? Can these researchers on their own initiative take this information to appropriate authorities for action? Doing so might lead to arrests and convictions, get some pushers off the street, make old ladies safer at night, mothers less worried about the welfare of their children, families less subject to a drain on meager funds, and everyone less likely to be the victim of a violent crime, at least temporarily. This would be an interesting inversion of Operation Anticipate. The project as planned may violate the principle of confidentiality primarily for the benefit of the "majority" community of upper and middle-class society. The new question is whether researchers can ignore usual procedures in order to protect and serve the law-abiding "minority" citizens.

Reporting this information to authorities would violate carefully developed standards for research, might undermine the research project itself, and might be detrimental for future research efforts. Perhaps it would be only a short-lived benefit, lasting only until a new "criminal element" replaced the old. But can it be justified? Is it even ethically required?

Employer-Employee Relations

The question of justice in research relationships goes beyond the treatment of research subjects. It may apply to the relationships of researchers themselves. As an example, let's ask about the responsibilities of the research firm and its employees.

Fritz Simmons is a high-ranking executive officer at Datatronics. His obligations to the firm and its stockholders include doing good work, promoting the organization, and making money. Operation Anticipate offers him a chance to accomplish these goals. He's probably also a loyal citizen, having served in the Office of Special Services during World War II. He may well feel that Operation Anticipate can be a great service to American society. There's no evidence that he thinks he is doing anything unethical or asking anyone else to do anything wrong. Covert operations are nothing new to an old OSS officer. If his former associates, now leaders in the federal bureaucracy, have approved the project, why should he question it?

But is this fair to his employees? He has committed the firm to the project without consulting his staff, and they can do the work or leave the firm. In a way, that makes sense. Companies can't hold a referendum every time they develop a new product or accept a new contract. Still, their employees didn't join Datatronics to do questionable research, and this project does raise questions. Project Camelot created a lot of controversy, and that was to be done on somebody else's turf. With Operation

Anticipate, we are looking at our own citizens, and it even combines research with police work. Fritz should anticipate that some of his employees will have trouble with this. Sacking hardworking staff because they have ethical scruples about this project hardly seems right. It seems to ignore the mutual commitments and manifest ingratitude for the employees' dedication to the firm in the past. Doesn't Fritz owe his employees more consideration, especially if times are hard and other jobs scarce?

Pam and Allen may have their own set of problems. They may not have any qualms about the revised project. They may be worldly-wise and a bit cynical and simply accept that this is the way things are. Or their exuberance over landing this big project and the excitement about doing a major and potentially useful study may have overwhelmed them so that they didn't even think about ethical issues. But it's also possible that they felt less comfortable after the "D'Anglis meeting." What if they don't approve of the new direction? What if they become concerned about ethics as the project progresses? They have responsibilities to the firm, but they have other commitments as well—to their families, to the community of social/behavioral scientists and their immediate colleagues, and to society. If they object, should they quietly resign from the firm? Perhaps Pam couldn't afford to leave the area to look for another job because of an invalid mother who is dependent on her; perhaps her husband would find it difficult to get a decent job somewhere else right now. Allen might be hard pressed to find a comparable job. Keeping his job could be very important if a new member of his family were on the way. Resigning would be a big sacrifice for ethics, but there are times when that is the responsible choice.

Or should Pam and Allen "blow the whistle" if they think something is basically wrong with Operation Anticipate? They might see the project as a dangerous step toward a police state and feel that it is their civic duty to protest publicly. But the people most likely to be hurt by that are Pam and Allen. The history of whistle-blowing is not all that favorable.[3]

They could go along with the project but try to sabotage it. That possibility has its own ethical perils. Could betraying the trust relationship with the firm to prevent an unethical research project from accomplish-

---

[3]Many of the reports on whistleblowing emphasize the costs that conscientious whistleblowers must pay, such as a dead end in their careers. Without minimizing the costs, one writer provides a more hopeful note. A study of ten such individuals found that almost all had rebuilt their careers and had found a meaningful future. See Myron Glazer, "Ten Whistleblowers and How They Fared," *Hastings Center Report* 13:6 (December 1983): 33-41.

ing its goals be justified? Is there any reasonable hope of success? Is likelihood of success a relevant factor in the moral valuation?

Finally, Pam and Allen could conclude that they are only doing a job; somebody else can decide whether the project is morally acceptable. "Following orders" does not relieve us of all moral responsibility, but usually we can and do carry out "orders" without asking questions. Social institutions couldn't work unless people felt justified in obeying orders most of the time.

Even if Pam and Allen have no ethical reservations, how about others working on the project? What about the sociologists and anthropologists who staff the field stations? Is Datatronics being unfair to them by deceiving them about the use to which their work will be put? Maybe Datatronics didn't lie, but certain employees have been kept in the dark about the project's purpose. Surely some of them would be distressed to know that they are unwittingly contributing to police files. Is there a violation of professional ethics in keeping the nature of the project from these colleagues? What about confidentiality? Did Datatronics make a "lying" promise that records will be handled confidentially? Or did the firm merely permit the field workers to *assume* that the usual standards of confidentiality applied? In any case, it seems probable that both the frontline researchers in the field and their subjects assume a confidential relationship that does not in fact exist.

Looking from the other side, do the field-station operators have any obligation to inquire about the use of their data, or can they be content merely to do the job they were hired to do, no questions asked? What is their obligation if they discover its real purpose midway through the project and they object?

Researchers at the Public Trough

Finally, let's ask about the relationship of scientists to the larger society that funds research. A host of issues can be raised; we can mention only a few. First, is there a right to do research?

We would argue that the freedom and autonomy that we value and that is so basic to our political system implies a right to engage in scientific research *without interference.* This right, like all other rights, has its limits. Is it just for society, through the state or through the pressure of public opinion, to prohibit researchers from undertaking Project Camelot or Operation Anticipate? Is "censorship" of these projects indefensible on the grounds of "academic freedom"? Because it may affect some people adversely, do the rights of those subjects override the rights of researchers in this case?

The "right to do research" could mean more than freedom from interference. It might be a claim to community resources to support research. Is such a claim valid? Again we have more questions than answers. Society does not simply permit people to seek a career in the sciences. We devote a great many resources to enabling individuals to prepare for that work. An appropriate response for the scientist is to use that training for the benefit of the community. But the giving is not one-sided. Researchers have devoted a great deal of personal energy and time to prepare themselves for that role. Has society made a kind of promise to them in providing the educational benefits, a promise that they will be able to exercise their skills? Encouraging people to pursue careers where they can't find a job seems unfair, especially if extensive and rigorous training is involved. From this perspective, it may seem that society has struck a kind of bargain that requires the funding of research.

But it is also clear that societal needs and the perception of needs change. Society and the economy move in fits and starts. Even in an economic system where freedom is compromised for the sake of centralized planning, the planning will never be exact. In our society, there may be more rough spots, but there is also a lot more freedom of career choice and location. The obligation of society to use the scientist's skills is certainly modified by the nature of this social/economic system.

Society funds research by supporting universities, by government grants and contracts, by the work of private foundations, and by research in industry. These social institutions will influence what research is done. Both the public and the scientific community have some role in setting funding priorities, and there is still latitude in many research grants for individual researchers to follow their own interests. The system is far from perfect, and perhaps some competent researchers are not utilized effectively. And, yes, some projects that are funded turn out to be suitable nominees for a Golden Fleece Award.[4]

This latter prospect raises yet another question. Do individual researchers have the responsibility to make judgments about the relative worth of particular projects? If Allen or Pam believed that Project Anticipate was an absolute waste of time, destined to expend an enormous amount of money and time without any meaningful result, do they have any responsibility to say so? There is the question of their own participation. Should they and their firm decline to participate in a worthless project? Do they have an obligation to share their assessment with the federal funding agencies? Or can they simply stand at the public trough and partake of whatever is poured?

---

[4]For many years Senator William Proxmire announced "Golden Fleece Awards" to call attention to projects that had "wasted" government funds in "frivolous" research.

Because resources are limited and money spent in one area may mean deprivation in another, wasting public funds can be an ethical issue. But whose job is it to identify and prevent waste? It may be unrealistic, unworkable, or inappropriate for researchers to make judgments that have been legally delegated to specific public officials. But such acquiescence perpetuates the inefficiency and waste for which the federal bureaucracy is so often criticized. How can this be resolved? No one, unfortunately, seems to have a good answer.

This issue and others that we have addressed in this chapter may apply to various types of research, not just experimental research. We have noted the responsibilties to different social groups and to society as a whole. We have noted how conflicts of values and responsibilties can confound an ethically serious researcher. These problems may be intensified in a multifaceted study like Operation Anticipate—an example of a large-scale contract—because so many people are involved. Do researchers face the same ethical quandaries in more narrowly focused social experiments? Let's look at another case in the next chapter.

12

Balancing the Equation:
Who Benefits
and Who Decides?

The preceding case raised ethical issues with broad political and social ramifications. In this chapter we will consider a much more limited study with implications primarily for the subjects themselves.

"IT SHOULD WORK"

"Let me sum up by saying the program is really simple. Because of our tests we'll know which students are most at risk for alcoholism and we'll be able to do something about it, before they wind up dead on the road or in the schoolyard like the tragedy last month. Ladies and gentlemen, the choice is yours."

Sue Rohrer knew she had this one in the bag. She had been waiting for an opportunity like this since she began as school psychologist in the Brookside School District more than a year ago. With more than a little satisfaction, she watched how members of the school board responded to her reference to the death of Jerry Emmons. Some squirmed uncomfortably. The junior high school principal blanched at the mention of the ninth grader's death from alcohol poisoning during a lunchtime drinking bout at his school. Referring to the Emmons incident might not have been fair, Sue thought, but it had worked.

Right then, Dr. Bowers, the president of the school board, rose. The room quieted, and she cleared her throat. "That was quite a presentation, Sue. I think we all agree that teenage drinking is a serious problem today and anything we can do about it is worth our consideration. Naturally, we'll have to study your proposal further. But speaking for myself and a few other board members here tonight, I think you should be making plans so you can get underway as soon as we take final action."

She looked up and down the table and saw the nodding heads and knew that her program of testing, treatment, and follow-up was going to be endorsed by the board. She knew this was her big chance. The social experiment would be important. Sue was convinced that it would work. If the students who demonstrated a proclivity for alcohol and drug abuse could be identified early enough, they could be carefully watched. Then, if needed, they would be brought in for intervention and treatment.

For Sue, this represented the goal of several years' thinking. She had gotten the idea from her thesis work in graduate school. She had assessed the psychological tests used to predict adolescent alcoholism and drug abuse. The idea of using the school system as a natural laboratory to test her plan of predictive intervention came right after she landed the job as school psychologist at Brookside.

Brookside was an ideal site for the study. It was a typical "bedroom community" for a moderately-sized midwestern city. As such, its population was fairly homogeneous. Like most such communities, Brookside had just sprung up, with many housing plots appearing almost overnight. Sue could easily divide Brookside geographically into control and experimental groups.

As school psychologist, Sue was frequently called in to "pick up the pieces." She was convinced that alcohol and drug abuse was the number one problem facing youngsters in Brookside. Everyone remembered the tragic automobile accident only two or three years ago: two members of the varsity soccer team died because during the ride home after a victory party, the driver was drunk. During a casual walk around the school yard, Sue soon learned, you could see many "dead soldiers" or empty wine bottles hastily discarded in the bushes. A week rarely went by that Sue wasn't called on for a substance abuse consultation. Usually a Brookside teacher was at wits' end over the misbehavior of a student. One interview with Sue would reveal that the student had a drug or alcohol problem. Sue remembered the hours spent in conference with Larry Byers, the Brookside police chief, who was besieged by complaints from the area residents about students who sat on their lawns smoking pot.

"No question about it," thought Sue, "the school and community want something done. And if I don't do it, the lunatic fringe might start pushing Chief Byers into making a big bust and that wouldn't do anyone any good. If we can head off trouble before it starts by identifying and treating youngsters with problems, we will be doing them and everyone else a favor."

As she predicted, the school board approved Sue's proposal at its next meeting and authorized the superintendent to proceed with the comprehensive drug and alcohol abuse program. Sue's subsequent meeting with the superintendent was straightforward. She was told to get a program underway in a hurry. Moreover, the project was hers; she was to report directly to the superintendent, who promised financial as well as administrative support. Sue told Dr. McMillan, the superintendent, that it would take about ten days to put the final touches on her plans. She already had the tests and the questionnaires written, and her job now was to complete plans for training the schools' staff.

The project was ambitious. It would involve testing more than two thousand students and following a large number over a five-year period. She would be working with staff from all the district's secondary schools. There was much the project could accomplish.

The project involved five stages: (1) universal testing; (2) staff training; (3) ongoing observation and documentation; (4) intervention and treatment as needed; and (5) follow-up. Each stage required Sue's careful supervision to ensure that the data collected were specific enough to meet the requirements of the experiment. Sue would have to solve some big logistical problems. If it could keep kids from getting into trouble with drugs or alcohol, Sue thought, it would be worth it.

The project entailed dividing the school district into halves. Since there were two junior high schools in the district, one would become the "experimental" group; the other would be the "control." All seventh graders would take a battery of tests. Children most likely to develop a problem with alcohol would be identified. In the "experimental" school, these students would take courses and attend treatment seminars. They would meet together weekly in small groups for intensive discussions. Students identified as "at risk" in the "control" school would *not* participate in these special programs. Sue's hypothesis was simple: the number of "at risk" students would be the same in the two schools at the beginning of the experiment, but by the experiment's end (graduation), *more* students from the control group would have developed alcohol and/ or drug problems.

Sue's head spun as she thought about the project. There was so much to be done! The testing was easy. When she thought things through, she realized the teaching wouldn't require too much effort either. The real problem was the observations. For the experiment to work, the staff would have to be trained to observe the "at risk" youngsters throughout their junior and senior high-school years. They would have to document evidence of a developing problem. A log would be maintained on each student involved in the experiment. Staff would be expected to make entries of their observations and impressions. Sue knew the school staff was behind her in the project, but unless they kept the logs, the experiment wouldn't work. Record keeping would become a problem after the initial enthusiasm for the project waned. Teachers and staff were already overworked; keeping records and attending staff meetings would be a burden for them. She would need to find some way to reward their efforts.

Other parts of the project fell quickly into place. Sue arranged for interview rooms with hidden videotape cameras and microphones where she could record parent-teacher conferences about "at risk" students. Moreover, Sue devised an interview schedule for these families in which she would seek information about behavior patterns. She hoped these interviews would provide more information about the dynamics of the family because this would help in intervention and treatment.

The family dynamics were especially interesting to Sue. She knew that much current work on alcoholism involved its "genetic" component. Here was a chance to do something that had not yet been done: observe the dynamics of families before a "public" identification of a substance abuse problem had been made. Thinking of the family aspect of her study made Sue recall recent research by a Dr. Jevitt in California. Jevitt's work had suggested that children of alcoholic parents produce different liver enzymes, a fact deemed exciting by the scientific community. Sue wondered if she could do blood tests on elementary-age children, identifying those with the unusual enzymes and tracking them for Dr. Jevitt. She could correlate these findings with the psychological tests she planned to give seventh graders. There wouldn't be much risk, since drawing a few cc's of blood wouldn't harm a child. "Well, let me get this thing started before I begin to solve the genetics problem," Sue chuckled to herself. She thought about how well things had been going and realized that she would have to slow down just a bit.

Sue reviewed her agenda once more before her first big staff meeting. The research instruments and design were ready to roll. Consent forms were ready, and the outlines for the training sessions were complete. She looked with pride at her letter from a data processing company; some of its staff were going to donate their services to the project. The training modules had been completed, and the log sheets were being printed. "Away we go, let's hope it all works."

IT MAY WORK, BUT IS IT ETHICAL?

Sue Rohrer is clearly excited about her project: It allows her to combine two things that she enjoys: being a researcher at the same time that she is a practicing school psychologist. Either task can be a full-time job, and probably most psychologists tend to go one way or the other. We can only hope that Sue hasn't let her energy and enthusiasm get out of hand and that she can maintain balance, doing both jobs well.

Both the idea and the design of this experiment have come from the researcher. Sue is going to effect a change in the lives of some students who are deemed at risk for a substance abuse problem, and she is going to measure carefully whether those changes make any significant difference in their lives compared to the control group.

Sue's dual role as researcher/school psychologist may make her even less likely to compromise the well-being of her subjects in the interest of scientific advance than if she were only engaged in research. Still, she needs to examine some ethical issues before she decides that her plan is ethically sound. Let's begin by looking at the positive side of the ledger.

The Benefits of Research

Up to this point we have referred to the benefits of scientific research almost in passing. Without some potential benefit, we would have no justification for doing any study that might have risks; we wouldn't even have any reason to spend time and money on such research. Of all the cases we have presented, this one probably has the greatest potential immediate benefit, so let's look at the issue now in more detail.

The ethical principle of *beneficence* goes beyond merely avoiding harm to others. It means promoting other people's well-being by positive action. If one has faith, whether theological or humanistic, in the ultimate goodness of life and corresponding gratitude for the benefits received, a willingness to serve others through positive actions seems an appropriate moral response. The responsibility to do positive good may be less stringent than the obligation to avoid harm, since it is unreasonable to think people ought to help others all the time. But the morally good life includes doing such good some of the time for some people. Deciding whom to help involves some discretion and judgment: judgments about whom we *can* help, given our place in life, our roles, our skills and knowledge, our resources; judgments about who most *needs* our help; and judgments about *risk* and *cost* to ourselves and to others for whom we have responsibility.

The decision about whom to help and how is not entirely open-ended. Positive duties might arise out of *specific situations.* We might feel that persons trained in CPR should use that skill when they come upon someone experiencing respiratory or cardiac arrest. We may be incensed that people can callously stand by and watch a crisis without offering any help. We were appalled by the story a number of years ago of Kitty Genovese, who was stabbed repeatedly over a period of an hour or more while dozens of people watched and did nothing to help, not even calling the police.

Most positive responsibilities are connected with specific *social roles.* The range of discretion is significantly reduced when the people who need our help are related to us in a special way. As school psychologist,

Sue Rohrer has the responsibility to help the students of the Brookside community. Would her role as researcher/scientist *alone* carry any positive responsibility? We have already expressed our judgment that scientists have a responsibility to *society at large* to exercise the skills they have acquired. Sue is accorded opportunities, resources, and status in her role as scientist; reciprocal service to society seems fitting. But her responsibility to help an *identifiable individual* is a function of the particular study and the relationships that become part of that study. A study of public records does not involve individual responsibility. A study like Sue's creates relationships that entail *some* responsibility to the research subjects, even if no prior relationship existed.

As we examine the potential benefits of social and behavioral researchers, we need to ask several questions. *What* benefits may result from research? *Who* is likely to benefit? *How likely* is it that a research project will be beneficial? *How important* are the potential benefits?

What are the potential benefits? Our earlier discussion dealt with the value of science. We count the increase in real knowledge as one "benefit" of research, even if the knowledge has no foreseeable practical application. This is often the only tangible benefit to which a researcher can point. The reasonably affluent, educated classes would probably be more inclined to consider the advancement of human knowledge a "benefit" than would the less affluent or less educated. Minorities who have been studied repeatedly with little or no improvement in their situation may not be very interested in contributing to science; they may want results that they can see and enjoy.

Sometimes social research can make life better—more pleasant, more fulfilling, more rewarding—immediately or in the foreseeable future. Sue's effort is noteworthy because it offers potential immediate and far-reaching benefits. First, the *programmatic* component of Sue's work may offer concrete benefits by reducing Brookside's alcohol-related problems by a "preventive medicine" approach. Moreover, a successful program could be exported to other communities.

The *scientific* portion of the study may also prove beneficial. Sue may help establish the reliability of those tests that predict a propensity for alcohol problems. If she is right that alcohol-related problems can be averted by intervention even *before* the drinking behavior begins, Sue may increase the understanding of the condition itself. Understanding alcoholism has great practical importance in designing new approaches to therapeutic programming. Sue's work could help ameliorate a staggering social problem created by the misuse of alcohol.

The potential practical benefits of Sue's work are part of the study design itself. Often a study's benefits depend entirely on other people's using the findings; and it is sometimes a matter of opinion as to whether the resulting actions are beneficial or harmful. Recall Sherry's study at Darkwoods Manor. Suppose her study included a careful examination of the medical treatment provided to the terminally ill at Darkwoods. She might discover that the "standard practice" included the omission of antibiotics to fight infection, the maintenance of comfort with high levels of painkilling medication even to the point of compromising breathing, and a policy of not sending dying patients to the hospital in the event of congestive heart-failure or other emergencies. Suppose an ambitious young journalist used this information to launch an attack on nursing homes, causing them to begin treating all patients aggressively for fear of bad publicity or even legal repercussions. Would this result be a benefit or a harm? Some people would consider this reversal of policy "good," marking an increased respect for the sanctity of life in the elderly. Others would judge the change a "harm" because it would deny patients "death with dignity."

Value judgments are always involved in determining that something is "beneficial." The administration and staff with whom Sue works would all agree that the prevention or interruption of alcohol or drug abuse is a benefit, both to the students and the school. The students who are involved, however, may not see it that way. At the time, at least, they may see it as a deprivation, an interference with their privacy, and an imposition of someone else's values on their personal lives, though someday in retrospect they may be grateful.

Identifying the benefits obviously entails identifying *who* the beneficiaries are. In Sue's case, the people who are likely to benefit most are the research subjects themselves—those students of Brookside who may avoid significant alcohol problems because of her program. Even those for whom prevention fails may still benefit, since their alcohol problem should be recognized and treated early. It is not always the subjects who gain the benefit of research, but it is easier to justify some risk to subjects if they have some possibility of direct benefit. Sue is dedicated to helping those students who are vulnerable; she understands her role as school psychologist to include dealing with the "number one" problem facing Brookside's youth.

But Sue faces a new ethical question if the special seminars work. Suppose Sue's hypothesis appears borne out: midway through the study, the program seems to be preventing alcohol problems in the experimental group. Will it then become *unethical* to *withhold* this "preventive treatment" from the control group so that the five-year study can be completed? Doing so may result in avoidable problems for some students in the control group. Can she deny students such a benefit? Or can she argue that she doesn't "owe" anybody these benefits, so it cannot be wrong to withhold it from someone. Before Sue came to Brookside, no one got this special attention. However, after deciding to offer this special program, is it fair, is it just, to provide it for some but not for all, if it appears to be working?

On the other hand, eliminating the control and providing the special services for all may reduce the value of the study; erroneous conclusions may result. Perhaps, for example, the special seminars are merely delaying rather than preventing the onset of alcohol problems. Without the control group, Sue will have no standard against which to measure the significance of a later manifestation of alcohol problems.

Thus far we've discussed potential benefits for Brookside *students,* but others may also benefit. *Parents* may be spared the agony and expense of seeing their children through an alcohol or drug abuse problem. The *school staff* may not have to undergo another Emmons tragedy and may find their jobs more satisfying if alcohol and drugs cause fewer discipline problems. *Classmates* may be spared some of the interruptions and distractions common in a school with drug and alcohol abuse problems. *Other students* in schools far from Brookside might benefit if Sue's program becomes a prototype for programs elsewhere.

Brookside itself may become a better community, less troubled by the social problems that accompany alcohol and drug abuse, including alcohol-related crimes. The effects may extend into the *region* around Brookside. Area highways may become somewhat safer, with fewer cases of personal injury and property damage, fewer insurance claims, and less need for medical services.

If her experiment is successful, *Sue,* too, will benefit. Her work will endear her to the school administration. She may get some publications out of her work, and a really successful program might launch her career in a new direction. Often professional acclaim for researchers depends on their successfully helping others, but not infrequently the *primary* beneficiary is the researcher—the books or papers published, the jobs landed, or promotions gained. In many cases, the research subjects continue living just as they did before the project began. Researchers should never become too complacent about this disparity.

A brief story may illustrate this point. Several years ago one of the authors attended a conference sponsored by the Department of Health and Human Services. Its focus was problems of doing research on the street. A few researchers had been invited to attend the meetings held at a five-star hotel in an exclusive section of Key Biscayne, Florida. Each room had a magnificent ocean view; the government had arranged for gourmet meals and daily cocktail parties. One couldn't help being struck by the incongruity between the lives of the genteel scientists seated around the green felt-covered conference table discussing their research and those people they had lived with in desperate situations while doing research. Ironically, while the scientists stayed in their lavish rooms at the conference, their subjects still suffered in their fetid slums and ghettos. Somehow, that fact did not and still doesn't feel right.

Researchers obviously have no magic wands with which to change the living conditions of their subjects. Neither is it reasonable to expect them to forgo the advancement and rewards that their research brings. But at least an awareness that their success depends in part on their subjects should make them more grateful to those subjects and increase their commitment to respect them and avoid offense or injury.

Identifying potential beneficiaries is important, but it is equally important to establish *how likely* those potential benefits actually are. Predicting the likelihood of benefits from research is often a bit like a preseason bet on the Super Bowl game. There are two levels of uncertainty. First, you're uncertain whether your team will even make the playoffs. Second, the outcome of the "Big Game" itself is remarkably unpredictable. So it is with research. You can't be certain what your research findings will be, and you can't know with certainty how those findings might be used—or misused—by others.

Recognizing that predictions are at best only educated guesses, we often must guess about the likelihood of alternative outcomes. Such predictions are essential in balancing benefits against other factors in the ethical equation. Researchers can more easily address the scientific importance of a project, but assessing the probability of benefits other than advancement of knowledge may prove difficult. Estimating the likelihood that subjects may benefit *directly* from the research is hard enough. If benefits are indirect and depend upon *someone else's* implementing recommendations arising out of a project, the problem of prediction is compounded. To what extent must the *scientist* make such assessments to justify a study? Can the researcher simply show the *potential* for benefit? Perhaps it is reasonable to ask that the researcher show what the benefits would be if the findings were applied or if a model program were to be replicated elsewhere. Asking researchers to assess the political climate and to guess how people unknown to them would apply their findings is asking too much, in most cases.

Funding agencies often consider the likelihood of benefit in making their decisions. Sometimes they will ask for projections about the number of people who will benefit directly from a study and the probable effects if its model were adopted by others. Researchers have no crystal ball that provides a clear vision of the future. They must simply be as forthright as possible in describing the prospects and implications of their studies.

Computing the value and cost-effectiveness of research requires determining the *importance* of a particular benefit. This assessment is often necessarily subjective and abstract, perhaps even an exercise in fantasy. How can one possibly "measure" the value of knowledge derived from studying a collection of lonely hearts or nursing-home residents or a socially deviant group like the Necrons? Even if we could accurately predict the outcome of research and its applications, assigning a value to that outcome often strains the imagination. Just as we have no calculus for figuring the degree of harm, so also we have no solid instrument for measuring benefits.

Sometimes calculations can be made in terms of cold cash; but that doesn't necessarily solve the problem. For example, the Brookside School Board will evaluate Sue's work and will probably do so in monetary terms. Her experimental procedure will make it easy for her and the school board to determine how many students have actually been helped and how much it cost. Simply dividing the cost of the program by the number of students helped will give the cost per student of preventing alcohol problems. But that figure alone will not tell the school board whether to discontinue the program or expand it. That decision requires a judgment about how much saving a youngster from alcoholism is worth.

Calculations can sometimes be made in percentages rather than dollars, but the problem remains. Sue might find that her program reduces alcohol problems in the school by 5 percent. Is that reduction sufficient to warrant the continuation of the program? If not, how about 10 percent? 25 percent? 50 percent? Some people would probably say that saving even a single student from serious problems would make Sue's efforts at Brookside worthwhile. Such people probably aren't responsibile for the school's budget, however. Others might be disappointed by anything less that a 50 percent reduction.

Inevitably, we must make judgments about the value of research projects. When we decide that a project is worth the time that we will have to invest in it, or when we decide that the benefits to be gained outweigh the risk of harm for ourselves (when we are research subjects) or for others (when we are investigators), or when we as members of review boards recommend approving a grant proposal, we are making a judgment about the value of a piece of research. But we must make these judgments for the most part without any meaningful quantifiable measurement of the benefit. Unfortunately, a study of ethical theory will not provide the means for that measurement.

Balancing Harms and Benefits

In the previous chapters we have often discussed the balance of harms and benefits. Such comparisons are at the very heart of utilitarianism. Even if we are not *strictly* utilitarian, there is probably some of the utilitarian in all of us. However useful for analytic purposes are the distinctions between approaches to ethics, in practice most of us probably operate with some kind of mixed ethic.

Harmful and beneficial consequences may be part of each of the several styles of ethics we have described. The importance for a *consequentialist* ethic is obvious. But what about a *rule* ethic? Rules embodied in such an ethic usually prohibit behavior that harms people, and the rules may require helpful acts. Recall some rules that prohibit harm: don't kill, don't cause pain, don't deprive of freedom, and so on. Even exceptions to the rules are probably related to an awareness of harmful or beneficial consequences. Harming others may be justified by some good. Killing might be morally legitimate in defending oneself, one's family, one's country. Causing pain is permissible if the purpose is to improve the person who experiences the pain, for example through surgery to reset a broken bone or remove a cancer. Depriving people of freedom through imprisonment may protect the public and maintain social order; involuntary hospitalization may be necessary to provide treatment for psychiatric illness.

Other styles of ethics also require weighing consequences. An intuitional ethic does not define its "method" of decision making as a risk/benefit calculation, but a sense of harmfulness and helpfulness certainly will influence one's reaction to a situation. Actions likely to produce intense suffering won't *feel* right in a "visceral" ethic unless the act seems counterbalanced by some equally strong intuitive feeling. Likewise, those whose style focuses on self-fulfillment and character development can't ignore the consequences of their actions—for good or ill—because "good people" want to help rather than harm people.

A relational ethic with its concern for the nature and quality of interpersonal and institutional relationships must be concerned about the effects of action on people. Thus, though different approaches to ethics may treat the matter differently, some consideration of harmful and beneficial consequences seems inevitable in any ethic.

Whatever one's approach to ethics, some weighing of good consequences against risks of injury is unavoidable. What are the risks of Sue's research? The most obvious is that of labeling. The tag "problem kid" or even "potential problem kid" may make life unpleasant for a student. Constant surveillance may make students feel caged by a world just waiting for a mistake. These students may suffer socially because of an imaginary Scarlet A (for "Alcoholic") emblazoned on their sweat shirts. The label could cause police officers to monitor their out-of-school behavior more closely or even harass them. Conversely, the designation might give these students new status with those for whom drinking and drugs are surrounded by the aura of excitement. Casting them in a role they feel bound to live up to could be the most harmful effect of labeling. For some students, the label might activate a self-fulfilling prophecy.

The research design should take this risk into account and attempt to minimize it. As extensive as the project is and with as many people as there are recording observations, it is unlikely that the purpose of the study can be kept secret. Creating a blind or even double-blind study might be one way to eliminate risks associated with labeling. The procedure might even improve the quality of the research.

Harm could also result if personal information became generally known because of the research. Thus the issue of confidentiality becomes a major concern.

Confidentiality

Confidentiality belongs to the same family as privacy. It is, however, a more narrowly drawn concept. Confidentiality restricts communication of personal information obtained because of special relationships unless the person gives permission to share it. It may be part of a professional relationship (physician/patient or lawyer/client relationships are classic examples) or purely personal relationships (as with an intimate friend). Let's look at this concept a bit more closely.

Sometimes the confidential relationship is part of the *deliberate commitments* we make to one another. We may implicitly or explicitly promise a friend or acquaintance that we will hold what we are told in confidence. We all need someone with whom we can talk freely without fear that the person will pass on to others what we say.

Sometimes confidentiality is *socially defined* as integral to particular roles. Several of the professions are premised on the assumption that "clients" cannot be served well unless they can talk with the professional without fear of public revelation of the information shared. A patient who is afraid to speak openly to a physician may not report an important symptom; a client who feels inhibited in talking with an attorney may not receive adequate legal representation; a parishioner who can't trust a minister to maintain confidences may be deprived of adequate spiritual and counseling guidance. School psychologists and classroom teachers are also aware that some information available to them must be kept confidential.

What about Sue Rohrer? Certainly her role as school psychologist includes expectations of confidentiality in relationships. But what about her role as behavioral scientist? If she were employed by Brookside only as a researcher, would her research role alone include confidentiality as a component? Confidentiality regarding personal information is generally assumed in most research settings, but the particulars may depend upon the agreements Sue negotiates with her research subjects. In dealing with sensitive areas such as drug and alcohol abuse, she is well advised to promise confidentiality (and to specify its limits) if she hopes to establish the kind of relationship that can give her the information she needs.

Please note that even well-established expectations of confidentiality are not necessarily accorded legal status when information is needed for a legal proceeding. In fact, "privileged communication" is very limited in most states. Unless a researcher has been accorded a special grant of immunity by a federal or state attorney general, a court is not likely to accept the existence of a "confidential relationship" as legitimate reason for a researcher's refusal to testify.[1] The result is that the researcher must either accept the court's order as justifying a breach of confidentiality or conclude that ethical obligations require resisting a legal mandate at the possible cost of being held in contempt of court.

Promising *confidentiality* will often increase the willingness of research subjects to share personal information. *Anonymity* is another technique that, when possible, may be even more effective because the subject does not have to trust the researcher to be discreet or rely on his or her integrity. Anonymity means that not even the researcher knows which individual respondents have reported what information because no names or other identification are included with the data. Sue might do an anonymous survey of alcohol and drug use in her schools to assess

---

[1]The 1968 Code of Ethics of the American Sociological Association specifically noted that sociologists do not enjoy privileged status under the law. The 1980 revision changed the tone by stating, "Confidential information provided by research participants must be treated as such by sociologists, even when this information enjoys no legal protection or privilege." The revision also dropped the earlier provision that "the sociologist has no obligation to withhold information of misconduct of individuals or organizations."

Congress has authorized the granting of confidentiality certificates for some research. These certificates relieve scientists from the obligation to testify in any federal or state court. Researchers may apply to the Department of Health and Human Services or the Department of Justice for such a certificate in certain research involving drugs, alcohol, and mental health. The Department of Justice is also authorized to grant immunity for research involving criminals that is funded through the Department. See Natalie Reatig, "Confidentiality Certificates: A Measure of Privacy Protection," *IRB: A Review of Human Subjects Research* 1:3 (May 1979): 1-4, 12.

the significance of those problems and compare it with a survey a few years later to measure the effectiveness of her program. But the experiment as described cannot be anonymous. Sue, or someone, must be able to identify the "at risk" students, the records must be kept for identifiable students, and she must be prepared with intervention and treatment capabilities for students who develop problems.

The most important point is that we need to be clear about what is being promised. If the researcher means that confidentiality will be protected for persons who can be identified, the word "anonymity" should not be used.

As with most such issues, the practice of confidentiality is much more difficult than the principle. What information should be considered confidential? Certainly not everything that one knows about one's client/patient/parishioner/subject is confidential. Much that one knows is public knowledge. Therefore, judgment is required in deciding that something ought to be treated as confidential. Is only what one obtains *from* a person confidential, or does confidentiality include sensitive material obtained *about* the person from another source? Because of personal observations, information received from others, and conclusions inferred by putting together information from several sources, a researcher may know things that the subject has never divulged. Researchers should not simply assume that confidentiality applies solely to what a person says.[2] But how much of Sue's information is confidential, and does confidentiality come in degrees? Are entries in the logs describing behavior observed in public as confidential as the information Sue obtains through counseling sessions? To what extent can information about students be shared among members of the school staff who are all "members of the team"? Who ought to have access to the logs? Should they be available to all staff who have some responsibility for the students? Should they be available only on a "need-to-know" basis? Should they be closed to everyone except Sue?

---

[2]As far back as the Hippocratic Oath one can find a provision prohibiting "spreading abroad" things that are known from the "professional" relationship. The Ethical Principles of American Psychological Association defines information about a research participant as confidential. Principle J states, "Information obtained *about* [italics added] the research participant during the course of an investigation is confidential unless otherwise agreed upon in advance." The Code of Ethics of the American Sociological Association refers only to "information *provided by* [italics added] research participants" in its treatment of confidentiality. The Principles of Professional Responsibility of the American Anthropological Association do not use the word "confidentiality" at all. The concept seems implied in its references to privacy and anonymity.

We believe that different roles and relationships call for different approaches to confidentiality. When a researcher gains access to a private portion of a person's life because of a trust relationship, the demands of confidentiality take on special importance. The trust calls for faithfulness in defending the well-being of the person by respecting confidentiality. Some people have concluded that confidentiality is an outdated concept, outdated not because the idea itself is too old-fashioned but because institutional complexity renders confidentiality impossible. For example, hospital staffs have become so large, and so many people need access to a patient's record, that assuring confidentiality is extremely difficult.[3] The computer may make it quite impossible. We are not yet prepared to accede to the judgment that confidentiality is outmoded, though it must be qualified, and we believe that researchers should still have a strong commitment to protect their subjects' confidentiality. It is equally important, however, that they be cognizant of the logistical problems in maintaining confidentiality and not make promises that are impossible to keep. Moreover, they should not lead subjects to believe that the duty of confidentiality is absolute, since protecting others or the individual himself or herself may require breaching it.

The practice of confidentiality is further complicated in Sue's case because her experimental subjects are minors. Does Sue have a right or obligation to share information with parents? Should she share information with parents anytime it is in the *best interest* of the student? Only when the welfare of the student is in *serious jeopardy?* Or should she *never* tell parents anything obtained in confidence without the student's permission?

Another Special Population

As we considered "Operation Anticipate," we noted the problems of special populations, like prisoners. Sue Rohrer's special population raises new questions. Studies of minors are at least as important for sociology and psychology as for medicine. Understanding social and psychological growth and development is one area of profound importance as we attempt to improve education and deal with a host of social and psychological problems. But minors also need to be protected. Besides relying on researchers themselves to have this commitment, informed consent procedures reduce the likelihood of harm.

---

[3]See Mark Siegler, "Confidentiality in Medicine—A Decrepit Concept," *New England Journal of Medicine* 307:24 (9 December 1982): 1518-21. Siegler's argument is not that the concept of confidentiality should be abandoned, but that patients need to be better informed about how widely information is disseminated within the health care team.

Presumably Sue plans to obtain the consent of the *parents* of her students. Should she also seek the consent of the *students?* They are not small children in elementary school. They are maturing junior high school students who will be followed through high school. They are developing independence and are steadily assuming responsibility for themselves. The question of their consent is an important one for much scientific research, especially for psychological studies on growth and development.

Many ethicists and scientists argue that the *assent* of minors (at least of adolescents) should be obtained. This means that a minor's agreement would not be sufficient to authorize proceeding (hence the term "assent" rather than "consent"), but the youngster would be given veto power. Assent should be tailored for the stage of development of the children studied. This procedure acknowledges a respect for developing autonomy without recognizing full autonomy.

Allowing a minor to veto research may make good sense if he or she does not have anything to gain from the research. But what if it could be beneficial? We wouldn't let young people veto necessary medical treatment. Sue Rohrer's experiment is linked closely with a treatment alternative for students discovered to need it. Is the possibility of diagnosing and treating alcoholism or drug addiction so "therapeutic" that youths should not be given veto power? Or is the "experimental" nature such that students' cooperation should be enlisted? And if students' *assent* is to be sought, do they need to be told as much about the procedures as their parents are to be when their *consent* is sought?

Parents in granting consent for students to participate in Sue's experiment must weigh the risks against the potential benefits. Those students identified as being at risk for developing an alcohol or drug problem may really benefit from Sue's program. But what if Sue decided to include some low-risk students in the seminars and other special programs to reduce the risk of labeling? Labeling might still occur; only now some of the "labeled" students might be mislabeled. Would parents be justified in permitting their "low-risk" youngsters to participate in a program where they might mistakenly be labeled as "problem kids" and suffer some discrimination because of the labeling? Should parents even be allowed to place their children at risk if there is no expectation that they might benefit?

This issue has been debated especially in the field of medical ethics. One well-known writer once argued vigorously that it is unethical for parents to permit medical research with their children if it is not for the child's benefit. The rationale for allowing parents decision-making authority for their children is that they will protect the interests of their children. Since research that can *only* benefit others will by definition not benefit the subjects, parents cannot morally give consent for their children to participate. The most stringent position would prohibit even the drawing of a small amount of blood for Sue's next project—the one on genetics and alcoholism—even though the risk is quite low. Few people would go this far. Even writers who accept the basic premise of the argument think that parents can rightly permit their children to participate in "low-risk" experimentation.[4] Medical research is, of course, somewhat different from social and behavioral research, but the question of harm and benefit to the child is the central issue in them all.

Implicit in this discussion is a fundamental question crucial in any number of decision areas. *Who decides?* Deciding who decides is itself an important ethical question. Some experiments would be so dangerous that researchers ought not to seek parents' permission and ought not to undertake the research even with permission, even with adults who consent, certainly not with children. In borderline cases, where people of good will may sincerely differ about the ethics of a procedure, who should decide? No matter who has the authority to make decisions, that person may make the "wrong" decision.

In the case of children, we must ultimately decide where the burden of proof lies. Are children basically the responsibility of parents, with society through the state intervening only when it is quite clear that the parents are acting contrary to the child's interest? Or are children essentially the responsibility of society, which pragmatically has assigned

---

[4]Paul Ramsey, in *The Patient As Person* (New Haven CT: Yale University Press, 1970) 1-58, makes the case for prohibiting parental consent for medical experimentation that does not benefit the child. He does not apply this principle to the noninvasive research encountered in the social and behavioral sciences, but his argument would seem equally applicable to such research. Richard McCormick introduces another concept into his response to Ramsey. McCormick suggests that it may be a moral duty (not a legal duty) to volunteer for some research, since we have all benefited from past research, and it could be justifiable to allow children to be used in low-risk research because of a moral duty. See Richard A. McCormick, "Proxy Consent in the Experimentation Situation," *Perspectives in Biology and Medicine 18:1* (Autumn 1974): 2-22. William Bartholome follows McCormick, but argues that if moral duty is what justifies the use of a child, then the child must be able to gain moral benefit from volunteering; hence the child must at least be old enough to assent. William G. Bartholome, "Parents, Children, and the Moral Benefits of Research," National Commission for the Protection of Human Subjects of Biomedical and Behavioral Research, Research Involving Children, Appendix (1977) DHEW Publication (OS) 77-0005. A condensation can be found in Thomas A. Mappes and Jane S. Zembaty, eds., *Biomedical Ethics* (New York: McGraw-Hill, 1981) 169-72.

parents the authority to make decisions, but only so long as they can demonstrate that they are serving the child's interest? The alternative we choose may make a great deal of difference in determining who makes decisions and possibly what decisions are made in a number of areas, including consent for social and behavioral research.

Historically, preeminence has been given to the family, with the state intervening only in the most extreme circumstances. The family has been seen as a basic social unit with an autonomy of its own. Parents make many decisions that affect their children profoundly—decisions about what schools they will attend, where or whether they will go to church, with whom they may associate, and so on. At this time a "children's rights" movement may be underway that may challenge the priority of parental authority and may lead to increased state intervention to "protect the interests of the child." The decline in family stability and a heightened mood of individualism may support this trend, for better or worse.

We have reached the end of our case presentations. The Sue Rohrer story, as with all the others, is left unfinished. You are perhaps wondering, "Well, did it work?" The answer is, of course, "We don't know, either." Each of our fictional cases leaves behind some unfinished business, and we have no intention of writing a sequel in which you will learn the result of Don's study of the Necrons or discover whether Linda's study of the lonely hearts led to fame, fortune, and promotion and tenure or to her dismissal from Riverbend College. Knowing the end of the story does not answer the moral questions. Our purpose in these vignettes has been to bring you face to face with a variety of ethical issues—some minor, perhaps almost trivial, some with profound impact on researcher and subject alike—that are part of social and behavioral research. We did not expect to arrive at conclusions so cogent and compelling that no rational person would dare dispute them, nor is it our hope that you have arrived at unambiguous answers for yourself about each of these cases. We merely hope that we have engaged your thinking about some very important concrete issues in the practice of social research. In the final section of the book, we want to address some more general questions about the researcher and the social context of research.

VI

THE
RESEARCHER
AND BEYOND

13

What Makes
a Good Researcher Good?

As we have presented and discussed fictional cases throughout the book, we have asked what our characters should do in their situations and what we can learn about more general problems in the ethics of social research through their example. There are probably some clues in the cases about the kind of persons our characters are, but we have not made it our business to look at that question extensively. As we come to the end of our study, however, it seems appropriate to make a few comments about the personal qualities of a good researcher.

THE VIRTUES OF A RESEARCHER

Treatises on ethics in the past would often contain a section on "the virtues," the praiseworthy qualities that characterize "the good life" in the broadest sense of that phrase. Though never completely ignored, that theme has been largely dormant for some time, especially in the writings of philosophers and Protestant theologians. Catholic writers have tended to retain more of that emphasis, and a number of non-Catholic writers have also recently joined a revival of interest in the virtues or "character" as an important component in ethics. A number of traits of character or virtues (such as compassion, diligence, and a sense of fairness) that are desirable in any person have special implications for researchers. Some qualities are especially fitting for work in a scientific field. Let's look at some virtues that befit the scientific investigator.

Tolerance and Respect

A degree of tolerance for differences in values, outlook, and life-style and respect for those who embody them seem essential for effective work in any of the social and behavioral sciences. Sue will not get far with the alcohol and drug problem at Brookside if she appears intolerant. If she projects a moralistic attitude and communicates a feeling that students who use alcohol and drugs are "bad" people, she will have the formula for failure. The people who need her most will turn her off. She will not be able to obtain needed information or offer assistance. Her program and her study will be failures, or so we predict. Even without being judgmental, she may "devalue" her students in other ways. She may treat students as if they are "dumb" or not worth her valuable time. This lack of respect will interfere with her function as school psychologist and as researcher. If she treats the teachers with disdain, she will soon lose their cooperation in her project.

Tolerance is most crucial when the scientist does research that depends on effective personal interactions. The participant observer, like Don for example, must be prepared to be tolerant of "deviant," "offbeat," or simply "different" attitudes, values, and practices of the people studied, without necessarily indicating approval of them. Likewise, if Sherry had appeared intolerant of Darkwoods's residents, the likelihood of any meaningful relationship developing would have been greatly diminished.

Even when the personal interactions are minimal, intolerant and disrespectful attitudes may affect the research adversely. In survey research, intolerance may lead to bias in framing questions for a survey instrument and distortion when conducting interviews. The surveyor who manifests shock, disgust, contempt, or perhaps even mild disapproval in the administration of an interview schedule may cause the respondents to alter their answers to avoid "offending" the surveyor, or they may become deliberately provocative to upset the surveyor.

Likewise, cooperation with research colleagues requires a measure of tolerance. Diversity of personality types, philosophical outlooks, and professional and personal values are a fact of life in our pluralistic society. This diversity is at least as evident among social and behavioral scientists as it is in the population at large. Tolerance does not require agreement nor does it prohibit disagreement or even heated debate. It does require a recognition of diversity and a willingness, within limits, to work harmoniously with others with whom we may disagree. This leads us to the next virtue, open-mindedness.

Open-Mindedness

Closely related to tolerance is the virtue of open-mindedness, a fundamental requirement for work in any of the sciences. Researchers must not become so wedded to their own ideas that they cannot entertain the thought of other explanations. Open-mindedness is more difficult to achieve than it might seem. All researchers claim to be open-minded, but blind spots are not easily detected. Sue is convinced that her project will work. She is confident that her tests can predict the risk of alcohol problems, and she is sure that she can help students avoid problems. She will have difficulty in recognizing and accepting failures if the project doesn't work.

Without openness to new ways of formulating questions and interpreting data, the scientist will be blocked from making new discoveries, even when they are right under the researcher's nose. Data may be unconsciously molded to fit existing patterns and firmly held convictions which are never examined. The ability to remain open to new ways of seeing is thus related to the virtue of imagination.

Imagination

The closed mind is fatal in scientific work because it prevents new ideas from even being considered. But real success in science goes beyond recognizing a good idea when one comes along; it requires the imagination to envision new ways of conceptualizing and new ways of formulating and testing a hypothesis. Several of our characters seem reasonably inventive, though none are among those truly creative individuals who introduce really novel approaches. Each has taken some existing idea or approach and applied it creatively to a new setting. Imagination at several levels is a first ingredient in research. But it must be accompanied by hard work. As Thomas Edison put it, "Genius is 10% inspiration and 90% perspiration."

Perseverance, Tenacity, Patience, and Energy

The idea and the inspiration are only the beginning. Translating an idea into a workable research protocol requires time, careful planning, sometimes tedious detail, and lots of energy. Most of our composite characters seem to have the qualities of patience and perseverance that will carry them through the sometimes trying periods of a research project. Sue, for example, has patiently bided her time, waiting for the right moment to introduce an idea that she had long before. When the time was right, she tackled the job with vigor and enthusiasm. We have left the story in the early stages. Whether Sue can sustain her interest, determination, and energy for the five years of the study remains to be seen. Studies like hers require a special kind of patience because their longitudinal nature means a long wait before any significant conclusions are possible.

Patience is also required when a project keeps running into dead ends or roadblocks that require retracing one's steps and trying a new direction. Working with subjects who do not share the same sense of importance of the project or the same sense of urgency may demand all the patience the researcher can muster. The need to persevere may even increase during the period of analysis following data collection. In some research, the fun comes in the process of gathering data. The process of analyzing it may become a burdensome chore, but obviously carelessness, laziness, and impatience at this stage can destroy the value of the whole study. The capacity to stay at the job energetically after the initial enthusiasm has long passed is essential for successful research. Likewise, the value of the research will never be recognized if the scientist lacks the tenacity to prepare and present the findings in such a manner that the report will be published and read. The "duty to publish" involves making one's work publishable.

Passion for Knowledge

The passion to know, to understand, to explain to oneself and others what makes the world work is the driving force behind the research enterprise. An unrelenting drive to find out "Why?" certainly promotes research activity and may keep a researcher hard at work when others flag. But it may also lead to impatience when results are not immediately forthcoming. It may encourage sharing knowledge through publication or another forum, but it may also generate impatience with constraints that appear to impede the search for knowledge, such as ethical restraints.

Honesty and Trustworthiness

We have already discussed the practice of honesty in the collection, analysis, and presentation of data; and we noted that honesty and trustworthiness are basic requisites for meaningful relationships. The practice of honesty and trustworthiness is grounded in the character of the practitioner. Shakespeare's advice rightly locates the source of honesty and faithfulness in honesty with oneself: "This above all, to thine own self be true, and it must follow as the night the day thou canst not then be false to any man." The admonition provides no recipe for instant integrity, but it does identify the ingredients of moral action in the character of the moral self. Character is the precondition for the *art* of morality.

Humility

Humility is seldom considered a professional virtue. The connotations of the term may even seem the very antithesis of our usual image of the self-confident professional. But humility does not mean thinking ill of oneself; humility in its noblest expression points away from self to others. Its opposite is not self-confidence but arrogance.

Genuine humility means recognizing one's limits as well as one's achievements and recognizing one's indebtedness to others. All scholars, if they think about it, should recognize that whatever vista they may have of the human landscape is theirs because they stand on the shoulders of giants. The richness of our intellectual heritage calls for humility, as does our relative ignorance of those yet unexplored regions of human experience. Humility is indeed an appropriate virtue for the scientist.

VIRTUE AND MORALITY

As we have described some of the "virtues" of the researcher, you may have been asking yourself, "What does this have to do with morality?" And rightly so. Some of these virtues, like honesty and respect for others, may have an inherent moral quality. But others, like imagination and perseverance, though "good" for researchers, can be equally useful in the service of evil causes. These virtues appear to be more "instrumental" virtues than moral virtues. But is there not some moral value even in the "honor among thieves"? Moreover, do not even instrumental virtues take on special moral meaning when placed within the context of a morally commendable activity? To the extent that social and behavioral research is directed toward the good of humanity, its diligent pursuit is a service to the human community, and the virtues that support the endeavor acquire a moral quality. Herein lies one of the greatest risks of the moral life, for the trappings of good can also mask the face of evil. Among the virtues that can support the best research are qualities that can also serve the cause of evil. We shall return to this ambiguity of the moral life in the concluding chapter.

14

Should They
or Shouldn't They?
The Pros and Cons
of Regulating Research

As we discussed the ethics of research, we often referred to the relationships on which we base our ethics and alluded to the professional community's role in setting standards for researchers. We also mentioned the role of government in regulating research. Now we will treat these subjects more directly.

THE AGE OF REGULATION

Historians often characterize periods of time with single adjectives. We had an "Age of Reason," an "Age of Innocence," and more recently an "Age of Anxiety." In this vein, our age might be described as the "Age of Regulation." Someone is always looking over our shoulders. Federal regulatory commissions scrutinize everything done for us and by us: our banking, foods and medicine, transportation, and communications. Even in a political climate where complaints are heard about "too much government," most people still seem convinced that a significant amount of regulation is necessary. The public has come to expect that commissions and agencies will make the world a safer, more pleasant place. Not surprisingly, research involving human subjects has become an area for regulation. We wish to examine briefly three levels of this scrutiny—review by the scientific community, regulation at the institute or institutional level, and reaction by the general public.

The Scientific Community

At the most basic level, work is reviewed in the scientific community by professional colleagues or peers. Researchers, as members of the professional community, are expected to subscribe to a set of standards governing their conduct. For instance, professional anthropologists would probably hold their colleagues to a different set of standards than they would expect of journalists; likewise, professional journalists wouldn't expect sociologists to subscribe to their rules and procedures. Professional groups establish written "Codes of Ethics" for their members. Writing such a code is usually one of the first steps taken by an occupational group in moving toward "professional" status. These codes are standards by which each profession defines the relationship of individual members to their colleagues, clients, and the public.

Most of the issues that have concerned us throughout the book are addressed directly or are alluded to indirectly in the ethical principles of sociological, psychological, and anthropological organizations; and we have noted some of these for illustrative purposes in footnotes. Those interested in a thorough examination should obtain and examine these statements of principles. Those entering one of these careers should study carefully the ethical guidelines provided by the professional organization representing that field because these guidelines represent the thoughtful consideration of numerous colleagues in the field. They provide part of the social framework within which researchers must interpret their task and responsibility.

The seriousness with which we urge consideration of these codes of ethics should not be interpreted, however, as implying that they are definitive or infallible. A great deal of interpretation is still required in the application of those principles, and it is possible that the principles themselves, or the interpretations provided by those professional groups responsible for their "enforcement," are in error. The process of professional formation is ongoing and invites continuing discussion within the profession regarding questions such as those raised in this book. Continued reflection with an open mind is essential for good ethics and good science.

Even though the professional "code" is not fixed for all time, the principles established by professional groups have great import for the practice of professional ethics because the organizations are perceived as representing their fields, even though not all practitioners hold membership in them. These organizations speak for the fields in creating and sustaining public expectations and support.

Since membership is not required to do research in sociology, psychology, or anthropology, the professional organizations have limited power to discipline unethical practice. The most serious formal sanction available to the organization, expulsion from the organization, will not necessarily have great effect on the individual. Unless colleagues in the research field take that sanction seriously as they consider whether to support promotions, relocations, honorary awards, or other advancements, professional codes will affect only the virtuous.

One way in which ethically questionable research may be flagged is in the review process of professional journals. We believe that these journals should refuse to publish work in which unethical research methods have been used. We think the day is approaching when each scientific report will have an "ethics" or "human subjects" statement as routinely as such reports now have a "methods" section. In this section, the author will describe the methods used to insure that ethical standards have been met.[1]

Institute and Institutional Review

Already a review of ethical issues is part of the research-planning process of institute supervision. The review process in the research institutes, such as the National Institutes of Health, is active and direct. Here the protection of human subjects is seen as serious business. The United States Department of Health and Human Services provides substantial funds each year to support research projects. As with any funding agency, research proposals are scrutinized carefully by a panel of experts. The panel assesses the scientific and technical merit of the proposal and the qualifications of the researcher to execute the project successfully. If human subjects are involved, the review committee also examines the mechanisms designed to protect them. This painstaking process includes a review of consent forms, a study of provisions for protecting privacy or confidentiality, and other relevant concerns. If the provisions specified in the proposal do *not* meet the approval of the committee, the proposal will not be approved for funding and will be returned to the investigator for more work.

---

[1]There is considerable debate about the morality of publishing material unethically obtained. There are some interesting variations on this theme. One possibility is suggested by a recent publication of a biography of Howard Hughes, based in part on secret memos written by Hughes and stolen in 1974. The biographer had no part in stealing the papers, but used them in writing the biography. See Tom Morganthau, "Biography of a Billionaire," *Newsweek* 105:4 (28 January 1985): 33. Could researchers legitimately use in scientific research such illegally obtained materials if they were not responsible for the theft? Second, is it ethical to cite unethical research that has been published? The question is raised most painfully in connection with Nazi medical research. Kristine Moe ("Should Nazi Research Be Cited?" *Hastings Center Report* 14:6 [December 1984]: 5-7) argues that it should never be done "without regret or without acknowledging the incomprehensible horror that produced [the data]." Nevertheless, she argues that it may be possible that "some good may be salvaged from the ashes."

In most cases, however, before a grant proposal will even be considered by a federal funding agency, the proposal must be approved by an *Institutional Review Board* (IRB) at the local level. This review is mandated in regulations from the Department of Health and Human Services and is imposed on institutions receiving federal funds.

These local human-subjects-protection committees review proposed research projects to ensure that the well-being and rights of those under study are protected; they also protect the interests of sponsoring institutions. Such committees usually include a broad range of people representing different academic and professional disciplines and usually include a lawyer and a community representative. Proposals for any research in which investigators will use their institutional affiliations to obtain data, funding, or publications are reviewed by these committees. They are concerned to protect subjects from harm, though the possibility of harm does not automatically mean disapproval of a project. If the research involves risk, the researcher must demonstrate that the subjects are sufficiently informed to make a rational choice whether to participate. Furthermore, the researcher must convince the committee that any risks are outweighed by the potential benefits and that the subjects' participation is voluntary, without excessive rewards of money, grade points, or class credit.

Institutional review committees look into the "nuts and bolts" of a project—for instance, the ways in which respondents' confidentiality will be protected. They may review the mechanism for giving questionnaires, making notes, and keeping records secure. The group usually examines forms and procedures for obtaining informed consent. While all of this might seem tedious, we should remember that the committee ultimately protects the researcher by protecting the subjects. Such committees can be a researcher's best friend in helping to avoid the ethical pitfalls of research. Our experience with these groups has been positive.

Much of the early concern that norms for medical research, where danger may be high, would be inappropriately applied to very benign social-science research has been allayed. The final guidelines published in 1981 either exempt most social-science research or permit an "expedited" review.

The IRB structure and procedures have been generally quite useful, but they should not be considered the absolute test of morality. The guidelines established by the Department of Health and Human Services need continual review. While striving to adhere to these guidelines, researchers have the responsibility to evaluate those procedures and to influence their continuing refinement. The review boards at the local level have been accorded a significant amount of authority and power. They deserve respect and should be heeded, but that does not mean that researchers should abdicate their own ethical responsibility to a committee. Committees can make mistakes. They can restrict research that is perfectly legitimate ethically. They can also err in approving morally objectionable research. In the first case, a researcher may feel a responsibility to work for changes in a decision or even in a procedure itself that unduly limits legitimate research. With the second, it should be obvious that a researcher should not use a committee's approval as a justification for undertaking a project that he or she knows is unethical.

Public Reaction

Research may ultimately be scrutinized by the public. Any project can be examined by the media and even by public officials. The media, much like sharks sensing a wounded fish, are quick to home in on discord and distress. Sound projects in which everything is done to ensure that both the researcher and subject finish the project feeling good about what has occurred are not newsworthy. Let people say, however, that they have been harmed by participation in a project they didn't consent to, perhaps naming a university or hospital in a large law suit, and a reporter will quickly appear to capture the full story. The step from media to "official" notice, as an elected or appointed official gets interested in the case, may be a small one. It matters little whether the researcher is a full professor or a graduate student. The fallout from a research scandal can be disastrous. Ethics and the protection of human subjects are serious business.

EXTERNAL REGULATION AND SELF-DISCIPLINE

The individual researcher nowadays faces the prospect of informal regulation and sanctions and regulation by more formal review mechanisms. But what has this regulation to do with morality? Is this regulation of research an illegitimate effort to legislate morality? If that well-worn maxim "You can't legislate morality" is true at all, it is because we can't make people act from proper *motives.* But we can clearly regulate *conduct* by legislation. We do it all the time. That's the whole purpose of criminal law. The real question is whether we *should* regulate *this particular area* or leave these matters for the moral judgment of presumably well-intentioned researchers.

Is This Regulation Necessary?

There are three kinds of reasons for defining guidelines or regulations. First, morally serious people are often genuinely perplexed and can benefit from external direction. Although a few people have a kind of sixth sense for moral issues that keeps them invariably on the right course, most of us ordinary people need some guidance worked out in a moral community. We do not accept those norms by blind faith; still, few of us feel competent to devise our own moral system in isolation from others. We realize that the "lone ranger" approach to ethics is risky business. We personally recommend that researchers take seriously the emerging guidelines and that they develop the habit of consulting with morally sensitive colleagues and friends as they think about their research programs.

The moral life is always life in a community. As we continue to test our basic principles and examine the validity of existing rules and apply guidelines to concrete research situations, we need to engage in ethical discourse with colleagues and sometimes with research subjects. Codes of ethics evolved by the careful, deliberate thought of professional groups and other regulators can be immensely helpful to many earnest researchers.

But besides helping researchers grapple with moral uncertainty, external regulations may provide a defense against any occasional moral lapses. Under the pressure of the moment, because of time constraints, because the research seems so important, there is sometimes a temptation to cut ethical corners. If Oscar Wilde's quip that "the only way to get rid of temptation is to yield to it" is correct, then we may need an external regulator so we won't have to rely solely on our own self-discipline to protect us from our own worst inclinations.

But finally regulation may be necessary because of the powerful human tendency to be more concerned for self than others. Sometimes the failure to recognize the rights of others is overt, deliberate, and self-conscious, the assertion of the unabashed ethical egoist: that is, a claim that moral obligation means pursuing self-interest as the highest, indeed the only, good. In its most blatant form it becomes the claim that "might makes right," which either upends all traditional moral claims or is a denial that there is any such thing as morality.

More commonly, egoism is defended by a more subtle argument that pursuit of self-interest will often promote the common good as well. Adam Smith with his "invisible hand" voices the economic version of this theory.[2] Numerous psychologists and philosophers have argued that

---

[2]In the classic passage in book 4, chapter 2 of *The Wealth of Nations,* Smith did not assert that egoistic behavior *always* led to the public good. " . . . by directing that industry in such a manner as its produce may be of the greatest value, he intends only his own gain, and he is in this, as *in many other cases* [emphasis added], led by an invisible hand to promote an end which was no part of his intention. . . . By pursuing his own interest he *frequently* [emphasis added] promotes that of the society more effectually than when he really intends to promote it." See Adam Smith, *An Inquiry into the Nature and Causes of the Wealth of Nations* (New York: Random House, 1937) 423.

egoism that is "enlightened" will realize that the responses of others to perceived selfishness is detrimental to the egoist. Thus, egoists must be "concerned" for others in order to protect their own welfare.

A major English philosopher in the late nineteenth century argued that egoism and utilitarianism frequently converge for just this reason. The egoist must be concerned for the "greatest good for the greatest number" because the egoist is finally happier that way. However, despite his best efforts to reconcile the two completely, that philosopher finally concluded that sometimes even enlightened self-interest and the public good do not coincide.[3]

A recent, highly acclaimed book on justice begins with an assumption of self-interest and constructs a hypothetical society in which that self-interest is best served. The result of this social contract theory of justice is a commitment to the well-being of the lowliest, least fortunate member of society, a conclusion far removed from the theory's egoistic starting point.[4]

However agreeable we may find the results of these latter views, we are not convinced that egoism is an appropriate place to begin a theory of ethics. These theories may be instances of T. S. Eliot's "highest treason," that is, they "do the right thing for the wrong reason." Yet there is a virtue in the very honesty of egoistic theories. They recognize the reality of the human condition. People are egoistic. To provide real guidance for real people in real situations, an ethic cannot deal solely with abstract ideals of the right and the good. Any ethic must implicitly or explicitly be guided by some "theory" about human nature and about human social institutions. To be effective, an ethic must hold a view of human nature that is realistic. Are people basically good, needing only to be educated in the ways of right conduct? Or are people basically evil, needing strong external control to prevent the exercise of that evil capacity? Or does the truth lie somewhere in between? Are social institutions flexible and malleable, subject to human manipulation to promote human good? Or do they take on a life of their own that resists a humanizing influence?

Some people want to regulate research because they don't trust others to do what's right unless they are coerced into doing so. Recalling Lord Acton's famous quotation, "Power corrupts, and absolute power

---

[3]Henry Sidgwick, *The Methods of Ethics,* 7th ed. (1874; reprint, London: Macmillan, 1963).

[4]John Rawls, *A Theory of Justice* (Cambridge: Harvard University Press, 1971). See also his essay, "Justice as Fairness," *The Journal of Philosophy* 54 (October 1957): 653-62.

corrupts absolutely," they insist upon some kind of external constraint that would limit the power of researchers.[5]

The most subtle corrupting effect of power is the distortion of moral vision. The human capacity for self-deception is enormous, and in their abuse of power most people can blind themselves to their own wrong-doing. The most horrendous evils can be committed in the name of the highest good. It is not simply that we can rationalize our actions to others. We deceive ourselves as well, a reality that social and behavioral researchers observe frequently in their subjects. The important moral lesson that researchers can learn from their subjects is that not even humane scientists are exempt from the distortion of moral perception. The nobility of the cause of scientific research should not obscure any ethical questions involved in a project.

Yet this important warning, rooted in a somewhat pessimistic assessment of human nature, is not the whole story. There is also an enormous capacity for good in humankind. The challenge for a social order is to permit and promote the free expression of those most noble impulses while restraining freedom, where necessary, to prevent the abuse of power.[6]

---

[5]Although he did not write about research ethics, the thought of Reinhold Niebuhr is instructive here. Niebuhr, perhaps the most influential American theologian in the twentieth century, was the intellectual mentor of countless people in and out of academe. For him, the most prevalent and destructive human sin is the sin of pride, which manifests itself especially in the abuse of power. Ethical theory requires not merely identifying wrongs, but also proposing ways to prevent them. Though he makes a strong appeal to individual responsibility and conscience, Niebuhr does not count on individual morality to ensure social justice. Promoting justice and social well-being will frequently require restricting the exercise of power, especially group power, by balancing the power of one group with the power of another. His work spanned several decades, and his writing was extensive. His classic work expressing his theological assessment of human nature and its ethical implications is *The Nature and Destiny of Man: A Christian Interpretation* (New York: Charles Scribner's Sons, 1941) vol. 1.

[6]Reinhold Niebuhr again is noted for his emphasis on both the corrupting and redeeming dimensions of human nature. His early book *Moral Man and Immoral Society: A Study in Ethics and Politics* (New York: Charles Scribner's Sons, 1932) is a monument to the pervasiveness of self-deception, as morally upright people feel virtuous in performing deeds on behalf of a group, like their nation, that they would consider immoral—perhaps atrocious—if done individually in their own name. Niebuhr's message is that we ought to be as critical of ourselves and our tendency to pursue our own interests while hiding behind the banner of some greater cause as we are critical of others whose selfishness is more obvious to us. No one, not even we ourselves, can be trusted with too much power. His defense of democracy, a political order structured on checks and balances,

Human Nature and Moral Failure

The human condition, we have been saying, predisposes us to seek our own interest, sometimes at the expense of others, and it is often impossible for us to see our own moral failures. A contemporary wit has added a new and insightful twist to the old adage about human failure and divine forgiveness: "To err is human. To blame somebody else is even more human." An ability to acknowledge one's errors and accept responsibility for them is a mark of maturity.

Treatises on ethics often deal only with issues that may provide moral guidance for future conduct and do not treat the experience of moral failure. But it seems important to discuss such failure in this context for two reasons. The first is that failure is educational. We can learn from our mistakes, but only if we can acknowledge that they are mistakes. The scientist who is unwilling or unable to admit errors in research method or technique may go on repeating the same mistakes over and over again. Besides learning from one's own mistakes, a researcher may even be able to help colleagues avoid those mistakes. In publication, for example, the researcher may sometimes make a greater contribution by pointing out his or her errors than may result from the reporting of research findings themselves. The same is true in the ethical realm as in the technical or scientific. An ability to acknowledge one's moral mistakes makes it less likely that the same mistakes will be repeated.

The second reason that it seems important to discuss moral failure is simply that it is a fact of the moral life *as lived,* and this is no less an issue in professional ethics than in the moral life in general. The capacity to feel guilty about moral mistakes is part of normal human existence; the absence of that capacity has even been defined as "pathological," in keeping with our current habit of "medicalizing" our social problems. But failure to deal effectively with feelings of guilt can also be pathological, as clinical psychologists know all too well from their work with people afflicted with overburdened consciences.

Researchers, like everybody else, need to be able to deal with moral failure, just as they must deal with any number of personal or professional failures. Feelings of guilt may result from making a wrong choice,

---

is rooted in his realism about the human propensity to misuse power, but also on his optimistic faith that human beings can accept limits in order to achieve a relatively just society. One of the most often quoted statements from his writings comes from his book on democracy, *The Children of Light and the Children of Darkness: A Vindication of Democracy and a Critique of Its Traditional Defense* (1944; reprint, New York: Charles Scribner's Sons, 1960) xiii. "Man's capacity for justice makes democracy possible; but man's inclination to injustice makes democracy necessary."

but many times these feelings may arise from situations in which none of the available choices seems right. Even if one knows intellectually that a choice was the best available, say in choosing to betray a confidence in order to prevent some serious harm, one may not *feel* good about it. Mark Twain's advice to do your duty today and repent tomorrow points to the ambiguity in the moral life.

There is probably as much diversity in how people deal with guilt as there is in their approaches to ethics. But part of the process for almost anyone is the interpersonal capacity to forgive and to accept forgiveness. Forgiveness, the experience of grace and mercy, has been part of the stock and trade of religion for millennia. But even for those not religiously inclined, some form of forgiveness seems necessary for psychological well-being and personal moral integrity, since some moral failure is inevitable. The experience of forgiveness will vary from person to person. One researcher, convinced that he has wronged some research subjects, may feel impelled to "confess" that error to a friend, a colleague, or even to the subjects themselves. Perhaps for some the feeling of forgiveness can flow from a purely inward acknowledgment of a wrong, especially when it was unintended, and a resolution to profit from that experience. Sometimes a person's sense of guilt is intensified immeasurably because the offended party can no longer be reached, as families sometimes experience after a death. Some belief in a gracious God (to use the language of traditional religion) or a beneficent "higher power" (in the language of Alcoholics Anonymous) or a forgiving and supportive human community (understood in the framework of humanism) may be essential for the health and wholeness of the moral life.[7]

Ambiguity and the Art of the Moral Life

Throughout the book our goal has been to raise questions, to stimulate thinking and discussion, and to provide some perspective on the ethical issues in social and behavioral research. Our intention was not to provide definitive answers even for the questions that we have raised, much less to provide a rulebook that can solve all the problems of research ethics. We hope that the perspective we have presented is illuminating as you think about these issues yourself. The moral life is fraught with ambiguity, and for that reason morality is more an art than

---

[7]The Principles of Professional Responsibility of the American Anthropological Association makes an interesting reference to the issue of forgiveness. "To err is human, to forgive humane. This statement of principles of professional responsibility is not designed to punish, but to provide guidelines which can minimize the occasions upon which there is a need to forgive."

a science. Discerning one's moral responsibility in complex circumstances lacks the certitude that we would all desire.

Each of the several styles of ethical thought and life that we introduced early in the book points to a different dimension of moral experience. The process of thinking about rules *and* consequences, of heeding one's immediate moral impulses *and* one's patterned habits of thought and attitude, all contribute to one's understanding of moral responsibility. The relational approach we have suggested is not a substitute for these other perspectives, but encompasses them in a broader framework that examines the demands of roles and relations, agreements and expectations, and the social or cultural context and institutional demands or limitations.

Most of the time our moral decisions are easy, often occurring without even conscious deliberation. Sometimes more thought is required, and we may want easy answers or some simple rules. Conceiving of ethics as finding the appropriate action within the network of the many factors we have described may seem to make decisions more difficult than they should be. We do not believe that there are easy answers to perplexing moral dilemmas. In our moral experience, we often feel the anxiety of ambiguity and the confusion that accompanies complexity. The moral life involves a measure of risk. To be a moral agent, no matter what system of ethics one adopts, is to take risks and assume responsibility for errors. No matter what one's style of morality, it is finally the individual who must decide and act, and the final appeal is to the individual conscience. This is not an endorsement of subjectivism, because we believe that the individual can be wrong. It is merely the acknowledgment that the individual cannot escape moral choice because even refusing to choose is itself a moral act. Since we cannot avoid moral choice, let us approach life as a gift to be lived with gratitude and with zest; and if error is inevitable, then, as Martin Luther put it, let us "sin bravely."

BIBLIOGRAPHY

Appell, George N. *Ethical Dilemmas in Anthropological Inquiry: A Case Book.* Waltham MA: Crossroad Press, 1978.

Beauchamp, Tom L., et al., eds. *Ethical Issues in Social Science Research.* Baltimore: Johns Hopkins University Press, 1982.

Barnes, J. A. *The Ethics of Inquiry in Social Sciences.* New Delhi: Oxford University Press, 1977.

_____. *Who Should Know What?: Social Science, Privacy and Ethics.* New York: Penguin Books, 1979.

Bermant, Gordon, Herbert C. Kelman, and Donald P. Warwick, eds. *The Ethics of Social Intervention.* New York: John Wiley & Sons, 1978.

Bulmer, Martin, ed. *Social Research Ethics: An Examination of the Merits of Covert Participant Observation.* New York: Holmes & Meier, 1982.

Diener, Edward and Rick Crandall. *Ethics in Social and Behavioral Research.* Chicago: University of Chicago Press, 1978.

Filstead, William J., ed. *Qualitative Methodology: Firsthand Involvement with the Social World,* part 6. Chicago: Markham, 1970.

Kelman, H. C. *A Time to Speak: On Human Values and Social Research.* San Francisco: Jossey-Bass, 1968.

Klockars, Carl B. and O'Connor, Finbarr W., eds. *Deviance and Decency: The Ethics of Research with Human Subjects.* Beverly Hills CA: Sage Publications, 1979.

Nejelski, Paul, ed. *Social Research in Conflict with Law and Ethics.* Cambridge MA: Ballinger Publishing, 1976.

Reynolds, Paul Davidsoon. *Ethical Dilemmas and Social Science Research.* San Francisco: Jossey-Bass, 1979.

_____. *Ethics and Social Science Research.* Englewood Cliffs NJ: Prentice-Hall, 1982.

Rynkiewich, Michael A. and James P. Spradley, eds. *Ethics and Anthropology: Dilemmas in Fieldwork.* New York: John Wiley & Sons, 1976.

Sieber, Joan E., ed. *The Ethics of Social Research: Fieldwork, Regulation, and Publication.* New York: Springer-Verlag, 1982.

_____, ed. *The Ethics of Social Research: Surveys and Experiments.* New York: Springer-Verlag, 1982.

Sjoberg, Gideon, ed. *Ethics, Politics, and Social Research.* Cambridge MA: Schenkman, 1967.

Wax, Murray L. and Joan Cassell, eds. *Federal Regulations: Ethical Issues and Social Research,* AAAS Selected Symposium 36. Boulder CO: Westview Press, 1979.

INDEX

Roles and ethics, 36, 52-53, 64, 70, 75,
91-92, 100, 111, 125, 126, 163, 183-
84, 190-93, 215
Ross, W. D., 28n, 98n
Rules, 27-28, 32n, 36n, 44-46, 50, 62,
92, 98, 102, 112, 139, 142, 189, 210,
215
Schwartz, T., 119n
Scientific ethic, the, 62-70, 171-72
Sidgwick, Henry, 211n
Siegler, Mark, 193n
Silverstein, S. J., 119n
Sissons, Mary, 119n
Smith, S. S., 119n
Smith, Adam, 210
Social contract, 86-87, 211

Solomon, Robert, 313n
Statistics, 67-68
Stress, research involving, 4, 124n, 168
Stricker, Lawrence, 117n
Subject pools, 114n, 117-18, 170-71
Suedfeld, P., 119n
Survey research, 52, 67-68, 73, 124n,
130, 133-47, 200

Utilitarianism, 28n, 30, 50, 61-62, 87,
189, 211; ideal utilitarianism, 61-62

Vidich, Arthur, J., 94n
Virtues. *See* Character

Warwick, Donald P., 120n
Weber, Max, 29n, 63n, 64, 163
Whistleblowing, 126, 174
Whyte, William, 94n